New Ways in Teaching With Humor

John Rucynski Jr., Editor

New Ways in TESOL Series

Innovative Classroom Techniques

TESOL International Association

www.tesol.org/bookstore

TESOL International Association

1925 Ballenger Avenue

Alexandria, Virginia 22314 USA

Tel 703-836-0774 • Fax 703-836-7864

www.tesol.org

Director of Publishing: Myrna Jacobs

Cover Design: Citrine Sky Design

Production Editor: Kari Dalton

Copyeditor: Sarah Duffy

Layout and Design: Capitol Communications, LLC

Printer: Gasch Printing, LLC

ISBN 9781942799818

Library of Congress Control Number 2016945978

Contents

I. Humor and Language Development

II. Wordplay and Puns

III. Comics and Cartoons

IV. Jokes and Joke Telling

V. Sitcoms and Movies

VI. Internet Resources and Digital Literacy

VII. Parody, Satire, and Sarcasm

ACKNOWLEDGEMENTS

Making this book has been a long journey, so I might as well go way further back and start with my journey of becoming a teacher. For this I have to thank my mother, Kathy Rucynski, for giving me the heart to enter the teaching profession, and my father, Jack Rucynski, for giving me the grit to put up with it.

I am also convinced that one doesn't continue as a teacher unless they have great teachers along the way to inspire them. For this I have to thank three people. While majoring in creative writing at the State University of New York at Oswego, Leigh Wilson taught me the important difference between childlike and childish. Later, while studying for my Master of Arts in TESOL at the School for International Training, Kathleen Graves taught me to articulate my beliefs about teaching into a consistent, professional methodology. Finally, while teaching at International Pacific College in New Zealand, John Fanselow taught me to forget everything I (think I) know about teaching and never rest on my laurels.

For the initial inspiration for this book, I have to thank the Ministry of Education, Culture, Sports, Science, and Technology of Japan. By approving my grant proposal for researching the role of humor in language education, they gave me the opportunity to seriously investigate my belief that humor in English language teaching means much more than just the occasional laugh. This book is the culmination of that 3-year grant, but I hope it is also just the beginning of investigating this theme.

There are also several people to thank at TESOL Press for making this book a reality. I would like to thank Carol Edwards for getting the ball rolling with the book and Myrna Jacobs for seeing it through to its completion. I also need to thank Sarah J. Duffy for her keen eye and copyediting skills. Sarah managed to take chapters written by teachers all over the globe and give the book a consistent, easy-to-read tone that all readers will be thankful for.

Finally, of course, this book wouldn't be a reality without all the wonderful contributors. I was mistaken in worrying that I wouldn't get enough ideas to make a complete book on using humor in English language teaching. Instead, the much bigger challenge was in narrowing the book down to the nearly 100 lesson plans you now have in your hands.

INTRODUCTION

When I mention my interest in using humor in the English language classroom, the types of questions I get show common misconceptions about the role and potential of humor in our field. *Does that mean you act like a stand-up comedian in front of the class? That only works for teachers with a good sense of humor, right? Isn't that only for really advanced students?* Of course, the answer to all these questions is no. Fortunately, we now have this book to illustrate this.

While the main aim of this book is to show the *how* of using humor in the English language classroom, it's important to start with the *why*. When it comes to the role of humor in English language teaching, much emphasis is placed on motivation and interpersonal benefits. The reality is that learning a foreign language is an extremely difficult endeavor that can result in a great deal of stress, anxiety, and shyness among learners. To complicate matters, for many students the study of English is a requirement rather than a choice. In such a challenging environment, it is easy to see why Cornett (1986) referred to humor as "one of our most powerful instructional resources" (p. 8). Used effectively, humor can make language learning more interesting and more memorable. In addition, a fun class atmosphere can greatly reduce the pressure of speaking in a foreign language. Ideally, the proper use of humor can also increase student motivation to study English.

Fortunately, the connection between language teaching and humor goes much deeper. After all, humor can be used to make learning more memorable and improve class atmosphere in almost any subject. When we consider Byram and Risager's (1999) description of the language teacher's role as "a professional mediator between learners and foreign languages and culture" (p. 58), the potential for humor in the classroom becomes even more evident. A great deal of humor is either culture bound or language bound, giving the language teacher a virtually endless supply of classroom material. Humor researchers including Gardner (2008) and Bell (2009) have thus argued for the use of humor as a tool for providing valuable insights into both language and culture.

Creating a positive classroom atmosphere and providing students with ample linguistic and cultural instruction are all part of the ultimate goal of our profession—equipping our students with the language skills and confidence to communicate smoothly and proficiently in English outside of the classroom. Krasner (1999) and Bell (2007) have argued that it takes more than just linguistic mastery to be proficient in a foreign language. When it comes to authentic cross-cultural communication in English, a deep understanding of English humor is essential. Humor is an integral part of communication, but researchers (e.g., Ziv, 1988) have found that some of the biggest cultural differences are based on uses and perceptions of humor. Communicating with someone from a different culture is greatly aided by an understanding of that person's style of joking, along with cultural references to humorous movies or TV shows. Because of the social isolation one might face when not understanding the humor used in social situations, Lems (2013) stresses that "an important part of learning a new language is learning to enjoy its jokes" (p. 26).

This brings us to the *how* aspect of using humor in the language classroom. I began this introduction by describing common misconceptions regarding the use of humor. Fortunately, there are also a great number of language teachers who make humor an integral part of their lessons. When giving presentations about humor in language teaching at conferences, I have been pleasantly surprised by the number of fellow teachers who have come up to me to make comments such as "I'm so glad to find someone else doing this!" or, more succinctly, "Finally!" So when the call for contributions for this book was posted, I was also overjoyed at the positive response. The end result you have in your hands is nearly 100 submissions from around the globe.

The lesson plans compiled in this book provide the reader with the whole gamut of possibilities for using humor in English language teaching. You can find ideas for beginning to advanced students, 5-minute activities to start a class on a humorous note to multiday projects, and silly English puns and jokes to activities for examining controversial social issues. What all these lessons have in common is that they all use humor to enhance the English learning experience and provide English language learners (ELLs) with the linguistic and cultural knowledge they need to become more proficient users of the language. Lesson ideas in this book are divided into the following categories:

I.   Humor and Language Development

II.   Wordplay and Puns

III. Comics and Cartoons

IV.   Jokes and Joke Telling

V.   Sitcoms and Movies

VI.   Internet Resources and Digital Literacy

VII. Parody, Satire, and Sarcasm

Obviously, many submissions fit more than one category. However, each submission was placed into the section in which that type of humor was most implicitly used. The book starts with ideas for a more general use of humor in the classroom and then proceeds to cover a range of more specific genres of humor.

The first—and biggest—section, Humor and Language Development, introduces lessons that integrate humor and language teaching. In other words, in this section you will find lessons in which the authors have creatively modified traditional language learnings tasks to give them a humorous component. This will give you many wonderful ideas on how to enhance the development of the four skills acquisition of their learners.

It is an obvious choice to have a Wordplay and Puns section in a book on humor in the language classroom, as this type of humor is arguably the most inherently connected with the teaching of a language. Introducing different types of wordplay into your classes is an excellent way of providing linguistic instruction in a fun and creative way. Puns, for example, are often dismissed as childish, corny, or even "the lowest form of humor" (Lems, 2013, p. 26), but the range of lesson plans here reveals the higher level linguistic awareness necessary to comprehend many puns. So there are interesting opportunities for students of all English levels. For those who still believe that puns are a simple form of humor, try translating "Linguistic humor is punny as hell" (Raphaelson-West, 1989, p. 130) into another language!

The Comics and Cartoons section presents another form of humor that offers an interesting window into the language and culture of English-speaking countries for learners of all ages and levels. As with other sections in the book, this section offers a wide range of lesson plans. As an extension of the previous section, comics can be exploited as material for discovering puns and wordplay. At the other end of the scale, students can examine how newspaper cartoons are used in some cultures as a forum for social commentary and political satire. Finally, another model suggests giving students the chance to create their own comics.

You will find two types of lessons in Jokes and Joke Telling: lessons on helping ELLs understand jokes of the English-speaking world and lessons on giving students the language skills and confidence to tell jokes themselves in English. Jokes are one of the most culturally bound forms of humor, as the content, type, and frequency of joke telling greatly varies from culture to culture. Fortunately, this section offers a number of interesting ideas for making the world of English jokes more accessible for your learners. While it is often said that dreaming in a foreign language is a sign of progress, telling a joke in English for ELLs is a great accomplishment, as "the ability to tell a joke, to be a good storyteller, on the part of the learner permits the bonding of speaker and listener, of joke teller with joke receiver or listener" (Schmitz, 2002, p. 104).

Sitcoms and Movies makes it clear that English-language entertainment is watched and loved around the world and thus also serves as interesting material for English language classes. Scenes from such resources not only offer a glimpse into daily life in the English-speaking world, but also provide valuable clues into how humor is used and what people find funny in the respective culture. The use of laugh tracks in sitcoms is an interesting way to compare perceptions of humor. As my students have written in their journals for my Humor and American Culture class, "I like the show and found it funny. However, the points at which I laughed were different from when the audience laughed." The English language classroom is a great place to break down scenes and develop student comprehension of English sitcoms and funny movies. Lessons in this section can provide students with a rich history of English humor, from the golden age of early sitcoms like *I Love Lucy* and *Leave It to Beaver* to the quirky sketch comedy of Monty Python to groundbreaking contemporary shows like *Modern Family*.

In recent years, English language teaching has been greatly enhanced by greater and greater access to the Internet. The number of students with smartphones and tablet computers makes English-teaching resources even more accessible. These resources of course include a treasure trove of humorous materials, resulting in this book's section Internet Resources and Digital Literacy. Just as ELLs might find that they are laughing at different times than the audience in English sitcoms, distinct differences can undoubtedly be found in the way in which people from different cultures use humor on social networking sites such as Facebook. This section thus provides useful guidance for students in navigating and comprehending the vast amount of English humor available on the Internet.

The humor genres in Parody, Satire, and Sarcasm were saved for the last section of the book as they can arguably be the most complex and controversial forms of humor. The latter two genres in particular provide further proof of Krasner's (1999) argument that linguistic knowledge alone is not enough to be proficient in a foreign language. Even though the vocabulary and linguistic forms in many satirical statements can be quite simple (think of George Costanza mocking Jerry Seinfeld with "Nice shirt!" when he wears the infamous puffy shirt), they can leave many ELLs completely confused, especially if sarcasm is not common in their native culture. Political or social satire can also prove to be quite complicated for students coming from cultures in which it is uncommon or taboo. Still, knowledge of these forms of English humor are important for the development of both linguistic and cultural knowledge.

As you can see, this book offers a little of everything. Schmitz (2002) claimed that "the advantage of humor is that it can be used with any language teaching approach or method" (p. 94) and this book is proof of the great potential of humor in the English language classroom. Whether you are an eager proponent or a wary skeptic of the role of humor in English language education, the great range of contributions to this book show that you don't have to be a comedian yourself to introduce your students to the fascinating range of the humor of the English-speaking world. Perhaps Bell (2009) summed it up best when she wrote, "Obviously we cannot prepare students for the spontaneous humor they will encounter, but we can provide them with new ways of thinking about and trying to make sense of humor . . . and a safe place to ask and experiment with it" (p. 250). The English language classroom is that safe place and the possibilities are endless. Happy teaching!

REFERENCES

Bell, N. (2007). How native and non-native English speakers adapt to humor in intercultural interaction. *Humor, 20*(1), 27–48.

Bell, N. (2009). Learning about and through humor in the second language classroom. *Language Teaching Research, 13*, 241–258.

Byram, M. S., & Risager, K. (1999). *Language teachers, politics, and cultures.* Clevedon, England: Multilingual Matters.

Cornett, C. (1986). *Learning through laughter: Humor in the classroom.* Bloomington, IN: Phi Delta Kappa Educational Foundation.

Gardner, S. (2008). Three ways humor helps in the language classroom. *The Language Teacher, 32*(6), 9–14.

Krasner, I. (1999). The role of culture in language teaching. *Dialogue on Language Instruction, 13*(1/2), 79–88.

Lems, K. (2013). Laughing all the way: Teaching English using puns. *English Teaching Forum, 51*(1), 26–33.

Raphaelson-West, D. (1989). On the feasibility and strategies of translating humor. *META, 34*(1), 128–141.

Schmitz, J. R. (2002). Humor as a pedagogical tool in foreign language and translation courses. *Humor, 15*(1), 89–114.

Ziv, A. (1988). Teaching and learning with humor: Experiment and replication. *Journal of Experimental Education, 57*, 5–15.

Humor and Language Development

Humorous Technique of Teaching Essay Development

Susan Olajoke Akinkurolere

Levels	*High beginner (can be adjusted up and down)*
Aims	*Increase awareness of paragraph types in essay writing*
	Develop paragraphs for essay writing
Class Time	*35–45 minutes*
Preparation Time	*15–20 minutes*
Resources	*Paper, pens, and markers*
	Chart of family members (see Appendix)
	Cardboard
	Pins

Mastering the composing process of an essay assists students in developing a full-length essay. Every ideal essay must have the basic components of paragraph types: introductory paragraph, transitional paragraph(s), and concluding paragraph. The types of paragraph that make up an essay could be likened and compared to family roles to amuse students and arouse their interest in essay development and writing. This activity helps students develop their essay writing through a cooperative writing process that is humorous.

PROCEDURE

1. Explain the three basic types of paragraph in an essay to the students.

2. Divide students into teams of five or six of mixed sex.

3. Bring each team to a table with chairs.

4. Write the topic to be developed on the board, and explain that each team will develop the essay topic as members of the same family.

5. Allow students on each team to appoint two parents. Other members of the team will be the children. The teacher can also assist in assigning roles.

6. The sitting arrangement should be in the order of Parent 1, Child 1, Child 2, Child 3, and Parent 2, depending on the number of students in a team. The students that are regarded as children should sit between the two parents. Hence, the sitting arrangement should be employed in explaining paragraph types' arrangement.

7. Fix stickers made from cardboard that indicate family positions to clothes to avoid confusion in the course of writing.

8. Draw students' attention to the chart on the board with different types of paragraph assigned to the parents and children (see Appendix).

9. The codes should be interpreted thus: Parent 1-I (introduction), Children-T1, T2, T3 (transitional paragraph 1, transitional paragraph 2, and transitional paragraph 3), and Parent 2-C (conclusion).

10. Each team should commence writing the essay in this way: The first parent writes the first paragraph and gives it to the first child, each child writes a transitional paragraph, and the last paragraph is completed by the second parent.

11. The essay is submitted to the teacher for assessment when each team finishes writing.

CAVEATS AND OPTIONS

1. The number of paragraphs you want students to develop will determine the number of students on a team.

2. You can give the same topic to all the teams.

3. The level of the students should determine topics that will be employed in the explanation and practice of essay development.

4. You could make the students practice another topic with different paragraph types from the initially assigned types in another class.

5. A family picture chart that demonstrates father and mother with children in between could be hung or drawn on the board.

APPENDIX: *Chart for a Team of Five Students*

1. Parent 1 (Introductory Paragraph)

2. Child 1 (Transitional Paragraph 1)

3. Child 2 (Transitional Paragraph 2)

4. Child 3 (Transitional Paragraph 3)

5. Parent 2 (Concluding Paragraph)

Spin the Yarn

Beena Anil

Levels	*Any*
Aims	*Develop narrative and creative skills through humorous pictures and stories*
	Enhance inter/intra-personality skills
	Develop communicative skills and confidence in public speaking
Class Time	*7–10 minutes*
Preparation Time	*10–15 minutes*
Resources	*Self-drawn pictures or pictures from Facebook, WhatsApp, newspapers, or magazines*

For ages, teachers have come up with unique ways to teach students, but the current trend is slightly modified from the teaching of discrete grammatical structures to the fostering of communicative ability. Multimedia is a boon in the classroom, and colorful visual presentations always attract students to learn a new concept in an infotainment manner. Applications like WhatsApp, Instagram, Twitter, and Facebook mesmerize youngsters and can help them learn English in an interesting and effective way. Visuals can be used to develop the correlative thinking skills of students. Students' creative, analytical, and productive skills can be honed by using colorful pictures or self-made stories. As a result, students' communicative skills can be improved as well.

PROCEDURE

1. You can draw simple humorous pictures and upload them to a computer as snapshots (see samples in the Appendix). Or you can download humorous pictures from applications like WhatsApp, Hike, and others that are available on mobile phones and can make the process of learning English interactive and interesting

2. Divide the class into small groups, and make students narrate the story or describe the given pictures.

3. Instruct learners to unleash their imaginative skills by looking at the fun-filled series of pictures that you provided.

4. Learners can narrate stories on their own by using their implicit knowledge of grammar.

5. Learners should not be restricted with one version of their interpretation but can be encouraged to give more versions, especially with a sting of humor.

6. Each narration or interpretation becomes original and eventually develops students' socio-psycho behavioral skills in the classroom.

CAVEATS AND OPTIONS

1. Monotonous interpretation should be avoided.

2. Students' level of interest or mood in learning should be considered.

3. Simple ideas should be used to minimize boredom among learners.

4. Picture interpretation or narration helps learners develop their interest in considering English as a language rather than a subject.

APPENDIX: *Sample Pictures and Stories*

Picture Story 1: The Umbrella Nest

Mary is happy to be in the rain, as her beautiful new umbrella keeps her dry. However, the umbrella is unable to withstand the power of a sudden storm. The umbrella flies away, but then a father crow gets a brilliant idea and takes it to his family to convert into a nest. Now, the crow family lives happily together in their new umbrella nest.

Picture Story 2: The Cat and the Mouse

A cat smells the presence of a mouse and wants to catch it. The mouse notices the cat and starts to run away. The cat tries to pounce on the mouse, but the mouse jumps to the nearby table. The cat continues to chase the mouse, but the brilliant mouse uses a magnifying glass that is on the table to frighten the cat. The magnified image of the mouse makes the cat fall from the table. Now, the mouse is safe and happy again.

Passive Pictures

Walton Burns

Levels	***Low-intermediate (but can be adapted to any level depending on the target language)***
Aims	***Understand and practice word order in the passive voice***
	Learn the meaning of the passive voice
Class Time	***20 minutes***
Preparation Time	***10 minutes***
Resources	***Paper***
	Pens or markers

Students often get confused when using the passive because the structure puts the grammatical object in the subject position. This method of presenting passive demonstrates how mistakes can lead to saying something unintended. In this way, it draws attention to the role of grammar as a mediator of meaning, rather than a set of dry rules. The fact that switching the subject and object of a passive sentence often results in a humorous image helps students remember the correct word order better. Used as an error-correction method, humor softens the blow of making a mistake.

PROCEDURE

1. Draw two pictures and hang them up in front of the classroom. One picture should illustrate the sentence "Sarah was eaten by the cake," while the other should illustrate "The cake was eaten by Sarah." Write the two sentences on the board.

2. Ask students to decide which picture illustrates which sentence. Draw attention to the fact that the only difference between the sentences is the position of the words "the cake" and "Sarah," the subject and object of the verb. Now ask which sentence is more likely to be a useful thing to say.

3. If necessary, repeat the steps with other pictures (see Appendix).

4. Put the students into groups and hand each group a set of sentences. Ask them to illustrate each sentence, and then have them share their sentences and pictures with another pair.

CAVEATS AND OPTIONS

1. After students illustrate the two sentences, they can hang their pictures up on the wall around the classroom. The other students can go around and guess which picture illustrates which sentence and which sentence is the more likely of the two.

2. You can keep the cake pictures in front of the class to remind students of word order in the passive voice. Pointing to these pictures makes for a mild form of error correction when students get the word order wrong in passive sentences.

3. For homework, students can write a story fitting one of the silly sentences into it, such as a horror story about a people-eating cake. This provides fun practice writing in the passive voice.

4. This method can be adapted to fit almost any grammar point. I have used it to target the difference between the past perfect and past simple as well as subjects and objects. It can also be used to target commonly mistaken words or common pronunciation issues, such as the dangers of failing to articulate p and b clearly, with pictures of "Barking at the peach" and "Parking at the beach."

APPENDIX

Sample sentence pairs to give students
The man was bitten by the dog. / The dog was bitten by the man.
The criminal was arrested / The policeman was arrested by the policeman. by the criminal.
The man was given a bicycle. / The bicycle was given a man.
Sean was bitten by a snake. / A snake was bitten by Sean.
The hamburger was cooked by my Mom. / My Mom was cooked by the hamburger.
Anna was hit by the ball. / The ball was hit by Anna.
My friend was brought by the book. / The book was brought by my friend.

Negotiating Meaning and Humor: Funny Caption Contest

Julie Dean, Zuzana Tomaš, and Rebecca Cornell

Levels	*High beginning, intermediate*
Contexts	*Any age*
Aims	*Engage in speaking practice by negotiating meaning and humor using set formulaic expressions*
	Write creative and funny captions to accompany images
Class Time	*30 minutes*
Preparation Time	*20–30 minutes*
Resources	*Printed images*
	Blank paper (small and poster size)
	Tape
	Scissors

This activity engages students in negotiating and creating humorous titles, quips, or dialogue to pair with interesting images, cartoons, and/or photographs. While such practice may appear frivolous on the surface, it is beneficial in a language classroom because it fosters an environment that has great potential to be rich with language use and engagement (Bell, 2009). The target language structures taught and practiced in this activity are preselected formulaic phrases useful in negotiating meaning in classroom and social contexts.

PROCEDURE

1. Collect funny or interesting pictures from any source (e.g., magazines, newspapers, Google, Pinterest). If using the Internet, search using terms such as "funny animals" or "funny kids." If images have captions, remove them by covering them with blank paper or cutting the caption off so that the image is free from any verbiage.

2. Model the activity by using one of the chosen images (perhaps one with the caption cut off), and elicit captions from students as part of a group brainstorm.

3. Teach and assist students in practicing the following discussion frames that are useful in negotiating meaning:

    a. What if we use the title _____?

    b. What if [character X] says _____?

    c. What if [character X] is thinking _____?

    d. Do you think it would be funny if [character X] says _____?

4. As a class, have students use the target formulaic phrases for negotiating meaning. Elicit captions, write them on the board, and have students vote for the best one. Show the caption, if available, from the original image. Discuss the reasons why certain captions are appropriately matched and humorous.

5. Place visuals around the classroom, each accompanied by a blank piece of poster paper.

6. Ask students, working in pairs or groups, to stand next to the image and, after discussing the visual, using the target formulaic phrases, write a funny caption or speech bubble for the image on the corresponding poster paper.

7. After 90 seconds give students a warning, and after 2 minutes ask them to move to the center.

8. After each pair has had a chance to produce a caption or speech bubble for every image, have them put a check next to the caption or speech bubble they like the most on each poster.

9. Tally the votes for each image, and congratulate students on their creativity and language use.

CAVEATS AND OPTIONS

1. Encourage students to find and bring in their own funny pictures.

2. Remember that some pictures by themselves, without captions, may not be particularly laughable but paired with an ingenious title may become quite funny. Remind students to push their imaginations and verbal creativity.

3. You can adjust the time spent on each image by allowing less time for more advanced learners and more time for less advanced learners.

4. This exercise can be played online using a group Facebook, Instagram, or Pinterest account. You could consider having students create fake hashtags for their uploaded image. Students could vote by using the "like" button to accumulate points for best picture-caption-hashtag combination.

REFERENCES AND FURTHER READING

Bell, N. D. (2009). Learning about and through humor in the second language classroom. *Language Teaching Research, 13*, 241–258.

Mad Headlines

Hilda Freimuth

Levels	**Intermediate and above**
Aims	**Write newspaper/magazine headlines**
	Write a newspaper article
Class Time	**60 minutes**
Preparation Time	**5 minutes**
Resources	**Newspapers and magazines**
	Scissors
	Glue sticks
	Paper
	Big bowl

This activity is a fun way to practice student writing as it combines humor with an authentic writing task. This activity will breathe new life into your writing class and reignite students' interest in English.

PROCEDURE

1. Begin class with a short news clip of a funny headline and news story.

2. Divide students into small groups.

3. Give each group a pair of scissors and some newspapers and magazines.

4. Tell students to cut nouns, adjectives, and verbs out of headlines.

5. When finished, students put the cutouts into the bowl at the front of class (on the teacher's desk).

6. Mix up the words and then ask one member of each group to come pull out a handful.

7. Each group gets several sheets of paper and a glue stick.

8. Groups get 5 minutes to create funny headlines with their cut-out words. Each headline needs to be glued at the top of the sheet of paper.

9. Students present their funny headlines to the class.

10. Collect the papers with the headlines, shuffle them, and ask each group to pull out a piece of paper.

11. Students in each group must work together to write a short *funny* newspaper article based on the headline they received.

12. One person per group then comes up to read the news.

13. The class votes on the funniest story.

CAVEATS AND OPTIONS

1. This lesson can be adapted to include only making funny headlines.

2. You can ask students to summarize their stories on an index card. One student becomes the news anchor and reads out the headlines and summaries while you videotape it.

3. The groups can illustrate their articles if there is time.

4. A class newspaper can be made with the compilation of all the stories.

5. If there is extra time, give each group a deck of Man Bites Dog, a funny headline card game.

Example:

Science Book Used in Classroom

After many years of no books in the science classroom, teachers have brought back the 'textbook.' Both teachers and students felt a textbook was a good idea for learning. Parents welcomed the decision.

Sentence Combination With Jokes

Scott Gardner

Levels	**Low +**
Contexts	**Junior high school +**
Aims	**Practice combining sentences utilizing interesting texts**
Class Time	**20–40 minutes**
Preparation Time	**5 minutes**
Resources	**Jokes suitable for students in terms of grammar and content**

Sentence combination and other grammar exercises run the risk of becoming boring. This activity utilizes joke texts—broken down into extremely simple sentences—to let students create "smooth," more natural versions of the jokes. They have an opportunity to see how repetition and ellipsis work, not only in English syntax, but in good joke telling. Working in groups, students can learn from each other and compare their work with other groups.

PROCEDURE

1. Prepare a minimum of three simple punch line jokes by reducing them to simple sentences (see Appendix for examples). These will sound awkward and repetitive, so the work of the students will be to return them to a more natural state. Three jokes are needed so that one joke can be used with the whole class and the two additional jokes can be used for small-group work, allowing groups to tell a new joke to others who have not heard or seen it yet. Jokes can be selected to emphasize certain grammar points, and simplification of sentences can be adjusted to match student level.

   Example of a simple-sentence joke

   There was a mother rat. She had a son. They were together one day. They were searching for food. They were in the kitchen. In the kitchen they met the cat. Suddenly the mother rat barked like a dog. She barked at the cat. The cat got scared. The cat ran away. The mother rat said something to her son. She said, "See? Now you can understand the importance of knowing a second language!"

2. Prepare two sets of handouts with two simplified jokes each. The first joke should be common to all handouts, and the second joke should be unique to either Handout A or Handout B. Allow a lot of open space around the text so students can edit freely and/or rewrite.

3. Divide the class into groups of two or three students and give them one copy of a handout per group. Alternate A and B handouts among groups, making sure all members in a group have the same handout.

4. Tell students to work in their groups to combine sentences as they see fit to make the language flow more naturally. Depending on the level of the students and their previous sentence combining experience, you may want to demonstrate with the first couple of sentences of the first joke. Encourage all group members' input to arrive at a good finished product.

5. When students are finished, let them compare with other groups to appreciate how many different ways the sentences could be combined. It is important here to have students *tell* the joke to others rather than just show it. This is to get them to pay attention to the flow of the sentences—and to practice joke telling—as well as to keep the second joke hidden from other students who may not have seen it yet.

6. After sharing, discussion, feedback, and error correction, tell students to work on the second joke on their handout. Point out that other groups have different jokes, so they should keep their discussion fairly quiet until they finish.

7. When they are finished improving their second joke, students should approach members of other groups and tell it to them, looking especially for students who worked on a different joke. After a sufficient amount of sharing, the newer jokes can be discussed as a class.

CAVEATS AND OPTIONS

1. Throughout both activities, it may be necessary to explain the humor of one or more jokes to students. This will depend of course on what jokes you select and on how well the students combine sentences. Hopefully at least one person per group will understand the joke and can explain it to others, but if you find that a joke requires explanation to many people time and time again, it may be wise to consider selecting a different joke the next time you do the activity.

2. If there is time and a desire among students, different student versions of the jokes can be rated for their humor, timing, and so on. Students can also practice telling the jokes in front of the class, acting as comedians.

APPENDIX: *Possibilities of Jokes for Sentence Combination*

A man is sitting in an airplane. He is looking out the window. He turns to his wife. He says, "Look at those people down there. They look like ants!" She leans over. She looks out the window. She turns to him. She says, "They *are* ants. We haven't taken off yet!"

A politician was in a rural town. He was in the town square. He was giving a speech. He saw an old woman. She was standing at the front of the crowd. She was watching him. He asked her, "Have you lived here all your life?" The old woman paused. She said nothing for a long time. Finally, she looked up at the politician. She said, "I don't know yet!"

Rude/Stupid/Crazy Questions

Hall Houston

Levels	Elementary and above
Contexts	Young adult to adult
Aims	Practice interrogatives
	Use appropriate and inappropriate questions
	Write dialogues
Class Time	1 hour
Preparation Time	10 minutes
Resources	Blackboard
	Chalk
	Pens
	Paper

This is a fun, enjoyable activity that motivates students to speak out. It can help students develop fluency by asking questions and writing a dialogue cooperatively. Furthermore, it gives students practice with assessing and categorizing questions, and putting questions into the context of a larger stretch of discourse.

PROCEDURE

1. Before class, prepare a brief lecture on a topic you know your students will find extremely boring. (When I do this activity, I teach them the alphabet, going into tedious detail about how to write and pronounce each letter.)

2. At the beginning of class, write three words on the board in big letters: RUDE STUPID CRAZY.

3. Tell the class that you want them to think of some questions that are rude, stupid, and crazy. Give them an example of each kind of question (e.g., a rude question: "Why are you so strange?"; a stupid question: "Do you have a nose?"; a crazy question: "Do you plan to fly under the Brooklyn Bridge yesterday?").

4. Next, put students in groups of four or five. Ask each group to write down at least five of each type of question.

5. When each group has produced enough questions, announce that you are going to give a lecture and you want students to loudly interrupt at any time with their questions. If you have a somewhat reticent class, you should emphasize that you expect them to interrupt you frequently.

6. Begin your lecture. Once the questions begin, you can either produce an answer or respond with an appropriate exclamation such as "How rude!" or "What a stupid question!" or "I can't believe you just said that!" As you continue your lecture, act progressively annoyed by the students until you stop the lecture entirely.

7. Call on several students to recall some of your responses to their questions. Write these on the board, making corrections if necessary. Also, ask students to come up with some additional responses. You can ask, "What would you say to an extremely rude question?" or "How would you respond to a stupid question?" Write their ideas on the board as well.

8. Next, divide the class into three groups. Assign each group one type of question. Each group sends a representative to visit the other groups to collect all the questions in their category. Then the groups each make a large poster that contains all the examples of one type of question. Ask the groups to put the posters up on the walls when they're finished.

9. Invite students to stand up and wander around, going to each poster and putting a check mark next to the three best questions on each poster (the rudest, stupidest, and craziest questions).

10. Take the two questions with the most checks from each poster (that's six questions in all) and write them on the board. Work together with the class to correct any errors. Drill the questions together with the class.

11. Ask students to work in pairs to practice asking each other the questions on the board. They can use some of the responses you put up on the board earlier.

12. Put students into pairs to create a short dialogue using some of the language used in the activity. However, students need to provide different roles and a different context for the dialogue. Call on a few pairs to perform their dialogues for the class.

CAVEATS AND OPTIONS

1. This activity encourages students to produce questions that are rude. Therefore, it's best for a class where student–teacher rapport is good and you are prepared to hear the students' rude questions. If you think the activity might result in offensive language or an out-of-control situation, then you might not want to use it.

2. You might want to make videos of the students reading out their dialogues. The videos can later be uploaded to YouTube or another video site for students to watch outside of class.

Note: This activity first appeared in the TESOL Spain newsletter in 2010. Reprint approved by TESOL Spain.

Harnessing Humorous Outbidding for the Rapid Generation of Content

Nick Kasparek and Matthew W. Turner

Levels	*Lower intermediate to advanced*
Contexts	*Middle school to university*
Aims	*Drill target forms to use to support opinions in later academic tasks*
	Automatize these forms and patterns of thinking for more thorough argumentation
Class Time	*30 minutes*
Preparation Time	*15 minutes*
Resources	*Handouts (see Appendices)*

This interactive activity encourages the joint creation and "topping" of humorous fantasy sequences (see Bell, 2011; Kotthoff, 2007) to engage learners in rapidly generating their own content. By encouraging humorous language play, it forestalls boredom and aids the creative automatization of not only target language forms (see Gatbonton & Segalowitz, 1988) but also fundamental habits of persuasive argumentation (see McCann, 2010). As the activity prepares students for a variety of academic tasks that require thorough argumentation, it is an effective focused preparation activity.

PROCEDURE

1. Pose a question with an apparently commonsense answer (e.g., Do you think school is good?). Assign students to small groups and ask them to discuss the question. Take notes of examples of students supporting their opinions or making comments like "It's common sense."

2. After 2 minutes, start your presentation. Acknowledge the difficulty of discussing such a commonly shared opinion, but emphasize that every opinion needs support. State that this lesson will provide useful phrases to ask for and give this support in the form of *reasons*.

3. On the board, present two questions to use in for asking for reasons: "Why do you think so?" and "Can you give me another reason?" Present three phrases for giving reasons: "It's mainly because (if) . . ."; "It's partly because (if) . . ."; and "Another reason is (if) . . . ." Emphasize imagining as many reasons as possible when explaining and supporting ideas. Explain that imagining reasons for the opposite opinion can make arguments even stronger. Provide a few silly examples for the opposite opinion (e.g., "I think school is bad. It's partly because if there was no school, we could sleep more. Another reason is if we slept more, we could save money by eating less."). Point out that we could then think of a stronger reason to disagree (e.g., "I don't think so. It's mainly because if we didn't go to school, we would probably have to wake up for hard work instead.").

4. Distribute the practice handout (Appendix A) to pairs of students. Go through its structure: target phrases to check off as students use them, numbered reasons to check off (in the empty circles), and an ideas bank for imagining even more reasons. Challenge each team to give at least five reasons for each side. Encourage them to use the ideas to imagine many possibilities, the funnier the better.

5. After this 5-minute practice and some brief feedback on their creative ideas and use of the phrases, distribute the template handout (Appendix B) to new pairs. Note that it follows the same structure as the previous handout. Its topic, on which there are divergent views (i.e., Should all school and university tuition be free?), is the one that will be used for a later academic task such as a group discussion, presentation, or essay.

6. Give students 5 minutes to think together of reasons for both sides. Remind students that silly reasons can also be helpful at this stage.

7. Ask students to decide their personal opinions.

8. Ask students to mingle with new partners to discover their opinions and reasons. Students will then be ready for the academic task that follows.

CAVEAT AND OPTION

1. This activity would also work well for numerous other forms of support for opinions, including examples, advantages and disadvantages, and reported and experiential evidence. For condensed units, multiple forms of support could be combined in the same activity.

REFERENCES AND FURTHER READING

Bell, N. D. (2011). Humor scholarship and TESOL: Applying findings and establishing a research agenda. *TESOL Quarterly, 45*, 134–159.

Kotthoff, H. (2007). Oral genres of humor: On the dialectic of genre knowledge and creative authoring. *Pragmatics, 17*, 263–296.

Gatbonton, E., & Segalowitz, N. (1988). Creative automatization: Principles for promoting fluency within a communicative framework. *TESOL Quarterly, 22*, 473–492.

McCann, T. M. (2010). Gateways to writing logical arguments. *The English Journal, 99*(6), 33–39.

APPENDIX A: *Practice Handout*

Target Phases

ο ο ο ο ο Why do you think so?

ο ο ο ο ο Can you give me another reason?

ο ο It's mainly because (if) . . .

ο ο ο It's partly because (if) . . .

ο ο ο ο ο ο Another reason is (if)

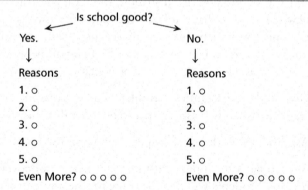

Is school good?

Yes.	No.
↓	↓
Reasons	Reasons
1. ο	1. ο
2. ο	2. ο
3. ο	3. ο
4. ο	4. ο
5. ο	5. ο
Even More? ο ο ο ο ο	Even More? ο ο ο ο ο

Ideas Bank

ο ο ο ο Friends   ο ο ο ο Job   ο ο ο ο Sleep   ο ο ο ο Pet   ο ο ο ο Farm   ο ο ο ο Crime

ο ο ο ο TV   ο ο ο ο Parents   ο ο ο ο Knowledge   ο ο ο ο Hospitals   ο ο ο ο Bully

APPENDIX B: *Template Handout*

Target Phases

○ ○ ○ ○ ○ Why do you think so?　　　　　　○ ○ It's mainly because (if) . . .

　　　　　　　　　　　　　　　　　　　　○ ○ ○ It's partly because (if) . . .

○ ○ ○ ○ ○ Can you give me another reason?　○ ○ ○ ○ ○ ○ Another reason is (if)

Should all school and university tuition be free?

　　　　←　　　　　　　　　→

　　　Yes.　　　　　　　　　No.

　　　↓　　　　　　　　　　↓

　　　Reasons　　　　　　　Reasons

　　　1. ○　　　　　　　　1. ○

　　　2. ○　　　　　　　　2. ○

　　　3. ○　　　　　　　　3. ○

　　　4. ○　　　　　　　　4. ○

　　　5. ○　　　　　　　　5. ○

　　　Even More? ○ ○ ○ ○ ○　　Even More? ○ ○ ○ ○ ○

When Headlines Go Bad

Adam Kavetsky and Zuzana Tomaš

Levels	Intermediate to advanced
Contexts	Any age, academic and non-academic contexts
Aims	Raise awareness of lexical and grammatical ambiguity
	Practice four skills
Class Time	25–35 minutes
Preparation Time	5 minutes
Resources	Sample headlines and stories (see appendix A)
	List of ambiguous headlines (see appendix B)

Studies on humor in the classroom have found that "humor appropriately used has the potential to humanize, illustrate, defuse, encourage, reduce anxiety and keep people thinking" (Torok, McMorris, & Lin, 2004, p. 14). This humorous, consciousness-raising activity expands these benefits further by tapping into language leaners' metalinguistic awareness while practicing all four skills. Learners are challenged to identify the source of grammatical or lexical ambiguity in headlines and demonstrate their understanding by producing a collaborative story that revolves around the unintended meaning of the headline.

PROCEDURE

1. Ask students to work in pairs.

2. Give each pair two stories and one headline (see Appendix A).

3. Working together, students decide which of the two stories is the intended story and which is a humorous one due to potential ambiguity. (Note: Allow students to use dictionaries, and make yourself available to clarify meanings.)

4. Lead a discussion on what linguistic issues pertinent to the headline make the meaning ambiguous.

5. Ask students to work in groups of three or four.

6. Give each group an ambiguous headline (see appendix B).

7. Students are challenged to figure out what aspect of the headline makes it ambiguous and to write a short story about the unintended meaning suggested in the headline.

8. Monitor closely and help when necessary.

9. Students present their work to the class or walk around the classroom and read their classmate's stories.

CAVEATS AND OPTIONS

1. Groups that finish before other groups can be challenged to write the "real" story or to create a visual accompanying the story.

2. If students enjoy competition, have them vote on the best story.

3. During the writing part of the story, have students focus on additional grammatical aspects such as past tense (for story writing) or particular vocabulary (e.g., provide a list of words to practice and require that students use a certain number of words from the list).

4. Headlines can be modified to meet the needs of younger learners.

REFERENCES AND FURTHER READING

Torok, S. E., McMorris, R. F., & Lin, W.-C. (2004). Is humor an appreciated teaching tool? Perceptions of professors' teaching styles and styles and use of humor. *College Teaching, 52*(1), 14–20.

APPENDIX A: *Sample Headline: "Hospital Sued by 8 Foot Doctors"*

Story A

St. Joseph Mercy hospital is reporting a lawsuit filed last Monday against them by a group of podiatrists who are complaining of unfair treatment.

Dr. Hal Ross was quoted as saying, "St. Joe's has been treating the whole podiatry department like the unwanted stepchildren."

Ross cites lower pay, unequal benefits packages and discriminatory promotion practices as the complaints of the lawsuit. The group of podiatrists is seeking $20 million.

Story B

St. Joseph Mercy hospital reported a lawsuit filed last Monday. This lawsuit was filed by Dr. David Tork and Dr. John Darion, who are complaining that the facility is unfit for their use and the hospital has refused to adjust the entrances and hallways for their access.

Drs. Tork and Darion are 7'10" and 8'1", respectively, and have complained that the hallways and doorways are too short for them.

The hospital has stated the cost of refurbishing the facility would be prohibitive and have expressed some speculation that Drs. Tork and Darion may actually be two men, standing on shoulders, thus making refurbishing unnecessary.

APPENDIX B: *List of Ambiguous Headlines*

Children Make Nutritious Snacks

Red Tape Holds Up New Bridges

Man Who Stole Clock Now Faces Time

Stolen Dog Found by Pole

Politician Wins on Budget, More Lies Ahead

Complaints About Referees Growing Ugly

Enraged Chicken Injures Farmer With Ax

Poetic Farewells: Humorous Epitaphs in the Literature Class

Hale Kizilcik

Levels	*Intermediate and higher*
Contexts	*Secondary school, especially schools whose curriculum incorporates literary texts*
Aims	*Develop interpretive skills, language awareness, critical and creative thinking skills, and higher order reading skills*
Class Time	*50 minutes*
Preparation Time	*5–10 minutes*
Resources	*Whiteboard*
	Markers
	Computer and projector (optional)

An epitaph is an inscription on tombstone or monument. It gives information about the person and frequently makes a statement about his or her life and death. (Booth & Skinner, 1981, p. 38)

As Carter (1996) suggests, the definition of a literary text can be expanded to include advertisements, puns, examples of word play, and jokes since these texts display creative uses of language that can be considered literary.

I have been using epitaphs in my literature classes for a number of reasons: Epitaphs are brief, cleverly written, and humorous and thus motivating. And epitaphs are good tools to exploit characterization and point of view in literature.

Using literary texts provides ample opportunities for teaching integrated skills (McKay, 2001). As with other forms of literary texts, by using epitaphs we can help develop students' interpretative skills (Lazar, 1993), language awareness (Lazar, 1993; McKay, 2001), and creative and critical thinking skills (Showalter, 2003).

Epitaphs are culture specific, and by integrating them into the curriculum, we can increase students' awareness of cultural differences.

PROCEDURE

1. Write the body of the first epitaph on the board or show it on a PowerPoint slide:

   Here lies Frank Pixley, as usual.

   Tell students that the line was inscribed on a very special place. Ask them to predict where they are likely to read a line like this. Elicit predictions. At this point, it is not important whether they can come up with the answer "tombstone." Encourage as many answers as possible.

   If any of the students gives the correct answer, ask them to share the clues in the text that helped them predict it.

   If they cannot predict the answer, write the title of the epitaph on the board or show it on the slide and encourage more predictions.

   On Frank Pixley, editor.

   Here lies Frank Pixley, as usual.

   If nobody gives the answer, tell them the answer. Ask them why people inscribe such lines on tombstones. At this point, you can provide the definition for an epitaph.

2. Now students will work in pairs. Tell them that they will work like detectives to figure out as much as possible about Mr. Pixley and the writer of the epitaph. Tell them to copy the following chart in their notebooks and use it to record their deductions.

	100% sure	Very likely	Maybe
Mr. Pixley			
The writer of the epitaph			

Elicit answers and ask for justification. Remind students that there are no right answers, but there are justified and unjustified answers.

Possible answers:

	100% sure	Very likely	Maybe
Mr. Pixley	dead, editor	lazy	
The writer of the epitaph	knows Mr. Pixley	writer, witty	works with Frank

3. Ask students to read the following epitaph and guess the profession of the deceased.

Stranger, tread

This ground with gravity

_____ *Brown*

Is filling his last cavity

Elicit predictions and ask for justifications.

Tell students to read the epitaph more carefully. They can use their dictionaries to find out the meanings of the words *tread*, *gravity*, and *cavity*. Students will need to choose the definition(s) that fits the context. Elicit answers.

Ask students to explain the joke in the epitaph. Ask them to work in pairs to analyze the poetic devices and creative language play in the epitaph. Elicit answers. (Possible answers: rhyme (gravity, cavity), cavity refers to both a hole in the ground and a hole in a tooth.)

Based on the two examples they read, ask students to list the features of a humorous epitaph.

4. Students write their own epitaphs for a hero of their choice. (In literature classes, I want students to choose a character from the texts in the syllabus.) Explain that the epitaph does not have to be about the character's profession.

As a prewriting task, ask students to brainstorm ideas using the following character chart.

Name of the deceased: _____

Major events in his or her life	Anything striking about his or her appearance
What do other characters think about him or her?	What do I think about him or her?

CAVEATS AND OPTIONS

By hiding the names of the characters, student epitaphs can be used as a "guess my hero" activity.

REFERENCES AND FURTHER READING

Bierce, A. (2006). Here lies Frank Pixley, as usual. In H. Rawson & M. Miner (Eds.), *Oxford dictionary of American quotations*. New York, NY: Oxford University Press.

Booth, D. W., & Skinner, S. (1981). *ABC's of creative writing*. Toronto, Canada: Globe/Modern Curriculum Press.

Carter, R. (1996). Look both ways before crossing: Developments in the language and literature classroom. In R. Carter & J. McRae (Eds.), *Language, literature, and the learner: Creative classroom practice* (pp. 1–15). London, England: Addison Wesley Longman.

Lazar, G. (1993). *Literature and language teaching: A guide for teachers and trainers*. Cambridge, England: Cambridge University Press.

McKay, S. L. (2001). Literature as content for ESL/EFL. In M. Celce-Murcia (Ed.), *Teaching English as a second or foreign language* (3rd ed., pp. 19–32). Boston, MA: Heinle & Heinle.

Showalter, E. (2003). *Teaching literature*. Malden, MA: Blackwell.

Recipe for Laughter

Sally La Luzerne-Oi

Levels	*High beginning +*
Contexts	*University*
Aims	*Practice process writing with a humorous twist*
Class Time	*Can be spread out over several classes*
Preparation Time	*20–30 minutes to write a model paragraph if necessary*
Resources	*A model "recipe for laughter" paragraph or essay*

Process writing, describing an activity in steps, is a common rhetorical style introduced in textbooks. Suggested topics in textbooks often ask students to write about how to use or make something, or how to change some type of behavior. Suggesting topics that are the opposite of what students and readers might expect can yield some funny pieces of writing.

PROCEDURE

1. Tell students that there are many "how to" books on the market, with topics like how to learn English in 7 days, how to lose weight while eating your favorite food, how to live longer, and so on. For this activity, they will write how to do something, but their topics should not be typical ones because one objective of this assignment is to produce a humorous piece of writing. Give some topics like the ones below. Have students choose one or brainstorm their own topics.

   How to fail a test

   Easy ways to lose a driver's license

   How to get distracted while studying

   How to get on your instructor's nerves

   A dinner that will convince your roommate to cook all the meals

   Surefire steps to having customers complain to the manager

   How to guarantee no second date

2. Show students a model process paragraph/essay. (You can use the sample paragraph in the Appendix, write your own, or use a student model after having done this assignment once.) Together, analyze the model for its topic sentence, supporting details, the imperative verb form, and transitional devices showing order.

3. Include prewriting activities, drafts, and feedback in the lesson.

4. Publish the final drafts or leave time for students to share them.

CAVEATS AND OPTIONS

If you are working with advanced students, a lesson on satire before the students start writing works well here.

APPENDIX: *Sample "Recipe for Laughter" Paragraph*

How to Change Roommates

Are you unhappy with your roommate? If so, you can be sure to have a different one next term by simply undertaking the following steps. First of all, have an imaginary friend. Be sure to discuss your daily activities with your imaginary friend when your roommate is present. If your roommate asks you about this, introduce her to this imaginary person, and try to have a three-way conversation. Second, act contrary to your roommate. If your roommate enjoys rap, play classical music. If your roommate likes fresh air, close all the windows. Perhaps your roommate cannot stand the smell of garlic. That is your signal to use a lot of garlic in whatever you cook. Finally, make a mess in your room. Leave wrappers, empty cans, dirty dishes, and leftovers on the furniture and floor. If the pile gets high enough, your roommate will not be able to see you in order to ask you to clean. If she does ask you to clean, tell her you do not think the room is dirty, or tell her to ask your imaginary friend to clean. Any one of these behaviors might annoy your roommate, but by doing all of them, you should be guaranteed a new "roomie" before long.

Timely Tongue Twisters

Sally La Luzerne-Oi

Levels	**Low-intermediate +**
Aims	**Practice forming sentences**
	Practice pronunciation
Class Time	**25 minutes**
Preparation Time	**None**
Resources	**Dictionaries**

Tongue twisters are commonly used for pronunciation practice in language classes. Having students make their own tongue twisters requires them to think about words with the target sound as well as sentence structure. These student-generated tongue twisters are often hilarious and fun to say.

PROCEDURE

1. Explain to students that some phrases and sentences are called tongue twisters because they are difficult to pronounce. Ask students to say one or more tongue twisters practicing a target sound, for example, *She sells seashells by the seashore* (see References and Further Reading).

2. Explain that the tongue twister *She sells seashells by the seashore* requires differentiating between the [ʃ] and [s] sounds. Then analyze the grammar together.

3. Ask students to work in pairs or small groups to make their own tongue twisters. Assign a sound that is problematic for the students to reproduce.

4. Show students how to write a tongue twister focusing on that sound by following a series of steps.

   a. Write subject + verb + object. For example, *Peter peeled a pear.*

   b. Add another subject + verb + object. For example, *Peter peeled a pear, and Paula picked a peach.*

   c. Add the word *while* and subject + verb + object. For example, *Peter peeled a pear and Paula picked a peach while Pam poked a piñata.*

5. Once all groups have finished, have them teach their tongue twisters to the class. Students should practice saying each tongue twister several times.

6. Compile the student-generated tongue twisters. Have students use their list of tongue twisters for practice. Add to them at regular intervals.

CAVEATS AND OPTIONS

1. Write a set of instructions that suits the level of your students. The tongue twister could end after step 4b for lower level students, or you might add a step 4d for higher levels: Add another subject + verb + object. For example, *Peter peeled a pear and Paula picked a peach while Pam poked a piñata and Penny pet the puppy.*

2. More advanced students can also think of words in which the target sound is medial or final (e.g., *The curb curves at the corner; I like pot pie but not pad thai*).

REFERENCES AND FURTHER READING

This Wikiquote page lists many tongue twisters in English as well as other languages: https://en.wikiquote.org/wiki/User:Adam78/List_of_tongue-twisters

English Avenue categorizes tongue twisters according to the sound they practice: http://languageavenue.com/teaching-ideas/english-tongue-twisters

Funny Misplaced Modifiers

Lisa Leopold

Levels	*Advanced*
Contexts	*University*
Aims	*Develop grammatical competence*
Class Time	*About 45 minutes (depending on class size)*
Preparation Time	*20 minutes*
Resources	*Handouts*

Modifiers are words, clauses, or phrases that add description to a sentence and should appear close to what they modify. When used correctly, modifiers can make a sentence more elegant, but misplaced modifiers can create confusion for readers. By analyzing humorous misplaced modifiers, learners can avoid the mistakes writers commonly make with modifiers.

PROCEDURE

1. Present every learner with a funny misplaced modifier on a slip of paper (which can be found at www.eddiesnipes.com/2011/07/funny-dangling -and-misplaced-modifiers). Examples include "I gave olives to my friend that I stabbed with my fork" and "Mrs. Jones was proud that on her first hunting trip, she was able to shoot several animals as well as her husband."

2. Have learners read their example aloud to the class and explain what makes it funny.

3. Teach learners that in order to convey the correct meaning, modifiers must appear close to what they modify. Present several other examples of misplaced modifiers, including adjectives or adjective clauses, adverbs or adverb clauses, absolute phrases, infinitive phrases, participle phrases, and prepositional phrases. Have learners identify what the modifier should modify and revise the sentence accordingly.

4. Have learners apply what they learned to revise the sentence they received at the beginning of class for accuracy, and check their responses as a class.

5. Divide the class into three or four teams. Present teams with a handout of 10–15 humorous misplaced modifiers (see Snipes, 2011; UW-Madison Writing Center, 2009). Teams should work as quickly as possible to revise the sentences, and the team that finishes first should call "Stop!" At that point this team will read aloud their revisions and earn one point for every correct sentence.

6. Ask if any other team has a greater number of revised sentences than the number of points the first team accrued, and if so, ask that team to share their revisions. The team with the greatest number of correct responses wins the game.

CAVEATS AND OPTIONS

1. The game may be played in a Jeopardy format, where differing point values are assigned to each question according to its difficulty. You can download a PowerPoint template from Educational Technology Network (2009) to create your own Jeopardy game with misplaced modifiers. Each topic area might cover a different type of modifier: adjectives or adjective clauses, adverbs or adverb clauses, absolute phrases, infinitive phrases, participle phrases, prepositional phrases. Teams take turns selecting questions to answer and earn the corresponding number of points for a correct response.

2. The game may be played using a deck of cards with a different point value assigned to each question. Before teams answer their questions, they select a card from the presorted deck of cards with the numbers 2–10 to discover the point value assigned to their question. They then take turns revising sentences displayed on the PowerPoint slides, earning between 2 and 10 points for every correct answer.

REFERENCES AND FURTHER READING

Educational Technology Network. (2009). *Classroom use of PowerPoint.* Retrieved from http://www.edtechnetwork.com/powerpoint.html

Snipes, E. (2011, July 8). *Funny dangling and misplaced modifiers.* Retrieved from http://www.eddiesnipes.com/2011/07/funny-dangling-and-misplaced-modifiers

UW-Madison Writing Center. (2009). *The best misplaced and dangling modifiers of all time.* Retrieved from https://writing.wisc.edu/Handbook/CommonErrors_BestMod.html

Sounds Good! Using Drama and Role-Play to Improve Intelligibility

Rolf I. Naidoo

Levels	*Beginning to advanced*
Contexts	*University, adult*
Aims	*Increase phonemic awareness and production*
	Develop understanding of the relationship between sound and meaning
	Use drama in the classroom
Class Time	*40–60 minutes or more*
Preparation Time	*20–30 minutes (may vary)*
Resources	*Blank paper for script writing*
	A sense of humor

Intelligibility is often difficult to address. Students prepare a humorous drama/role-play script and perform it for the class. The method raises awareness through the usage hypothesis (Tomasello, 2009) and the noticing theory (Schmidt, 1990) to improve intelligibility in students. By producing and considering (in the form of drama) both correct and erroneous forms of individual sounds, learners can pay attention to their own speech, thus raising intelligibility where needed. The use of drama and role-play in ESL/EFL contexts is highly documented and offers a unique application to address the issue of pronunciation. This not only allows students to focus on correct forms for greater intelligibility but also allows for deeper processing by getting students to pronounce the incorrect forms using humorous contexts and to take notice of the difference. Adult learners will pay attention to the correct forms as a tool to consciously improve language. Pronunciation is a source of pride and accomplishment in any language learning experience. The goal is not to produce parrots but rather to reduce anxiety by using humor as a context for a judgment-free learning tool and context. This results in an ingrained class culture of accurate sound articulation that translates to improved intelligibility outside the classroom. Learners are often unaware of the sound–meaning relationship and the potential confusion it can cause. They need to be made aware that they control the meaning conveyed by correct sound production and that any significant variation can lead to misunderstandings. This goes beyond minimal pairs and contrasts any sound whether intelligible or unintelligible. In the South Korean context /b/ and /v/, among others, are used interchangeably, for example, *movie* versus "*mobie,*" where we understand *movie* but "*mobie*" is unintelligible and carries no meaning in English (Naidoo & Im, 2014).

The following are some sounds that prove difficult for learners in regard to intelligibility and producing accurate sounds:

/b/ vs. /v/ (*berry* and *very*)

/l/ vs. /r/ (*lake* and *rake*)

/th/ vs. /s/ (*thin* and *sin*)

/z/ vs. /j/ (*zoo* and *Jew*)

/p/ vs. /f/ (*pull* and *full*)

PROCEDURE

1. Inform students they need to form groups of two or three.

2. Students prepare a short role-play script based on a humorous exchange between characters.

3. Students perform the role-play for their classmates (see Appendix for examples).

CAVEATS AND OPTIONS

1. Move between the groups, assisting with the language or providing guidance where needed regarding technical or further explanation.

2. Beginners may struggle a bit, but encourage them to use simple case scenarios. If you like, you could provide them with a situation such as the confusion that results if someone has trouble with /p/ and /f/ sound production (e.g., a customer wants a fork to eat with but instead gets more pork). They must also provide an explanation for the confusion and an explanation of the sounds based on what they learned in class.

3. For large classes, groups of four are recommended to reduce anxiety and have a more manageable number of performances of greater quality.

4. You may record video of the performances for feedback later. If no video equipment is available, student cellphones may be used to record video clips.

5. Length of the role-play may be determined by the level of learners in the class. Higher levels will come up with longer complicated scenarios than lower levels.

REFERENCES AND FURTHER READING

Naidoo, R. I., & Im, S. C. (2014). Cognitive linguistics and pronunciation: The case for intelligibility. 언어과학연구 [*Journal of Linguistic Science*], *68*, 103–120.

Schmidt, R. W. (1990). The role of consciousness in second language learning. *Applied Linguistics, 11*(2), 129–158

Tomasello, M. (2009). *Constructing a language: A usage-based theory of language acquisition*. Cambridge, MA: Harvard University Press.

APPENDIX: *Excerpts From Student Work*

/th/ vs. /s/

> S1: My mouse was sore yesterday so I couldn't come to class. I'm sorry, teacher.
>
> Teacher: Thank you for letting me know. Did you take him to the vet?
>
> S1: No I went to the dentist . . .

Student has a puzzled look on face; teacher is also confused. Group then explains the sound difference.

/l/ vs. /r/

> S1: Yesterday I prayed with my nephew and he got hurt.
>
> S2: Really?! How did that happen?
>
> S1: He let go of my hand.
>
> S1: Huh?

Group then explains sound difference.

/z/ vs. /j/

> S1: I went to the Jew today.
>
> S2: Why? Don't you have class?
>
> S3: Dude, that is racist. Do you mean the jewelry store clerk?
>
> S1: No, the place they have many animals, the Jew!!

Group then explains sound difference.

Giant Dreams

Paula B. Newbill

Levels	High-intermediate
Contexts	Upper elementary or middle school
Aims	Strengthen narrating skills targeting grammar, vocabulary, and spelling when writing
Class Time	30–40 minutes
Preparation Time	15 minutes
Resources	The BFG *by Roald Dahl*
	Paper and pencil

In *The BFG*, Sophie is snatched from her bed by the Big Friendly Giant, or BFG. Unlike the other giants from his land, he does not eat human "beans." The BFG catches and distributes dreams and speaks in a strange manner. For instance, when Sophie asks him why he does not reveal himself to humans, he answers, "They would be putting me into the zoo or the bunkumhouse with all those squiggling hippodumplings and crocadowndillies" (Dahl, 1982, p. 31).

Students generally find the BFG's strange way of speaking humorous, especially if the teacher reads with expression. When I recently read the "Dreams" chapter aloud to a pull-out group of English language learners (ELLs), I added lilting intonation, a gruff voice, eyebrow movement, and even hunched shoulders to the parts where the BFG talks. My students really enjoyed hearing me read like the giant! They also enjoyed correcting the giant's English. This activity allows ELLs the opportunity to critique someone's language without correcting a classmate or being corrected.

This lesson is geared toward students who are capable of written narration but are still fine-tuning word choice, grammar, and spelling. Pairing a monolingual English speaker with an ELL works best so that the ELL has confidence when presenting the finished product. This task provides an opportunity for the ESL teacher to collaborate with the classroom teacher because many upper elementary and middle school reading classes already read this novel.

PROCEDURE

1. Pair an ELL with a monolingual speaker.

2. Using the "Dreams" chapter of *The BFG*, allow each pair to choose a dream to edit. Students revise the giant's language, paying attention to verb conjugations/tenses, other grammar points, spelling, and vocabulary. Students may take turns writing the edited version.

3. Students then draw a picture to represent the dream.

4. When done, pairs may compare their edited passage and picture with another pair that edited the same passage.

CAVEATS AND OPTIONS

1. Some dream sequences in the chapter are longer than others. You may have students edit only a portion of the dream.

2. ELLs might not be able to read the entire book on their own or even with assistance. However, this is a great book for a read-aloud in the ESL pull-out class or the regular classroom that contains ELLs.

3. This book also has excellent examples of literary devices for figurative language study, especially similes. This is a common standard in fifth-grade reading.

4. As an extension activity, students could narrate in written form a dream they had.

REFERENCES AND FURTHER READING

Dahl, R. (1982). *The BFG*. New York, NY: Scholastic.

All Mixed Up: Humor With Scrambled Sentences

Sara Okello and Jolene Jaquays

Levels	Intermediate
Contexts	Any
Aims	Practice writing different types of clauses and sentences
Class Time	10 minutes
Preparation Time	5 minutes
Resources	Three different colors of paper

Grammar instruction has undergone a change from focus on form to focus on *forms* (Nassaji & Fotos, 2004). This instruction emphasizes using the form in communicative, meaningful contexts and can lead to automatization for students (Spada & Lightbown, 2008). One area in which many students struggle with form is identifying and writing types of sentences and clauses. Not only can students struggle with grammar and writing, but learning a second language can also cause anxiety in students. Humor has been shown to be an effective method to reduce tension that some language learners experience (Deneire, 1995). This activity combines humor and a forms-focused approach to help students practice sentence and clausal types in an amusing, engaging format.

PROCEDURE

1. Review the three main types of sentences (simple, compound, and complex) as well as the two main types of clauses (independent and dependent).

2. To practice the compound sentence, give students one strip of red paper and one strip of green paper. Have them write one independent clause on the red strip and the other independent clause (with the coordinating conjunction at the beginning) on the green strip. Students then read their sentences aloud to the class. Then collect the strips of paper and scramble them. Each student chooses one red strip and one green strip and read the resulting sentence. The resulting sentences should be humorous, especially if they do not make sense (see Appendix for examples). This activity is guaranteed

to elicit some laughs from students, especially on the sentences that are not logical.

3. To practice the complex sentence, give students one red strip of paper and one yellow strip of paper. Have them write a sentence, writing the independent clause on the red strip and the dependent clause on the yellow strip. Students then read their sentences aloud to the class. Then collect the strips of paper and scramble them. Have each student choose one red strip and one yellow strip and read the resulting funny sentences aloud (see Appendix for examples).

CAVEATS AND OPTIONS

1. Make sure students write the clauses on the correct color of paper in order to ensure that the scrambled sentences correlate syntactically and grammatically.

2. You can use this activity to introduce each type of sentence and clause or as a practice or review for the sentence and clause types.

3. Students can write compound-complex sentences using two red strips of paper for the independent clauses and one green strip of paper for the dependent clause (see Appendix examples).

4. Check the sentences students write for accuracy and appropriateness before students read their sentences to the class.

5. A possible follow-up activity is to have students write compound, complex, and compound-complex sentences as an in-class activity or as a homework assignment. You could give a prize to the student with the funniest sentence.

REFERENCES AND FURTHER READING

Deneire, M. (1995). Humor and foreign language teaching. *Humor, 8,* 285–298.

Nassaji, H., & Fotos, S. (2004). Current developments in research on the teaching of grammar. *Annual Review of Applied Linguistics, 24,* 126–145.

Spada, N., & Lightbown, P. M. (2008). Form-focused instruction: Isolated or integrated? *TESOL Quarterly, 42,* 181–207.

APPENDIX: *Examples of Sentence Types and Humorous Sentences*

(Adapted from authentic sentences from students)

Compound

I like chocolate (red), but I study in university (green).

I will eat pizza (red), and I will pass the TOEFL (green).

I have free time (red), or I have a lot of money (green).

Complex

I'm going to the store (red) because I want to complete my education (yellow).

Because I'm out of milk (yellow), I'm living in the United States (red).

I won't complete my education (red) if I eat pizza (yellow).

Compound-Complex (Optional)

I like chocolate (red), and I eat it every day (red) because I want to go to university (green).

I won't drive a car (red) if I get fat (green), but I will walk or run (red).

If I'm not studying (green), I'll go on a diet (red), or I will eat some ice cream (red).

TOEIC Part 1 With Funny Pictures

Stephen M. Paton

Levels/Contexts	*Lower level students preparing for the TOEIC or TOEIC Bridge*
Aims	*Have fun learning and practicing test-taking strategies for Listening section Part 1 of TOEIC and TOEIC Bridge*
Class Time	*30 minutes or more*
Preparation Time	*15–30 minutes*
Resources	*Internet connection*
	Computer with a projector or large screen

Part 1 of the TOEIC involves candidates looking at photographs, hearing four short statements for each, and choosing which statement best describes what is seen in the picture. Distractors and traps usually consist of similar-sounding words (cat/cap) or appropriate lexical items in contextually incorrect sentences.

The photographs are typically mundane and uninteresting, and students can't be blamed for quickly becoming bored looking at images of dull everyday life. Such disinterest can get in the way of effective test-strategy and test-awareness instruction.

To overcome students' boredom, teachers can easily create instructional material using funny, bizarre, weird, and ridiculous images from the Internet. Rather than using pictures of secretaries filing papers, why not show a man casually reading a book, apparently unaware that he is being eaten alive by a crocodile? Rather than a photo of a salesperson working at a checkout counter, why not a woman riding a horse while balancing a wheel-barrow on her head? Or a heavily tattooed man playing a flame-shooting sousaphone while skateboarding? Or a cow leaping through ocean waves alongside a dolphin?

These kinds of pictures are so easy to find on the Internet, and a teacher can maintain student engagement and interest by making example test items with them.

PROCEDURE

1. Find a funny image you think is appropriate and that can be described in a short sentence at the language level of your students. A simple Google search can yield good images.

2. Identify the key words of the picture. For example, if you've found a picture of a woman riding a bicycle underwater alongside a shark, the keywords might be *woman, shark, bicycle, ride, swim,* and *water.* (It's a good idea to have verbs as well as nouns.)

3. Think of a short, simple sentence that accurately describes the picture, or an aspect of the picture. One example might be *The woman is riding a bicycle.* Another might be *The shark is swimming.* You can tailor these to the level of your students.

4. Come up with three (or fewer) "incorrect" sentences that are lexically or phonemically similar to what the picture depicts, with only one element in the sentence making it wrong. For example, *She's riding a bicycle near a park,* because *park* is phonetically similar to *shark.* Perhaps *The shark is riding a bicycle in the water,* as it's the *woman,* not the *shark,* that should be the subject of the sentence. Becoming aware of and learning to avoid these sorts of traps is the point of the lesson and will help students in the test.

5. Come up with as many of these as you'd like for your lesson. Four or five pictures is usually plenty and provides a good chance to experience the strategy instruction with new high-interest images coming up often enough to maintain engagement.

6. In class, display the picture on the screen, and then read out your four (or three) sentences. With response cards, or some other kind of response system (e.g., *rock, scissors, paper* gestures), students can indicate which of the sentences they think is the correct one. Repeat each sentence as many times as necessary, or include the text alongside the image for extra initial support.

7. Once students are familiar with the style of this section of the test, creating test items of their own is good practice. Have students find funny images themselves, or provide some more that you've found. Writing one "correct" sentence and three "incorrect" sentences for each gets them to think like a test-item writer. Quizzing each other can be a fun revision exercise in subsequent lessons.

CAVEATS AND OPTIONS

1. In most countries, copyright images can be freely used in educational institutions for educational purposes, provided they're not reproduced outside of the classroom. Be aware of the policy in your country and school.

2. Photographs have much more impact than illustrations. Inexplicable photographs are powerfully memorable.

3. If computer projection equipment can't be used, the pictures can be photocopied and distributed on paper, again with the sentences being read out by the teacher.

Using Humor to Uncover Details in Course Description Documents

Janice G. T. Penner

Levels	*Any*
Contexts	*English for academic purposes*
Aims	*Read the vital "fine print" in the course description*
	Begin to develop rapport on the first day of class
Class Time	*Varies with length of document; I prefer to give it for homework*
Resources	*Course description*

In English for academic purposes courses at postsecondary institutions, instructors are required to provide English language learners (ELLs) with the objectives, attendance, grading and academic honesty policies, and so on. Many ELLs experience academic culture shock because requirements often differ between institutions and even between instructors within the same institution. Rather than overwhelming the ELLs by having them read this information during class time, it's more interesting and time-efficient to have them skim and scan and answer questions individually. The relatively mundane chore of reading through a four- or five-page document can be more interactive by adding a humorous element. In addition, the instructor can be sure the ELLs have read the most important points.

PROCEDURE

1. After you complete your course description, determine which aspects students may be unfamiliar with or the policies your institution requires you to inform them about.

2. Develop *true*, *false*, and *don't know* statements based on the content of the course description.

3. Add in as many funny statements as you wish. They can be designated as *don't know*. (See Appendix for examples.)

4. Make some statements partially true or vague so that ELLs engage in critical thinking.

5. During the debriefing time, be sure to emphasize and explain the statements they got wrong.

CAVEATS AND OPTIONS

1. When discussing the "answers," be sure that students understand that you are joking.

2. I find that ELLs who "get it" start expressing their sense of humor earlier in the term.

APPENDIX: *What's This Advanced Reading/Writing Course Section All About?*

Part A: Read the course outline and decide if the statements are true, false, or you don't know.

- Circle T for true, F for false, or DK for don't know.

- If the statement is false, add the correct information to make the statement true.

Example: *Thursday*

_F_ This class meets on Monday, Tuesday, Wednesday, and ~~Fridays~~ at 10:30–12:30.

T F DK   1. Each week, we should take turns bringing chocolate for the instructor.

T F DK   2. The instructor will lend me books, so I will have to give my passport as a deposit.

T F DK   3. We will spend the first 5 weeks writing paragraphs, so we'll do essays after the mid-term.

T F DK   4. Only the instructor will evaluate my progress.

T F DK   5. We will do "timed readings" during every class period.

T F DK   6. In essays, each paragraph should have a topic sentence.

T F DK   7. Some homework will not be graded because it is preparation for the class activity.

T F DK　　　8. Sometimes we will do group activities, so I will have to speak and listen in this class too.

T F DK　　　9. If my birthday is during this term, I should tell the teacher so I can give everyone a gift.

T F DK　　　10. I must bring my bilingual dictionary to class.

T F DK　　　11. I will get one report that shows all my grades at the end of the course.

T F DK　　　12. I should hand in my homework at the beginning of class on the day that it is due.

T F DK　　　13. If I hand in my homework late, it will not be accepted.

T F DK　　　14. In this class I will learn how to plagiarize, which means putting someone else's idea into my own words.

T F DK　　　15. I will fall in love with one of my classmates this term.

T F DK　　　16. If I come to class every day and do all my homework, I am guaranteed a B grade.

T F DK　　　17. We will have an exam during the college's exam week.

T F DK　　　18. The final in-class writing and reading tasks will be worth 8% of the final grade.

T F DK　　　19. If my WPM word-processing speed does not improve, I will fail the course.

T F DK　　　20. If I come to class every day, the instructor guarantees that I will improve my writing.

T F DK　　　21. If I speak my first language during class time, I will have to drop out of the course.

T F DK　　　22. If I am late for class, I should not come because it is a rude interruption.

T F DK　　　23. We will have approximately 5,500 tasks to complete this term.

T F DK　　　24. I will receive a letter grade of A, B, C, D, or F in this course.

T F DK　　　25. If I plagiarize a second time, I will be able to do the assignment again.

Part B: Fill in the blanks.

1. What time does this class meet on Wednesday, and in which classroom? _____

2. What is the instructor's name? _____

3. Where is the instructor's office? _____ When are the instructor's office hours? _____

4. What's the instructor's e-mail address? _____

5. "AWL" probably stands for _____

6. "WPM" probably stands for _____

Limericks for Fun Pronunciation Practice

James M. Perren

Levels	*Beginning to low-intermediate*
Contexts	*Pronunciation or other skills class with an academic focus*
Aims	*Learn about rhyming techniques for pronunciation practice*
Class Time	*35–45 minutes*
Preparation Time	*15–20 minutes*
Resources	*Background information provided on a handout from one teacher resource book:* Teaching American Pronunciation *(Avery & Ehrlich, 1992), and several websites.*
	Handout 1—Two limericks on an 8.5 x 11 sheet of paper or pdf file located on the class Google website for viewing on a mobile device. Limerick A—Irish 'Listowel Writers Week' Winner, Limerick B—'Mouse in Stew Limerick' (Avery & Ehrlich, 1992, p. 213).
	Wikipedia Website: http://en.wikipedia.org/wiki/Limerick_%28poetry%29
	Children's Limerick YouTube Video website: http://www.youtube.com/watch?v=k-rN3DGMCsE
	Worksheet 1—Write a 'Collaborative Limerick' with a partner. Use this framework to match the strict rhyming sequence (scheme) 'AABBA' for guidance. Use this website: http://www.kidzone.ws/poetry/limerick.htm Handouts

Using limericks for studying pronunciation and rhythm fosters student analysis of hearing and production of sounds. Using limericks for language study may also influence grammatical accuracy in academic speech by focusing on phrasing and chunking as components of rhythm.

This activity is designed for use in pronunciation classes as a fun confidence-building exercise that raises awareness of stress prominence in content words. This activity should progress in short phases after the teacher provides background information about limerick creation.

PROCEDURE

1. Provide students with some background information about limericks from Wikipedia: https://en.wikipedia.org/wiki/Limerick_(poetry).

2. Students can be asked to follow a guiding reading sequence to become familiar with the content of the web page (introduction, form, origin, etc.). Begin reading from the top of the Wikipedia Limerick page (introduction), paying specific attention to the information regarding the strict rhyming sequence (scheme) AABBA and the use of humor.

3. Show the YouTube video of the "The Limerick Song" (www.youtube.com /watch?v=k-rN3DGMCsE) and ask students to pay attention and take notes. This video clip can be repeated and shared with students on the class website.

4. Next, organize students' chairs into two rows facing each other. Each student must read their limerick to their partner (examples A and B) from the handout in Appendix A. They have only 2 minutes (1 minute per student) for completion.

5. Instruct limerick partners to use the worksheet in Appendix B to write their own pair Collaborative Limerick using the Wikipedia information about the contents.

6. Share the Collaborative Limericks with the class by posting on the class website or passing them around in a larger "super group" limerick-sharing class activity, or have students turn them in for grading.

CAVEATS AND OPTIONS

1. You may also point out that limericks can be associated with other language purposes, but the lesson focus is socially appropriate humor.

2. Step 4 can be repeated by having students stand up and move down the row to be matched with a new limerick partner if time allows. Make sure that students move on again after a minute.

3. Step 4 can also require listener students to take notes depending on the amount of class time available. You can also require one writer/speaker to work with two listeners who each must take notes.

4. Technology can also be utilized by having student listeners use mobile devices to type what they hear as a dictation activity. Writers/speakers can also record their speaking with a device such as a DVR or smartphone voice app for reflection.

5. As a follow-up activity, students can select their own video about limericks from the Up Next menu choices available to the right of "The Limerick Song" YouTube page. They can show the video clip to their partners or in groups, analyzing the content, reasons for selecting the clip, and importance for English learning. This can be used as an activity for students who have completed the Collaborative Limerick writing task quickly (from Step 5) and require additional learning tasks.

REFERENCES AND FURTHER READING

Avery, P., & Ehrlich, S. (1992). *Teaching American pronunciation*. Oxford, England: Oxford University Press.

Collins, B., & Mees, I. M. (2008). *Practical phonetics and phonology*. New York, NY: Routledge.

Field, J. (2005). Intelligibility and the listener: The role of lexical stress. *TESOL Quarterly*, *39*, 399–424.

Jenkins, J. (2004). Research in teaching pronunciation and intonation. *Annual Review of Applied Linguistics*, *24*, 109–125.

Levis, J. M. (2005). Changing contexts and shifting paradigms in pronunciation teaching. *TESOL Quarterly*, *39*, 369–378.

APPENDIX A: *Handout—Two Limericks: Examples of Limerick Structure*

Limerick A: Irish "Listowel Writers Week" Winner

1. Writing a limerick's absurd,

2. Line one and line five rhyme in word,

3. And just as you've reckoned

4. They rhyme with the second;

5. The fourth line must rhyme with the third.

Limerick B: "Mouse in Stew" Limerick

1. There was an old lady from Crewe,

2. Who found a large mouse in her stew,

3. Said the waiter, "Don't shout,

4. And wave it about,

5. Or the rest will be wanting one, too!"

APPENDIX B: *Worksheet—Writing a Collaborative Limerick With a Partner*

Part A: Introduction to Limericks

Name: _____

A limerick is a silly poem with five lines. They are often funny or nonsensical. Limericks were made famous by Edward Lear, a famous author who wrote the "book of nonsense" in the 1800s. This was an entire book of silly limericks.

How to write a limerick:

- The first, second, and fifth lines rhyme with each other and have the same number of syllables (typically eight or nine).

- The third and fourth lines rhyme with each other and have the same number of syllables (typically five or six).

- Limericks often start with the line "There was once . . ." or "there was. . . ."

- Example of an 8, 8, 5, 5, 8 syllable limerick:

  1. There once was a wonderful star

  2. who thought she would go very far

  3. until she fell down

  4. and looked like a clown

  5. she knew she would never go far.

Part B: Now You Can Write Your Own Limerick

There once was a . . .

_____ 8 syllables

_____ 8 syllables

_____ 5 syllables

_____ 5 syllables

_____ 8 syllables

Sorry, My Dog Ate My Homework: Using Humor as an Apology Strategy

Anne Pomerantz

Levels	Advanced
Contexts	ESL or EFL; adolescents and adults
Aims	Learn forms and functions of common apology strategies
	See how apology strategies can be done in a humorous key to manage relationships
Class Time	1.5–2 hours (can be done over 2 days)
Preparation Time	30 minutes
Resources	Whiteboard
	Chart paper
	Markers
	One or more videos of humorous apologies
	Situation cards (see Appendix)

Knowing how to apologize forms part of one's communicative competence. Research on apologies has shown that this speech act tends to be realized through the use of one or more of the following strategies (Cohen & Olshtain, 1981; see also Ishihara & Cohen, 2010):

- expression of apology (e.g., "I'm sorry")

- acknowledgement of responsibility (e.g., "It's my fault")

- account or explanation (e.g., "I thought the payment was due next week")

- offer of repair (e.g., "I will call the company to explain")

- promise of nonrecurrence (e.g., "It won't happen again")

Yet apologies serve as more than just expressions of contrition. They also help to mitigate tensions and to restore goodwill between people when something has gone wrong. This lesson introduces learners to the forms and functions of common apology strategies and shows how these strategies might be done in a humorous key to manage relationships (Bell & Pomerantz, 2016).

PROCEDURE

1. Begin the class by asking students to brainstorm some situations in which they might apologize. Then ask them to generate at least 10 expressions that they tend to use in such situations (e.g., *I'm sorry, My bad*). Write expressions on the whiteboard.

2. Introduce students to the five apology strategies listed above. Then, in small groups, ask them to categorize the 10 expressions they have just generated accordingly (e.g., *I'm sorry* = expression of apology; *My bad* = acknowledgment of responsibility). Direct students to write their responses on chart paper. Nominate two or three groups to share their results with the class and discuss any points of contrast. Also, note any expressions that don't fall into the five categories and ask students to reflect on why this might be the case.

3. Invite students to consider when and why people use particular apology strategies. Some possible questions include the following: What is the purpose of adding an account or explanation to an expression of apology? When do you make a promise of nonrecurrence? How do you feel when someone makes an offer of repair?

4. Highlight that apologies serve as more than just expressions of contrition. They are also used to manage relationships. Apologies can help to release tensions and restore rapport. Humor can also serve similar functions. To illustrate this point, show a video of an apology sequence that shows one of the strategies done in a humorous key. (One example is this short scene from the movie *A Fish Called Wanda*: www.youtube.com/watch?v=m7mIy97_rlo.) Ask students to comment on how the use of humor functions in the video. Some possible questions include the following: What's different about this apology? Why do you think the apologizer chose to use humor? How did the recipient react to the use of humor in this apology? What do you think will happen next time these people interact with one another?

5. Put students into small groups. Ask each group to come up with three situations in which a humorous apology would diffuse tensions and lead to better rapport between interlocutors and three situations in which it would not. Direct students to record their situations on chart paper. Ask three or four groups to share their examples and the reasoning behind their examples with the class. Discuss these as a class. Note points of convergence and divergence across different class members' perceptions about the appropriateness of humorous apologies in particular situations. Remind students that attitudes toward humor vary both interculturally and intraculturally.

6. Divide the class into pairs. Give each pair two or three situation cards that involve making apologies (see Appendix). Ask students to decide which

situations warrant serious apologies and which might be open to the use of humor. Then give students an opportunity to practice acting out the situations on the cards.

7. Invite two or three pairs of students to act out their situations in front of the class. Ask the class to comment on whether they thought the use (or non-use) of humor in these situations was successful in terms of releasing tensions and restoring rapport.

CAVEATS AND OPTIONS

1. If students have trouble coming up with 10 expressions, you can supply additional examples.

2. You do not need to introduce all five apology strategies during the course of the lesson. You may limit the focus to two or three strategies.

3. If humor is not a typical feature of apology strategies in the students' first language, you may want to offer more examples of humorous apology sequences before moving on to Steps 5–7.

REFERENCES AND FURTHER READING

Bell, N., & Pomerantz, A. (2016). *Humor in the classroom: A guide for language teachers and educational researchers.* New York, NY: Routledge.

Cohen, A. D., & Olshtain, E. (1981). Developing a measure of sociocultural competence: The case of apology. *Language Learning, 31*(1), 113–134.

Ishihara, N., & Cohen, A. D. (2010). *Teaching and learning pragmatics: Where language and culture meet.* Harlow, England: Pearson.

APPENDIX: *Possible Situations*

You arrived late to work. Apologize to your supervisor for keeping a client waiting for 30 minutes.

You promised to meet a friend for coffee, but forgot about the date. Apologize to your friend for not showing up.

You turned an assignment in after the due date. Apologize to your professor for the late submission.

You borrowed $20 from a friend. Three months go by before you finally return the money. Apologize to your friend for the delay.

Trivia Contests in English Classes: Points for Interesting and Funny Answers

Barnaby Ralph

Levels	Tertiary
Aims	Work on listening skills, speculation, imagination, humor, small-group interaction, and plenary discussion
	Develop and contextualize vocabulary
Class Time	45–90 minutes
Preparation Time	1–2 hours for research and question writing
Resources	Blackboard or whiteboard
	A prize (optional)
	"Buzzers" (optional)

A number of pedagogically valuable aspects are apparent in this activity. The first is that students are encouraged to make interesting guesses and speculate, and can gain a high score without ever coming close to a correct answer. It encourages them "to interact, to perform, and especially to think" (Minchew, 2001, p. 67). The second is that students are able to succeed by making people laugh, including the teacher. This allows for humor based on both teacher and student input, a pairing that has been identified as positive for coping strategies (Torok, McMorris, & Lin, 2004, p. 15). The humor generated in this activity comes largely from the students, neatly sidestepping the frustration of missing a joke made by the teacher, as noted by Wulf (2010, p. 156) and others. Such an approach would help to "involve students in the process" (Minchew, 2001, p. 60). This leads to the third point, which is the reduction of classroom anxiety via the use of humor, an effect explored by Garner (2006, p. 180) and others. There is also the additional benefit of enhancing a positive view of the teacher from students' perspective (Bryant, Comisky, Crane, & Zillmann, 1980).

PROCEDURE

1. Put students into groups. Generally, groups of four to eight work well.

2. Begin by explaining the rules. You ask a question and groups have to try to guess the answer within a predetermined period of time (usually a few minutes). They can discuss, then may make an attempt at the question. Everything must be done in English.

   Scoring

   Correct: 5 points

   Answer that generates laughter: 5 points

   Interesting but wrong: 3 points

   Uninteresting but wrong: *Minus* 3 points

   You decide the scores. Groups may answer more than once in the allotted time.

3. Distribute "buzzers" of some sort, such as whistles, horns, or other noise-makers. Simply using something that makes an unusual or startling noise can itself be a source of amusement.

4. The group with the most points at the end is the winner and gets the prize.

CAVEATS AND OPTIONS

1. Sometimes, one group might try to dominate by offering many answers to questions. In that case, limit the number of responses to one or two per group. Also, do not allow smartphones and other such devices.

2. Buzzers provide more opportunity for laughter when they are noisemaking devices. Asking students to make sounds with their voices can fall flat.

3. Scoring can be modified to suit your aims, and the level of questions can be adjusted. Obscure questions that students have little chance of answering correctly are fun. An ideal question is easy to understand, but hard to guess the correct answer. A sample question, plus actual responses, is given in the Appendix.

REFERENCES AND FURTHER READING

Bryant, J., Comisky, P. W., Crane, J. S., & Zillmann, D. (1980). Relationship between college teachers' use of humor in the classroom and students' evaluations of their teachers. *Journal of Educational Psychology, 72,* 511–519.

Garner, R. L. (2006). Humor in pedagogy: How ha-ha can lead to aha! *College Teaching, 54*(1), 177–180.

McMahon, M. (1999). Are we having fun yet? Humor in the English class. *The English Journal, 88*(4), 70–72.

Minchew, S. S. (2001). Teaching English with humor and fun. *American Secondary Education, 30*(1), 58–70.

Pomerantz, A., & Bell, N. D. (2011). Humor as safe house in the foreign language classroom. *Modern Language Journal, 95*, 148–161.

Torok, S. E., McMorris, R. F., & Lin, W. (2004). Is humor an appreciated teaching tool? Perceptions of professors' teaching styles and use of humor. *College Teaching, 52*(1), 14–20.

Wulf, D. (2010). A humor competence curriculum. *TESOL Quarterly, 44*, 155–169.

Yair, G. (2008). Can we administer the scholarship of teaching? Lessons from outstanding professors in higher education. *Higher Education, 55*, 447–459.

APPENDIX: *Sample Question, Answers, and Student Responses (with scoring)*

Question: Which country has the *second* most productive film industry?

Actual answer: Nigeria, producing about 50 films a week as of 2015. Known colloquially as Nollywood, it is second in output only to India's Bollywood.

Answer 1: We think the first most productive must be America, so we think the second is India. (Obvious but wrong, so –3 points*)

Answer 2: We think it is YouTube. There must be thousands of films made every day. (3 points, as this is interesting and has some justification, but YouTube is not a country!)

Answer 3: It's Japan, because we film ourselves doing stupid things all the time with our smartphones. (5 points, as the other students laughed at this answer)

Answer 4: We think it's the Vatican, which is the smallest country in the world. Even if they only make one film a year, then they must still produce the most relative to population. (Interesting and clever, so 3 points)

*Note that, with additional justification or some humor, this answer could gain a positive score.

Acting Out: Participial Adjectives

Julie Riddlebarger

Levels	Intermediate
Contexts	All
Aims	Develop understanding of and use participial (-ed/-ing adjectives) appropriately in a humorous way
Class Time	15–20 minutes
Preparation Time	10–20 minutes
Resources	Computer and printer, or paper and pen
	Card stock and laminator (optional)

This activity gives students a fun and engaging way to work with -ed/-ing adjectives, through drama and physical movement. Many ESL/EFL students struggle with these adjectives, often mixing them up. With this activity, students act out one of a pair of -ed/-ing adjectives, while others guess at the word. If you model with humor, students will probably follow your lead!

PROCEDURE

1. Make a list of -ed/-ing adjectives (see Appendix for ideas), including especially ones your students have misused in the past. Put one of each pair on a card. Cards can be computer-printed or handwritten. Lamination will preserve cards for future use.

2. Explain the activity: Students get a card with an -ed/-ing adjective on it. They have 1 minute to act out the -ed/-ing adjectives. Classmates have to guess the word being acted out.

3. Demonstrate (or have a student demonstrate) the activity. *Boring* is always a favorite word for students to call a teacher!

4. Pass out the cards. Give students no more than 1–2 minutes to plan.

5. Students take turns acting out their words.

6. Other students have to guess the correct participial adjective. For example, if Student A slumps in his chair, looks around the room, and yawns repeatedly, Student B might say, "He is bored." Similarly, Student B might pretend to be a clown, making the class laugh, and Student C could say, "She is amusing."

CAVEATS AND OPTIONS

1. Instead of only one pair of -ed/-ing adjectives, put both on the card and allow students to select which one they want to act out.

2. Choose words that your students know. You may also want to project the list of words on the board or refer students to the word wall, if you have one.

3. In a large class, put students in teams and give them some time to plan a strategy. Make sure all students have a chance to participate, though—everyone on the team should take part in the acting, which may become a skit.

4. Be careful with the time; consider using a timer to keep students from going over 1 minute.

5. Make the activity competitive by giving points for guessing the word first or having teams compete against each other for successfully acting out the most words.

REFERENCES AND FURTHER READING

Braunstein, L. (2006). Adult ESL learners' attitude toward movement (TPR) and drama (TPR storytelling) in the classroom. *CATESOL Journal, 18*(1), 7–20.

Rieg, S. A., & Paquette, K. R. (2009). Using drama and movement to enhance English language learners' literacy development. *Journal of Instructional Psychology, 36*(2), 148–154.

Royka, J. G. (2002). Overcoming the fear of using drama in English language teaching. *Internet TESL Journal, 8*(6). Retrieved from http://iteslj.org

APPENDIX: *List of Possible -ed/-ing Adjective Pairs*

amazed/amazing

amused/amusing

annoyed/annoying

bored/boring

confused/confusing

depressed/depressing

disappointed/disappointing

discouraged/discouraging

disturbed/disturbing

embarrassed/embarrassing

encouraged/encouraging

excited/exciting

exhausted/exhausting

frightened/frightening

frustrated/frustrating

horrified/horrifying

inspired/inspiring

interested/interesting

irritated/irritating

overwhelmed/overwhelming

puzzled/puzzling

relaxed/relaxing

surprised/surprising

tired/tiring

worried/worrying

Exploring Humor and Memory

Jacob Schnickel

Levels	*Intermediate to advanced*
Contexts	*University*
Aims	*Develop autonomy and awareness of the learning process*
Class Time	*Variable*
Preparation Time	*Variable*
Resources	*List of target vocabulary words*

The value of this activity is rooted in the notion that humor has a positive impact on memory (see, e.g., Lippman & Dunn, 2000; Schmidt, 1994). Put differently, it seems that when events are associated with humor, they are more memorable. In the field of language education, Stevick (1996) writes that "any elements of vividness, bizarreness or humor will tie in with some of the learner's deeper and more general needs. . . . The resulting networks may be richer as well as more complex, and may therefore remain effective longer" (p. 124).

A key feature of this activity is framing it as an experiment, an investigation into the way memory works in general and, more specifically, the ways in which humor may impact memory. This may be a refreshing change in perspective for some students, and it may lead to more metacognitive forays that lead ultimately to more effective language learning.

PROCEDURE

1. Explain to the learners that they are going to investigate the impact of humor on their ability to recall vocabulary words. Invite them, in small groups or as a class, to explore possible connections between humor and memory. If the group can handle this in English, guide them to do so. If not, and if it is a homogenous group, invite them to speak in their first language.

2. Explain that learners are going to create humorous associations with target vocabulary words as a means of assessing the impact of humor on memory. Students will likely be familiar with the concept of using mnemonic devices to aid memory. Here, however, stress that the humorousness of the

mnemonic is essential to the research focus. Demonstrate the use of humorous mnemonics so that everyone is clear on the concept. The following, my own example, illustrates the connection between humor and memory.

> The Japanese word for "arrest" is *taiho*. My daughter thought the Seven Dwarves, rather than "heigh-ho, heigh-ho," were singing, "*taiho, taiho*." The image, which to me was hilarious and inexplicably appropriate, of the dwarves being carted off to prison, all in handcuffs and singing, burned a new Japanese word into my memory.

3. Guide learners to begin creating their own humorous mnemonics for some vocabulary words they are learning. Remind them that humor is the key to the experiment. Based on class size, number of target vocabulary words, and personal preference, you can decide how to organize this phase of the activity. For instance, small groups could be assigned different sets of words, the mnemonics for which could be shared with other groups at a later time. Alternatively, each group could have the same set to work with. These conversations should be lively, with a good amount of laughter.

4. Once the humorous mnemonics have been established, inform students that there will be a quiz on the vocabulary words. Be sure to frame the quiz as being an important part of the experiment. Ask students to study the words with the memory cues they created and to log their study sessions in their notebooks. You may choose to specify the length and frequency of these sessions (e.g., 10 minutes every day until the quiz), again being sure to stress how this measure makes for a more tightly controlled experiment.

5. On the specified date, administer the quiz, and check them immediately. Have students discuss the effectiveness of the humorous mnemonics in small groups, and then invite learners to share salient points with the whole class.

6. To conclude the activity, have learners write about their experiences with the humorous mnemonic experiment in a learning journal or as a single assignment. This can be an unstructured assignment, or you can give learners prompts such as the following:

- How does the use of humorous mnemonics compare to your previous method of memorizing vocabulary words?

- What did you learn about the way memory works through this experiment?

- Can you think of a way to improve the humorous mnemonic technique?

- Can you think of other ways to use humor to learn English more effectively?

CAVEATS AND OPTIONS

For an additional level of complexity, perhaps if you have an understanding of statistics, a rating system can be employed, as in Schmidt (1994) and Lippman and Dunn (2000). For this variation, have students assign a humor value of 1 to 5, with 1 being *not funny at all* and 5 being *very funny*. Once a reliable rating has been established—through group discussion, survey responses, or some other method—students, with your assistance, can determine the extent to which humor rating impacts vocabulary learning.

REFERENCES AND FURTHER READING

Lippman, L. G., & Dunn, M. L. (2000). Contextual connections within puns: Effects on perceived humor and memory. *Journal of General Psychology*, *127*(2), 185–197.

Schmidt, S. R. (1994). Effects of humor on sentence memory. *Journal of Experimental Psychology: Learning, Memory, and Cognition*, *20*(4), 953–967.

Stevick, E. W. (1996). *Memory, meaning, and method: Some psychological perspectives on language learning* (2nd ed.). Boston, MA: Heinle & Heinle.

Practicing Imperatives Through Company Warning Labels

Elena Shvidko

Levels	Beginning, low-intermediate
Contexts	ESL and EFL
Aims	Compose positive and negative imperative forms
Class Time	30 minutes
Preparation Time	1 hour
Resources	Pictures with humorous, absurd, or silly company warning labels that have imperative forms
	Several small items (e.g., clothes, household items, food packages, toys, office supplies)
	Computer and projector, or paper

Imperative forms are probably one of the least challenging principles of English grammar. This gives teachers the opportunity to design a variety of activities and games that achieve the learning objective without putting learners under cognitive pressure.

This activity can be used as practice, that is, after imperative forms have been introduced. By using humorous warning labels, the teacher creates a positive and relaxed atmosphere in class and helps learners practice imperative forms in a fun and interactive task.

PROCEDURE

1. Before class, do an Internet search to find several pictures of funny warning labels that have imperative forms (e.g., www.womansday.com/life/11-funny -fine-print-warnings-114710), or you can prepare pictures with labels by using the following examples: http://rinkworks.com/said/warnings.shtml. Prepare PowerPoint slides: one picture with its label per slide. If PowerPoint is not accessible in your setting, print them out.

2. Show learners the pictures (either on the projector or on paper copies). Give them time to read the labels. (There will be some laughs at this stage of the activity!)

3. Draw learners' attention to the grammatical aspect of these warning labels—negative and positive imperatives.

4. Divide the class into pairs or small groups and give each group one of the items that you have prepared for this activity. Ask learners to create a humorous warning label for their object. Encourage them to be creative. If time allows, you can ask learners to create two labels for their object: one with a positive and the other one with a negative imperative construction.

5. Have learners present their warning labels to the whole class.

CAVEATS AND OPTIONS

1. For homework, ask learners to create a humorous label for one school or classroom item (e.g., textbook, pencil, piece of chalk, teacher's desk) and bring it to class (along with a picture of the object). In the next class, you can collaboratively create a poster (or use a bulletin board if available) with their labels. If printing is not easily accessible to learners, they can draw a picture of their object.

2. You can also use humorous warning labels with a group of advanced learners, for example, when you teach a lesson on business. After showing learners the labels, let them share their opinions as to why some companies and manufacturers of consumer products come up with such absurd and silly warning labels for their products.

REFERENCES AND FURTHER READING

Warning labels can border on absurd. (1995, October 3). *Lakeland Register.* Retrieved from http://news.google.com/newspapers?nid=1346&dat=1995 1003&id=DPEvAAAAIBAJ&sjid=-PwDAAAAIBAJ&pg=4019,3018207

Humorous Advice for Unusual Problems

Kristin Tenney, Zuzana Tomaš, and Ariel Robinson

Levels	*High beginner, intermediate, advanced*
Contexts	*Any age*
Aims	*Engage in reading and grammar practice relevant to the function of advising*
Class Time	*20–40 minutes*
Preparation Time	*5 minutes*
Resources	*Sample problems (Appendix A)*
	Advice tweet handout strips (Appendix B)
	Tape

The use of humor in teaching allows second language (L2) learners to make great developmental strides linguistically and socially (e.g., Bell, 2009; Torok, McMorris, & Lin, 2004). The use of humor is particularly helpful when teaching grammar, an area that teachers often struggle to contextualize in meaningful ways. Humor provides a viable vehicle to situate grammar points in an engaging context, thus increasing learner motivation and interest in the lesson.

PROCEDURE

1. Activate L2 learners' prior knowledge on the concept of giving advice in order to engage students in practicing this useful linguistic structure (e.g., *you should*; *you ought to*; *if I were you, I would* . . .)

2. Before introducing the steps for the activity, ensure that students are familiar with the hashtag (#) symbol that is used in popular social media.

3. Using the board or projector, display an exaggerated problem that is one to two sentences long (maximum of 140 characters) from either Appendix A or your imagination.

4. Distribute the advice tweet handout (Appendix B) to each student then discuss possible advice students could give.

5. Model how to use the advice tweet handout. First, select a piece of advice discussed and write it on the board. Then, ask the students which vocabulary words, idioms, or sayings the advice reminds them of. Place those words or sayings after the hashtag symbol (e.g., #helpful).

6. Have students get into pairs. Display at least three to four more unusual problems, and have the pairs create advice tweets. Each advice tweet should be at least one to two sentences long and have at least two hashtags filled out with related vocabulary words, idioms, or sayings.

7. Once the pairs finish writing advice for each problem, have pairs combine to make groups of four. As a group, students must decide which of their advice tweets is the best for each of the problems (the funniest, the most appropriate, etc.).

8. After they have decided on the best advice tweet, the group tapes the winner on the board upside down (so the other groups cannot read it) next to the problem.

9. After all the groups have contributed, read the advice tweets aloud to the students. Ask students which advice tweet was their favorite and why.

CAVEATS AND OPTIONS

Instead of paper strips, if all students have access to a Twitter-enabled device, you can create a closed Twitter group where students can respond to the problems you create.

REFERENCES AND FURTHER READING

Bell, N. D. (2009). Learning about and through humor in the second language classroom. *Language Teaching Research*, *13*, 241–258.

Torok, S. E., McMorris, R. F., & Lin, W.-C. (2004). Is humor an appreciated teaching tool? Perceptions of professors' teaching styles and use of humor. *College Teaching*, *52*(1), 14–20).

APPENDIX A: *Sample Problems*

Option A provides a statement. Option B requires the student to provide original written advice to a situation posted on social media.

1A: You and three friends run into a bear in the woods. You are the only one holding food. What should you do?

1B: Oh my goodness. I am in the woods with my friends and we just saw a bear. I am holding a plate of hamburgers. What should I do? #scared #help

2A: Your friend calls and tells you that their stomach hurts after eating 12 candy bars. What advice would you give?

2B: My friend just ate 12 candy bars and is holding his stomach in pain. What should I do? #regret

3A: Your friend wants to buy a gold collar for her dog and a dog house made of diamonds, but her parents gave her only enough money for one. What should she do?

3B: My cute puppy wants a gold collar and a diamond dog house. My parents are mean and will not give me enough money to buy both. #problem

4A: Your piece of cake is bigger than your friend's piece. What should you do?

4B: My piece of cake is bigger than my friend's. She is mad. What should I do? #piece of cake

5A: Your friend wants to sleep for 9 hours instead of the recommended 8, but he is worried that he will not graduate if he spends too much time sleeping. What should he do?

5B: I am so tired. I want to sleep for 9 hours instead of 8 hours. Will I die or get sick if I get more than the recommended amount of sleep? #curious #exhausted

6A: Your friend calls and tells you her parents found out she has been keeping 12 cats in their basement. Her mother hates cats. What should she do?

6B: My parents finally found the 12 cats I have in the basement. Mom hates cats and wants to get rid of them. They are so cute though! #cats out of the bag

APPENDIX B: *Advice Tweet Layout*

_____

_____

_____

_____

\#_____   \#_____

\#_____   \#_____

....

Reluctant Parents

Gordon West

Levels	*Intermediate to advanced*
Contexts	*Middle school to adult*
Aims	*Develop negotiation ability, especially proposals and refusals*
Class Time	*20–30 minutes (depending on number of students)*
Preparation Time	*5–10 minutes*
Resources	*Request cards*

This activity is intended to give students speaking practice in a situation that mimics a real-life situation and forces them to use language to negotiate. It is inspired by theater games created by Augusto Boal (1992). This activity, along with quickly becoming hilarious by creating unlikely scenarios, uses turn taking to force students to think creatively in English.

PROCEDURE

1. Prepare request cards. These should be things that children would request from their parents. They can range from the plausible to the highly unlikely (e.g., a pet, a car, spending money). The humor comes in making cards that are less likely or unexpected (e.g., a pet crocodile, permission to go on a date with a celebrity, a roll of toilet paper).

2. In class, explain the rules of the game, which are that a child has two parents who are very strict and must refuse the child's request. They must take turns, meaning that if one speaks, that person cannot speak again until the other two have spoken.

3. Give students request cards. They have a few minutes to silently prepare what they will say when they request the item from their parents.

4. Select three students to begin the role-play. Two students play the parents, and one plays the child. Any student may begin the role-play. The child may make the request first, or the parents may welcome the child into the room and ask what they want.

5. The parents of the child must continue to refuse the child's request, which should become more and more desperate, until given a signal from the teacher or until they feel they can no longer refuse.

6. Once the child's request has finally been granted, students rotate. The child becomes one parent, the first parent takes the second parent's role, and the second parent rotates out. A new student is chosen to play the child. In this way, each student has an opportunity to play all three parts. They also have a chance to get "revenge" by being a strict parent after having played the child.

CAVEATS AND OPTIONS

1. In most cases, you should begin the role-play as the child and rotate through all three roles to give a model for the students to follow. The more ridiculous the situations are and the more you play up the part, the more hilarity will ensue and the more students will get into playing the parts.

2. You may want to get students to create the request cards during class by asking them to write on simple notecards something silly for a young person to ask their parents for. You might want to give some examples. Toilet paper, for instance, becomes quite funny because no reasonable parent would deny a request for something like this. If students make the cards, depending on age, you should screen them for inappropriate items before the game by simply collecting them and reading them before redistributing them.

3. Family configurations should not be limited to mother, father, and child. There should always be three—two authority figures and a child—but students should be encouraged to alter the configurations as they feel comfortable or as fits their context or experience. For example, there may also be mother, mother, and child or grandparent, father, and child configurations.

REFERENCES AND FURTHER READING

Boal, A. (1992). *Games for actors and non-actors*. New York, NY: Routledge.

APPENDIX: *Sample Dialogue*

Child: Mom, dad. Um, I have a question for you.

(Parents are pretending to watch TV.)

Mom: What is it, honey?

Child: Can I have a pet crocodile?

Dad: What?! NO!

Child: Please, I really want one!

Mom: No, he would eat our dog!

Child: But the dog is so boring. We need a new pet.

Dad: Who will take care of the crocodile? You never walk the dog now. No.

Mom: Yes, I always have to walk the dog. Will you walk the crocodile? How will it get exercise?

Child: Please, please, please! I promise I will walk the crocodile, and feed the crocodile, and do everything!

Dad: We live in a tiny apartment. How can it live here?

Child: I will build a pool on the roof.

Mom: You can't do that! What about our neighbors?

Child: They will love playing with the crocodile! It can be everyone's pet!

Dad: No way, it's too dangerous.

Child: (begging on knees) Please, just a small crocodile, a baby crocodile! I will take care of it. I will build the pool. I will talk to the neighbors, and I will feed it every day so it is not hungry. Then it will be safe. Please! If it is trouble, I will take the crocodile back to the pet store.

Mom: Well, maybe, since you really want it . . .

Dad: One week. You can try it for one week, but only a baby crocodile.

Child: Wow! Thank you so much! I'm going right now!

Unusual Greetings

Jocelyn Wright

Levels	Any
Aims	*Break the ice*
	Develop awareness of various ways to perform greetings as well as confidence and flexibility using them
Class Time	*5–10 minutes*
Preparation Time	*0–5 minutes*
Resources	*Greeting prompts*

Greetings, which I take to include salutations and possibly introductions and small talk, are notable in spoken discourse because of their prominence and social importance (Eisenstein Ebsworth, Bodman, & Carpenter, 1995). Eisenstein Ebsworth et al. (1995) identify them as complex and creative because they "involv[e] a wide range of [verbal and nonverbal] behaviors and a sensitivity to many situational and psychosocial variables" (p. 89). Their research shows that language learners seem to have a limited repertoire of greetings, or at least that they do not show great ease in using them in appropriate ways. Informal register, speedy greetings, and prosody are areas learners especially seem to struggle with. The fun suggestions provided here can be used to develop flexibility in using greetings and also engage students at the beginning of class. Humorous greetings can be done individually, taking turns in front of a class (if group dynamics are good), in pairs, or in groups, while seated or mingling.

PROCEDURE

1. Choose (or have a students choose) a prompt and assign it to the class.

   - prosody: Greet each other using only sounds, by not opening your lips. Others interpret.

   - prosody: Greet each other emotionally or as if you were robots.

   - audibility/intelligibility: Greet each other, whispering, shouting, speaking quickly, speaking really slowly, speaking with a low voice, speaking with a high pitch, etc.

- intensive/extensive speech: Greet each other as if you were in a hurry or as if you had not seen each other in a while and wanted to get caught up.

- nonverbal communication: Greet each other using only body language. Others interpret.

- syntax: Greet each other, saying everything backward (e.g., Morning good! Today great feel I! You about how?)

- question syntax: Greet each other, finishing each turn with a question. Keep the conversation going as long as possible.

- register: Greet each other, taking on roles (e.g., as if you were a queen or a hip-hop artist).

- functions: Greet each other with a pickup line, a funny request, a white lie, an unusual invitation, etc.

- gender awareness: Greet each other as if you were a member of the opposite sex.

- cultural awareness: Greet each other as if you were from another culture.

- culture: Greet each other with a song, researched in advance (e.g., "Good Morning" from *Singing in the Rain*, "Hello, Goodbye" by the Beatles), or prepare your own.

- culture: Greet each other with a joke.

- motivation: Greet each other with words of encouragement.

- creativity: Greet each other, saying something you have never said before.

2. Students greet each other according to the instructions in the prompt.

CAVEATS AND OPTIONS

1. Students randomly select prompts and perform greetings.

2. After conversing, students guess which prompts the others chose.

3. For greater challenge, specific scenarios could be assigned. Students have to guess the details of the situation (see examples in Appendix).

REFERENCE AND FURTHER READING

Eisenstein Ebsworth, M., Bodman, J., & Carpenter, M. (1995). Cross-cultural realization of greetings in American English. In S. Gass & J. Neu (Eds.), *Speech acts across cultures: Challenges to communication in a second language* (pp. 9–107). New York, NY: Mouton de Gruyter.

APPENDIX: *Sample Situational Greeting Prompts*

1. Students perform these situations without explicitly stating the words on the cards:

Greet your partner(s) as if a baby were sleeping in the next room. (Goal: to practice volume)
Greet your partner(s) as if you were in a noisy club. (Goal: to practice volume)
Greet your partner(s) as if you were in a rush to get to an important meeting. (Goal: to practice speed)
Greet your partner(s) as if you they were aliens from another planet who only understand slow English. (Goal: to practice speed)
Greet your partner(s) as if you were a robot. (Goal: to raise awareness about stress and intonation)
Greet your partner(s) as if you had a bad case of laryngitis (lost your voice). (Goal: to raise awareness about nonverbal communication)

2. Other students guess the details of the situation.

Note: The above greetings are excellent as a warm-up activity on presentation day.

Part II

Wordplay and Puns

Scientific Conference: Who's Coming?

Jean L. Arnold

Levels	*Advanced*
Contexts	*University, especially fun for science majors*
Aims	*Interact with classmates*
	Use scientific and other cultural knowledge and deductive reasoning to find partners
	Develop awareness about vocabulary used to introduce reported speech
	Have fun
Class Time	*15–20 minutes*
Preparation Time	*2 minutes*
Resources	*Strips of paper with the subject separated from the rest of the sentence (see Appendix)*

Getting students up and moving increases their energy level. This partner-match activity is great for getting students to mingle with other class members whom they might not yet have interacted with much. Recent brain research states that exercise not only is good for the body, but "makes the brain function at its best" (Ratey, cited in Randolph, 2013). Additionally, engaging students' background knowledge with these examples of famous scientists and allowing them to help each other discover why these statements are funny increases their confidence in reading between the lines and expands their English vocabulary. Also, the challenge of solving a word puzzle is enjoyable. Thus, this activity uses several of the five Es that McPherron and Randolph (2014) encourage teachers to use in the classroom: emotions, examples, energy, exercise, and euphoria.

This activity also encourages students to talk with everyone since they don't know who will have the information they need. Increasingly, students interact with each other less and less. It's common these days to see classrooms full of students fully engrossed in their own mobile device, waiting for the teacher to arrive. This activity helps students interact with each other in a nonthreatening way and forge connections with their peers. The hope is that they will increase real-life communication and continue to engage their peers with more frequency.

PROCEDURE

1. Print the sentences in the Appendix and cut sentences so they're on individual strips. When you know how many students are in class that day, snip enough sentences in two so that each student will get a slip with half of a sentence on it.

2. To introduce the topic of the scientific conference, ask students to name some famous scientists or inventors and what theories or devices they developed or discovered.

3. Next, explain the procedure of the partner match to students: They will each draw a slip of paper that contains half of a sentence about a person, usually an inventor, and a reference to that person's creation. Students have to stand up, go around the class, say to other students what their slip of paper says, and find the person who has their match.

4. After finding their match, have students sit with their newfound partner and discuss the sentence, discover why it's funny, and prepare to explain it to the class (e.g. "Newton said . . . he'd drop in" is funny because Newton discovered the theory of gravity, purportedly when an apple fell from a tree under which he was sitting).

5. Have each pair tell the class what their sentence is and explain the humor of the statement.

CAVEATS AND OPTIONS

1. In the sentences that have reporting verbs, you may want to ask students to notice the verb tense used. You could ask why the verb tense is different in the direct quote from the reported speech examples.

2. Lower level students can be catered to by changing the content of the sentences used. For example, another humorous partner-matching activity could be created with ironic profession/name combinations. Some real examples: Sue Yoo, lawyer in New York; Storm Field, retired meteorologist; Sgt. Law Power, Royal Canadian Mounted Police officer; Gary Wood, creator of custom-made furniture; Cardinal Sin, pastor; Dr. Russell Brain, neurologist; Richard Rich, business teacher.

REFERENCES AND FURTHER READING

McPherron, P., & Randolph, P. T. (2014). *Cat got your tongue? Recent research and classroom practices for teaching idioms to English learners around the world.* Alexandria, VA: TESOL.

Randolph, P. T. (2013, Summer). The magic of movement: Exercise's phenomenal impact on the language learner's brain. *ITBE Link.* Retrieved from http://www.itbe.org/newsletter.php

APPENDIX: *Scientific Conference Activity Strips*

Newton said	he'd drop in.
Descartes said	he'd think about it.
Ohm	resisted the idea.
Boyle said	he was under too much pressure.
Darwin said	he'd wait to see what evolved.
Pierre and Marie Curie	radiated enthusiasm.
Volta was	electrified at the prospect.
Pavlov positively	drooled at the thought.
Ampere was	worried he wasn't current.
Audubon said	he'd have to wing it.
Edison thought	it would be illuminating.
Einstein said	it would be relatively easy to attend.
Archimedes was	buoyant at the thought.
Dr Jekyll declined; he said	he hadn't been feeling like himself lately.
Morse said,	"I'll be there on the dot. Can't stop now, must dash."
Gauss was asked to attend	because of his magnetism.
Hertz said	he planned to attend with greater frequency in the future.
Watt thought	it would be a good way to let off steam.
Wilbur Wright accepted,	provided he and Orville could get a flight.

Smart Answers

Jean L. Arnold

Levels	Intermediate and up
Contexts	Teen to adult
Aims	Learn to think outside the box and solve language puzzles
	Understand literal vs. figurative language
	Interact with peers
	Practice telling jokes
	Break the ice
Class Time	15 minutes
Preparation Time	2 minutes
Resources	Strips of paper with questions and answers (see Appendix)

When I was learning German, I was determined to "get" the jokes on a recording of a German comedian. I spent hours listening and re-listening to Otto Walkes jokes until I succeeded, or at least until I learned *when* to laugh. Humor reveals something of the culture in which it occurs and "getting" the humor teaches one not only about the language, but also about the society that uses it. I felt like an insider when I could understand not only the words, but also why the joke was funny. This exercise increased my confidence and motivated me to keep working on improving my language skills.

Ziyaeemehr, Kumar, and Faiz Abdullah (2011) studied the use of humor in academic ESL classrooms and found that its benefits were manifold. Psychological benefits included motivation, relaxation, and mirth. The social benefits were that using humor lowered fear of speaking up, attracted students' attention, and increased participation. The pedagogical benefits of including humor in the classroom were that it promoted learning and understanding and improved retention of material. Even if you're not the type of person who usually uses humor with your students, you can do this activity with them.

PROCEDURE

1. Copy the questions and answers in the Appendix and cut them into strips so that each student will have either the question or the punch line.

Alternatively, use your own jokes, or find others at http://prairiehome.org/jokes; A particularly good place for easy, yet funny jokes is the "Third Grader Jokes" section (e.g. Q: "What happened after the cannibal wedding?" A: "The congregation toasted the bride and groom.").

2. Have students take a slip of paper at random.

3. Then all students have to stand up and mingle, showing their phrase or saying it until they find their match.

4. Give students a chance to discuss the joke and figure out why it's funny.

5. Have pairs circulate around the classroom until all students have told their joke to all other pairs and have heard everyone else's joke and tried to guess the answer.

CAVEATS AND OPTIONS

As a follow-up, students can go to http://prairiehome.org/jokes and find a joke they like. Have a joke-telling competition and vote for the best joke or best teller.

REFERENCES AND FURTHER READING

Ziyaeemehr, A., Kumar, V., & Faiz Abdullah, M. S. (2011). Use and non-use of humor in academic ESL classrooms. *English Language Teaching*, 4(3), 111–119. doi:10.5539/elt.v4n3p111

APPENDIX: *Question-and-Answer Jokes*

Where was the Declaration of Independence signed?
At the bottom of the page.

What is the main reason for divorce?
Marriage.

What can you never eat for breakfast?
Lunch and dinner.

What looks like half an apple?
The other half.

If you throw a red stone into the blue sea, what will it become?
It will become wet.

How can a man go eight days without sleeping?
No problem, he sleeps at night.

How can you lift an elephant with one hand?
Don't worry about it; you will never find an elephant that has only one hand.

If you had three apples and four oranges in one hand and four apples and three oranges in other hand, what would you have?
Very large hands.

If it took eight men ten hours to build a wall, how long would it take four men to build it?
No time at all; the wall is already built.

How can you drop a raw egg onto a concrete floor without cracking it?
Any way you want; concrete floors are very hard to crack.

Puns for Fun!

Niery Grace Bardakjian

Levels	*Intermediate to advanced*
Contexts	*14 years old and above*
Aims	*Exploring some nuances of the English language*
Class Time	*25–45 minutes*
Preparation Time	*15 minutes*
Resources	*Slips of paper with puns (see Appendix)*

Teachers get accustomed to teaching the same materials over and over again. It is time-consuming to create something new, not to mention something fun! This lesson plan can easily be incorporated into a variety of lesson plans for a range of English levels. It will add a refreshing element of fun to the lesson by creating opportunities for communication while exchanging information.

PROCEDURE

1. Ask students to get in pairs. Give them the slips of paper with the beginning and ending of the puns all shuffled (see Appendix).

2. Ask students to match the halves of the puns in pairs.

3. Ask pairs to join another pair and check the answers by reading the puns to each other.

4. Ask students to discuss what makes the pun funny in pairs. Next, they share their ideas with another pair. Then discuss it as a class.

5. Discuss each pun as a class, explaining what makes it funny. *Optional:* If the classroom is equipped with technology, ask students to search the Internet for puns. Find one that they like and use that one for the following steps. Or students can search for their own puns outside of class time.

6. Ask each student to memorize one pun and tell it to one other student. The students must now memorize the pun they just heard and tell it to another student.

7. Tell them they have 5 minutes to tell and memorize the puns. They should try to approach as many students as possible.

8. The student that has managed to approach the most students during the set period of time wins. Or the student/pair/group that remembers and tells the class the greatest number of puns wins.

CAVEATS AND OPTIONS

Visual support can greatly assist students in uncovering the meaning of puns. By doing a Google Images search of the key words in each, you can find interesting images that fit each pun. You can also provide each group of students with the pictures and ask them to match each picture with the corresponding pun.

APPENDIX: *Beginnings and Ends of Puns*

Beginning of pun	End of pun
Let's talk about rights and lefts.	You're right, so I left.
Time flies like an arrow.	Fruit flies like a banana.
When a clock is hungry	it goes back four seconds.
Two fish are in a tank. One says to the other,	"Err . . . so how do you drive this thing?"
I went to buy some camouflage trousers yesterday	but couldn't find any.
Being struck by lightning	is a shocking experience!
Without geometry,	life is pointless.
A chicken crossing the road	is truly poultry in motion.
The roundest knight at King Arthur's table was Sir Cumference.	He acquired his size from far too much pie.
Two antennas met on a roof, fell in love, and got married.	The ceremony wasn't much, but the reception was brilliant!

Pickup Lines in Courtship Rituals: Identifying and Classifying Them

Joseph Dias

Levels	*Intermediate and above; mature learners*
Aims	*Learn about pickup lines as a type of formalized opening gambit in courtship*
	Classify types of pickup lines
	Rate proposed traits of individuals likely to use selected pickup lines
Class Time	*45–60 minutes*
Preparation Time	*Minimal*
Resources	*List of pickup lines (see Appendix A)*
	Categories of pickup lines (see Appendix B)
	Likert scales to rate imagined users of such pickup lines (see Appendix C)

The frequent occurrence of pickup lines in everyday settings means that learners—particularly those who might find themselves on the receiving end—should be aware of them, if for no other reason than to be prepared to give them short shrift. Although much maligned as crass, "canned" speech, lacking in originality, those at the less crude end of the spectrum can be appropriate to introduce to more mature learners as an awareness exercise and for their noteworthy linguistic, pragmatic, and rhetorical breadth.

Kleinke, Meeker, and Staneski (1986) identified three basic types of lines: flippant, direct, and innocuous. In the case of flippant lines, interest is expressed through humor (e.g., You must be tired, because you've been running through my mind all day), while direct expressions signal interest less circuitously and with apparent sincerity (e.g., You leave me speechless, but I'd like to talk to you). Innocuous lines might include "What do you think of the music?" or "Do you have the time?" Senko and Fyffe (2010) found that males were "judged more sociable, more confident, and funnier when using the flippant line than when using [other sorts of] lines, but also less trustworthy and less intelligent" (p. 660).

PROCEDURE

1. Introduce learners to the phenomena of pickup lines and contexts where they might occur (at a club, laundromat, gym, etc.). There can be a discussion of whether pickup lines are used in the culture that the learners represent and, if so, the forms they take and the opinion learners have of those who use them. Have learners look over the list of pickup lines in Appendix A and ask: Can you infer anything about the contexts where the expressions are likely to be used?

2. Distribute a handout to learners that displays the categories of pickup lines that are listed in Appendix B. Ask learners to place the pickup lines from Appendix A in the appropriate categories. Some of them may fit into multiple categories. Afterward, learners compare their answers and discuss the differences. You could encourage learners to create additional categories.

CAVEATS AND OPTIONS

Using selected examples of flippant, direct, and innocuous pickup lines, ask learners to rate the imagined traits of users of these lines on a 7-point likert scale (see Appendix C). This simulates the study conducted by Senko and Fyffe (2010). After learners make their ratings, a discussion can ensue, followed by your account of the Senko and Fyffe findings, detailed above.

REFERENCES AND FURTHER READING

Kleinke, C. L., Meeker, F. B., & Staneski, R. A. (1986). Preference for opening lines: Comparing ratings by men and women. *Sex Roles, 15*, 585–599.

Senko, C., & Fyffe, V. (2010). An evolutionary perspective on effective vs. ineffective pick-up lines. *Journal of Social Psychology, 150*, 648–667.

APPENDIX A: *Examples of Pickup Lines*

It's a good thing that I have my library card. [Why?] Because I am totally checking you out!

I'm no photographer, but I can picture us together.

Excuse me, if I go straight this way, will I be able to reach your heart?

Can I borrow a kiss? I promise I'll give it back.

If I received a nickel for every time I saw someone as beautiful/handsome as you, I'd have five cents.

Know what's on the menu? Me-n-u.

Do you believe in love at first sight, or should I walk by again?

Darn! Something is wrong with my cellphone. [Oh, really? What is that?] It's just that your number isn't in it.

My mom's ugly. My dad's ugly. So how do you explain this piece of work you have in front of you?

Are you a parking ticket? Because you've got FINE written all over you.

Do I know you? 'Cause you look a lot like my next [girl/boy]friend.

You are so sweet you could put Hershey's [any manufacturer of confectionery] out of business.

Do I remind you more of Forrest Gump or Rain Man?

I'm not trying to impress you or anything, but I'm Batman/Wonder Woman!

Did it hurt when you fell from heaven?

I'm sorry, were you talking to me? No? Well then, please start.

Oh, excuse me, I think you dropped something . . . (after a second or two, hand her/him a piece of paper with your phone number)

Shall we talk or continue flirting from a distance?

APPENDIX B: *Categories of Pickup Lines (not exhaustive or mutually exclusive)*

Word play

Know what's on the menu? Me-n-u.

Are you a parking ticket? Because you've got FINE written all over you.

Question followed by prepared response (no response from interlocutor expected)

Do I know you? 'Cause you look a lot like my next [girl/boy]friend.

Can I borrow a kiss? I promise I'll give it back.

Mysterious statement inviting a question that is followed by prepared response

Darn! Something is wrong with my cellphone. [Oh, really? What is that?] It's just that your number isn't in it.

Rhetorical question

Did it hurt when you fell from heaven?

Shall we talk or continue flirting from a distance?

Statement followed by physical act (such as handing the interlocutor something)

Oh, excuse me, I think you dropped something . . . (after a second or two, hand her/him a piece of paper with your phone number)

Utterance beginning with an exclamation or apology as an attention getter

Darn! Something is wrong with my cellphone. [Oh, really? What is that?] It's just that your number isn't in it.

Excuse me, if I go straight this way, will I be able to reach your heart?

Narcissistic (thinking [too] highly of oneself)

I'm not trying to impress you or anything, but I'm Batman/Wonder Woman!

Do you believe in love at first sight, or should I walk by again?

Self-effacing (ostensibly modest; critical of oneself)

My mom's ugly. My dad's ugly. So how do you explain this piece of work you have in front of you?

Do I remind you more of Forrest Gump or Rain Man?

APPENDIX C: *Rating Imagined Users of Selected Pickup Lines*

trustworthy

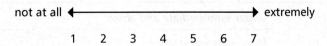

not at all ←――――――――――→ extremely

    1   2   3   4   5   6   7

intelligent

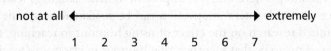

not at all ←――――――――――→ extremely

    1   2   3   4   5   6   7

sociable

not at all ←――――――――――→ extremely

    1   2   3   4   5   6   7

funny

not at all ←――――――――――→ extremely

    1   2   3   4   5   6   7

confident

not at all ←――――――――――→ extremely

    1   2   3   4   5   6   7

Learning New Words via Puns

Feifei Han

Levels	*Upper intermediate and above*
Aims	*Learn new vocabulary*
	Understand English puns
	Practise oral skills in storytelling
Class Time	*45 minutes*
Preparation Time	*30 minutes*
Resources	*English puns*
	Sample stories using puns

Language learning is a difficult task with demanding amounts of memorisation and repetition. Therefore, it is important to make language learning classes a fun place so that learners' motivation can be sustained over time. Although there is limited research on the effect of using humour in teaching, the general conclusion seems to be that incorporating humour in classroom teaching serves as an effective tool (Chiasson, 2002). Using humour can create an enjoyable classroom atmosphere, build positive student and teacher rapport, and foster effective learning (Chiasson, 2002). Despite the multiple benefits resulting from using humour in teaching, there are relatively few books about using humour in the English teaching classroom. This lesson plan recommends using English puns as a manifest of humorous teaching for students to learn new vocabulary and, at the same time, practice oral English via storytelling.

According to Merriam-Webster, *pun* is defined as "the usually humorous use of a word in such a way as to suggest two or more of its meanings or the meaning of another word similar in sound." Used effectively, puns "can be an effective communication tool in a variety of situations and forms" (Junker, 2013, p. 18). There are two reasons for using puns in English vocabulary teaching. First, using puns to learn new words can reduce boredom caused by rote memorisation and repetition. Second, using puns may increase the depth of processing of the to-be-learnt new words (Craik & Tulving, 1975). This means that, through some activities, the new words can be processed more deeply and, as a result, the new words will become more likely to be retrieved from memory in later time. This makes for more effective vocabulary learning.

In this activity, the teacher prepares some new words that have potential to be used via puns and gives one or more examples of how each new word is turned into a pun through a humorous story. Then students create funny stories with the other new vocabulary items using puns.

PROCEDURE

1. Explain the definition of puns.

2. Give students an example of a pun using words that they know. For example, *ketchup* and *catch up*:

   One Sunday, Ms. Tomato and her three little pretty daughters (One, Two, and Three) were well dressed up in red. They were walking towards downtown for a tomato reunion party. While walking, the youngest girl often stopped and picked up some flowers on the side of road. Little by little, the little tomato was lagging far behind. When Ms. Tomato saw the youngest girl was far away from her two sisters, she was angry and yelled to her: "Three, you'd better catch up, otherwise, I'll make you ketchup when we get back home."

3. Show students one of the new words that they are going to learn in class, for example, *hijack*.

4. Explain the meaning of *hijack* (to stop and steal a moving vehicle).

5. Tell students a pre-prepared humorous story in which the pun of *hijack* is used. (e.g., Jack went to meet his dad at the airport last night. His dad was so excited to see him, and as soon as he saw Jack he shouted loudly, "Hi, Jack!" To his surprise, a group of police ran towards him and arrested him, as they thought he attempted to hijack an aircraft.)

6. Write on the board a few words that are new to students and explain the meaning of these words.

assault and *a salted*

> Possible joke: Daddy Peanut and Mommy Peanut went to the market to buy groceries. Daddy Peanut bumped into a big Walnut. The Walnut was very angry and punched Daddy Peanut. Daddy Peanut stared at the Walnut and shouted, "If you assault me again, I will make you a salted walnut!"

finished and *Finish*

> Possible joke: In the college library, Student A was reading a book. Student B wanted to borrow the book. So he politely asked Student A, "Are you finished?" To his surprise, Student A replied with a smile, "Very good guess, but I'm not, I'm Danish."

7. Divide students into a number of groups according to the number of new words.

8. Assign each group one or more new words, and encourage students to think of puns for each word and to make up a funny story from them.

9. Ask a representative of each group to tell the story they have made up in front of the class.

CAVEATS AND OPTIONS

Instead of group work, you can make this activity pair work so that each student may have more opportunities to talk.

REFERENCES AND FURTHER READING

Chiasson, P. (2002). Using humour in the second language classroom. *Internet TESL Journal, 8*. Retrieved from http://iteslj.org

Craik, F., & Tulving, E. (1975). Depth of processing and the retention of words in episodic memory. *Journal of Experimental Psychology: General, 104*, 268–294.

Junker, D. (2013). In defense of puns: How to use them effectively. *Public Relations Tactics, 20*, 18.

Puns Venn Diagram

Jacob Huckle

Levels	*Advanced*
Aims	*Develop vocabulary*
	Understand the meaning of homophone, homograph, and homonym
	Understand how puns work
Class Time	*25–30 minutes*
Preparation Time	*10 minutes*
Resources	*Pun cards (Appendix A)*
	Venn diagram (Appendix B)

Nonnative speakers often find puns difficult to access because they require a rich understanding of words, including their multiple meanings and uses. Having some understanding of how they work—and the concept of homophones, homographs, and homonyms—can make puns much more accessible to learners. An awareness of such concepts will improve students' pronunciation, enrich their vocabulary knowledge, and allow them to access the hidden meanings contained in puns.

PROCEDURE

1. Use the example below, taken from Lewis Carroll's *Alice in Wonderland*, to introduce students to the idea of puns. Ask students why this quotation is funny and how the joke works.

   "And how many hours a day did you do lessons?" asked Alice, in a hurry to change the subject.

   "Ten hours the first day," said the Mock Turtle, "nine the next, and so on."

   "What a curious plan!" exclaimed Alice.

   "That's the reason they're called lessons," the Gryphon remarked, "because they lessen from day to day."

2. Explain that puns often use words that are homophones, homographs, and homonyms. Ask students to guess the meaning of these words from the prefix *homo* and the root words. Use some simple examples to illustrate these concepts, such as *too, to,* and *two*. Explain the relationship between homophones, homographs, and homonyms using the Venn diagram in Appendix B.

3. Ask students to pair up and study the example pun cards in Appendix A. Some students may need to use their dictionaries. Ask students to explain to their partners what the pun is and how it works.

4. Students work with their partners to categorize the puns as homophones, homographs, or homonyms, placing the pun cards into the correct section of the Venn diagram.

5. As a follow-up/extension task, encourage students to create their own homophonic, homographic, and homonymic puns.

CAVEATS AND OPTIONS

1. The pun cards could be replaced with easier puns, or students could be provided with two definitions for each underlined word, to make the activity more accessible. Alternatively, students could each be provided with a pun card prior to the lesson to read and understand.

2. As an extra challenge, students could bring their own English puns for other students to categorize.

REFERENCES AND FURTHER READING

Carroll, L. (1865), *Alice's adventures in wonderland*. Retrieved from http://www.gutenberg.org/files/11/11-h/11-h.htm

APPENDIX A: *Pun Cards*

	This new whiteboard is **remarkable**!	Atheism is a non-**prophet** organization.	"Your children need your **presence** more than your **presents**." (Jesse Jackson)
What do you mean I have to pay $100? The sign says, "**Fine** for parking here."	"You can **tune a** guitar, but you can't **tuna fish**. Unless, of course, you play **bass**." (Douglas Adams)	I can eat this whole cake in only 60 seconds! That's easy, it's so **minute**!	Q. How did the math teacher kill his victims? A. Using **axes**.
The fisherman's **net** worth was very high.	Q. Why do pandas often spend time alone? A. They can't **bear** being with others.	A boiled egg every morning is hard to **beat**.	"Time flies **like** an arrow. Fruit flies **like** a banana." (Groucho Marx)
The Sahara is so hot that all the soldiers will **desert**.	The pediatrician was always getting angry with the people in his hospital because he had little **patients**.	Q. Why do celebrities never feel hot? A. They have many **fans**.	We'll have 10 classes today, 9 classes tomorrow, 8 classes the next day, etc. That's why they're called **lessens**.

APPENDIX B: *Puns Venn Diagram*

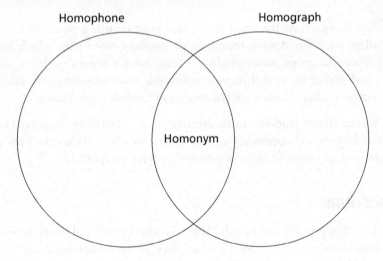

Homophone   Homograph

Homonym

Understanding and Creating English Puns

Sara Peterson and Aaron Shayne

Levels	Intermediate to advanced
Contexts	Middle school to adult
Aims	Develop listening and speaking skills
	Learn to analyze how puns are formed
	Build linguistic awareness by practicing rhyming and alliteration in the form of puns
	Create original puns
Class Time	1 hour
Preparation Time	Less than 30 minutes
Resources	Worksheet (see Appendix)
	Writing utensils
	Dry erase or chalk board

In this lesson, students learn about and practice using puns. Much of the vocabulary used has double meanings or involves word play, which requires sophisticated language understanding. Using humor lowers students' affective filters and makes them feel more comfortable understanding and interacting with native speakers. This is part of an overall English conversation class.

This lesson allows students to be creative while practicing English. They are motivated to use old vocabulary and learn new words. It allows students to collaborate and specialize in skills in which they have an aptitude.

PROCEDURE

1. Write this pun on the board: "Why did the bicycle fall over? It was two-tired." Warm up the students when they arrive by talking about this pun. Walk them through the duality of *two/too* and *tire/tired*. Introduce the lesson.

2. Ask students if they have heard puns before. Write known puns on the board.

3. Introduce the two types of puns, homophonic and homographic. Homophonic puns are those that rely on words that sound alike. Homographic puns use words that have two or more meanings.

4. Ask students to categorize the 8 example puns. Do the first few together, and then let students go in groups or on their own once they feel comfortable. Check for student understanding.

5. Read the example puns and focus on vocal inflection, emphasizing the pun words. Ask students to practice reading the puns to each other.

6. In groups, have students write their own puns. Once they have finished they can "perform" them in front of the class, focusing on proper inflection.

7. Students can be evaluated based on their understanding and application of the taught material. They could also be observed for their contributions to their group.

CAVEATS AND OPTIONS

This lesson has been altered to suit various levels with great success.

1. *Advanced:* Higher level students will be able to describe the picture more accurately, with better vocabulary. If the class is at a high level, more complicated pictures can be used.

2. *Low Level:* Students can be paired or grouped in Step 4 to help each other pick out the syntax points. During the description activity, students can choose a role that fits them best, be it speaking, writing, or listening and drawing. Easier pictures can be used for lower level classes.

APPENDIX: *Worksheets*

Puns

A bicycle can't stand on its own because it is two-tired.

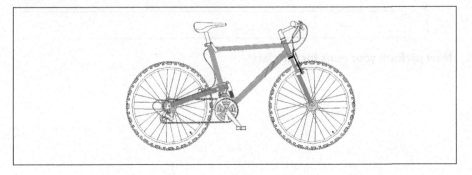

Puns are jokes based on words that sound or look alike. There are two basic kinds:

Homophonic Puns	Homographic Puns
Meaning:	Meaning:
Examples: a + f. *What's purple and 5,000 miles long? The Grape Wall of China!*	Examples:

Are the following puns homophonic or homographic? Match the puns and write them into the boxes above.

a. What's purple and 5,000 miles long? b. Why is ten scared? c. Two silk worms had a race. d. How does a lion greet the other animals in the field? e. I went to a pet store and saw a cute cat. f. Why are teddy bears never hungry? g. How do celebrities stay cool? h. How do turtles talk to each other?	a. They are always stuffed. b. "Nice to eat you." c. I had to paws to take a picture. d. They have lots of fans! e. They use shell phones. f. The Grape Wall of China. g. They ended up in a tie. h. Because seven eight nine.

Read and explain the following puns in your group.

    a.   One horse said to another, "Your face is familiar but I don't know your mane."

    b.   What does a clock do if it's hungry? It goes back four seconds.

    c.   It rains cats and dogs but it doesn't reindeer.

Now try writing some puns together. Here are some starters if you need help:

What's a dog's favorite food?

What do students like?

Did you see what happened on the news?

    a. _____

    b. _____

    c. _____

Now perform your puns for the class!

Did You Hear the Joke About the Plane? Never Mind, It's Over Your Head.

Nadezda Pimenova

Levels	Intermediate to high-intermediate
Aims	Increase awareness of word play in jokes
	Develop reading strategies
	Learn new vocabulary
Class Time	10–15 minutes
Preparation Time	15–20 minutes
Resources	Any book or website for English puns (see Appendix A)

Word-based jokes present serious challenges for comprehension and translation (Schmitz, 2002). Awareness plays an important role in L2 comprehension (e.g., Leow, 2001; Pimenova, 2011). According to Ballard, plays on words help make students aware of how the meanings can be construed and misconstrued (as cited in Schmitz, 2002, p. 110).

The think-aloud strategy allows teachers to model how a good reader thinks about text while reading. Then teachers can move from modeling think-alouds to students' independent use of them to monitor their comprehension (Wilhelm, 2001). As students think out loud, verbalizing their inner speech, they gradually develop into reflective and independent learners.

Humorous texts, according to Muhalcea and Pulman, "show frequently occurring words from classes that signify human-centric vocabulary (e.g., pronouns), use negations and negative polarity words ('wrong,' 'error'), mention professional communities (lawyers, programmers) and negative human traits ('ignorance,' 'lying')" (as cited in Hempelmann, 2008, p. 340).

PROCEDURE

1. Model a think-aloud using a pun (see example in Appendix B).

2. Match students in pairs.

3. Give three or four puns to each pair of students.

4. Tell students to read a pun and think aloud about it.

5. Have students share what was funny (or not) and what new words they learned.

CAVEATS AND OPTIONS

There are different types of puns. Most common are sound-alike puns based on homophones, lookalike puns (homographs or polysemous words), close-sounding puns (words that sound similar), texting puns (alphabetic, numeric, and simplified spelling), and puns inside idioms (Lems, 2013). (See Appendix C for some examples.) Choose appropriate puns for the think-aloud task. Have some extra puns for students who finish early. If you choose puns inside idioms, make sure that idioms are familiar to your students.

REFERENCES AND FURTHER READING

Hempelmann, C. F. (2008). Computational humor: Beyond the pun? In V. Raskin (Ed.), *The primer of humor research* (pp. 333–360). Berlin, Germany: Mouton de Gruyter.

Lems, K. (2013). Laughing all the way: Teaching English using puns. *English Teaching Forum, 51*(1), 26–33.

Leow, R. P. (2001). Attention, awareness, and foreign language behavior. In R. Ellis (Ed.), *Form-focused instruction and second language learning* (Vol. 4, pp. 113–155). Malden, MA: Wiley-Blackwell.

Pimenova, N. (2011). *Idiom comprehension strategies used by English and Russian language learners in a think-aloud study* (Unpublished doctoral dissertation). Purdue University, West Lafayette, IN.

Schmitz, J. R. (2002). Humor as a pedagogical tool in foreign language and translation courses. *Humor: International Journal of Humor Research, 15*, 89–113.

Wilhelm, J. D. (2001). *Improving comprehension with think-aloud strategies: Modeling what good readers do.* New York, NY: Scholastic Teaching Resources.

APPENDIX A: *Recommended Books and Websites for English Puns*

Jokes in English for the ESL/EFL Classroom (A Project of *Internet TESL Journal*). (1998–2005). Retrieved from http://iteslj.org/c/jokes-puns.html

Keller, C. (1986). *Waiter, there's a fly in my soup! Restaurant jokes.* New York, NY: Prentice-Hall.

Moger, A. (1979). *The complete pun book.* Secaucus, NJ: Citadel Press.

Terban, M. (1992). *Funny you should ask: How to make up jokes and riddles with wordplay.* New York, NY: Houghton Mifflin Harcourt.

The alphaDictionary language resource site. (n.d.). Retrieved from http://www.alphadictionary.com/fun/pun.html

Young, F. (1993). *Super duper jokes.* New York, NY: Farrar, Straus and Giroux.

APPENDIX B: *Think-Aloud Pun Example*

Two pencils decided to have a race. The outcome was a draw.

> Two pencils were competing. "To draw" means to make a picture. It was not a drawing competition but a race. When two people compete, one wins. But sometimes there can be no winners. Oh yes, I was reading a text about a soccer game, and the teams had equal scores; it was a draw. A draw is when neither side wins. That's funny.

APPENDIX C: *Pun Categories and Examples*

Sound-alike Puns

> When my wife saw her first strands of gray hair, she thought she'd dye. (Moger, 1979)

> What do they call the man who abandoned his strict diet? Desserter. (Terban, 1992)

Lookalike Puns

> Have you tried the meatballs? Yes, and I found them guilty.

> I want a steak and make it lean. Which way? (Keller, 1986)

Close-Sounding Puns

What do you call spiders who just got married? Newlywebs.

What do you call a rich watermelon? A melon-aire. (Young, 1993)

Texting Puns

Why is 10 scared? Because 7 8 9.

Peek a boo—ICU! (Lems, 2013)

Puns Inside Idioms

The first telephone conversation was only 18 feet apart. It was a close call. (Moger, 1979)

Who never cries over spilled milk? A cat. (Terban, 1992)

Wordplay Relay

Gregory Strong

Levels	*Lower intermediate*
Contexts	*Young adult, university*
Aims	*Develop appreciation of word play in English in the form of alliteration, fractured nursery rhymes, and situational irony in storytelling*
	Expand speaking and writing ability while developing examples of word play
Class Time	*15–30 minutes over three classes*
Preparation Time	*Varies*
Resources	*Examples of wordplay*
	Blackboard or overhead projector

Explaining wordplay in English and helping students develop their own examples helps increase their interest and enthusiasm for language learning. Dörnyei (2001) lists humor and games as types of activity that lower student anxiety toward language learning.

PROCEDURE

1. To start a wordplay relay, show several examples of each type of wordplay described in the Appendix. Students should try to make their own examples first, with you checking them.

2. Divide the class into groups to make alliterative phrases or fractured nursery rhymes. (It is hard for individual students to come up with many good examples. Also, through group work, students can learn from each other.)

3. Once they have done this, the wordplay relay begins. In their groups, students list as many alliterative phrases or fractured nursey rhymes as they can develop in a given period of time (e.g., 5 minutes). Once time is up, show the class each group's list. The group with the most phrases wins the relay.

4. A slightly different approach is used with situational irony, which is best played by individual students competing against each other in small groups.

In this case, each student has a time limit in which to produce the next twist or turn in a story.

5. Several different versions of the game can now be played. For the next round, students might be allowed to create phrases using only a particular letter. In another round, the contest might be to write the longest sentence in the class. Another round might be about making a sentence related to something or someone in literature, film, or the news. Ideally, several different groups in the class should have the chance to win a round of the game.

CAVEATS AND OPTIONS

Once students become better at these examples of wordplay, then small groups of students might compete with each other instead of as a whole class. The students will have to react more quickly and the game will become more intense.

REFERENCES AND FURTHER READING

Dörnyei, Z. (2001). *Motivational strategies in the language classroom*. Cambridge, England: Cambridge University Press.

APPENDIX: *Types of Wordplay*

Alliteration

An important part of the pleasure and humor in making an alliterative phrase is that it must make sense. Students probably would recognize this through a well-known tongue twister: "Peter Piper picked a peck of pickled peppers." These types of alliterative phrases are fairly easy to develop: "Beautiful Barbara Boxer baked the best brown beans," "My mother makes me muffins most Monday mornings," and "Sad Sally sat by the sea and sold salads to seniors."

Fractured Nursery Rhymes

For this type of wordplay, explain how to create a rhyme in English. Then challenge student groups to think of new rhymed endings for well-known nursery rhymes, for example, "There was an old woman who lived in a shoe":

She must have been tiny for this to be true.

She met an old man who lived in a can.

Situational Irony in Storytelling, or "Good News, Bad News"

This type of word play relies on describing the ironic or surprising twists and turns in a story. The humor arises from the degree of complication in the events in the story. The following is an example of a "good news, bad news" story:

> A woman had to get to New York City by Monday, but when she got to the airplane ticket counter, she learned that all the seats were sold.
>
> The good news was that someone who had bought a ticket hadn't shown up for the flight, so she could buy that ticket.
>
> The bad news was that the seat was at the back of the airplane and had the roughest ride.

The plane can catch on fire, the woman can escape with a parachute, and so on. The competition between groups is to keep the story going. Sets a time limit, perhaps 30 seconds, for each round.

Play Riddles With Grammar

Mohamed Yacoub

Levels	High beginning +
Aims	Increase knowledge of vocabulary
	Develop grammar awareness
	Strengthen sentence structures
	Develop cross-cultural humor sense
Class Time	45–60 minutes
Preparation Time	10 minutes
Resources	Blackboard and chalk, or whiteboard and markers
	Dictionary (optional)

Riddles play a twofold role. First, they introduce students to grammar in a motivating way. Second, they make student initiate the need to learn something out of curiosity. Riddles are different from jokes in that jokes make students laugh while riddles make them think of an untraditional answer to a simple question. This method encapsulates three major components—grammar (with all its tenses, subject-verb agreement, etc.), vocabulary, and sentence structure (syntactical, morphological, etc.)—in a way that makes students learn more effectively.

PROCEDURE

1. Get a cross-cultural riddle from any website (see Appendices).

2. Write a riddle on the board and make sure that all students understand every word in it.

3. Ask students what a good funny answer might be to this riddle.

4. Do not limit the answer to the riddle to just one possibility; any good answer is acceptable.

5. Discuss the grammatical rules that are included in the riddle.

6. In the next class period, ask students what they remember from the riddle and what they learned from it.

7. Repeat these steps to introduce different riddles when you have time in class.

CAVEATS AND OPTIONS

Some students are one-track-minded and do not like new ways of learning language. With a bit more effort, you can help them get used to this way. One of the positive ways you can catch students' attention is to translate the riddles that they already know in their language. This will be students' first time to hear them in English, so it will be fun. Another option is to give the translation of the local riddles as homework. You then compare different translations and pick up one that makes the most humor sense.

APPENDIX A: *Sample Riddles*

Q: What did the big chimney say to the little chimney?
A: You're too young to smoke!

Q: Why are frogs so happy?
A: They eat whatever bugs them!

Q: What do you take before every meal?
A: A seat!!

Q: Why do birds fly south in the winter?
A: Because it's too far to walk!

Q: What did one fish say to the other?
A: If you keep your mouth closed you will not get caught!

Q: Why are fish so smart?
A: Because they live in schools! (*schools* here means groups of fish)

Q: Why did the student eat his homework?
A: Because his teacher said it was a piece of cake!

Q: Why was the student's homework in her father's handwriting?
A: She used his pen!

Q: What is the longest word in the English language?
A: *Smiles*: there is a mile between the first and last letters!

Q: What starts with e, ends with e, and only has one letter?
A: An envelope.

APPENDIX B: *Suggested Riddles Websites*

Funology: http://www.funology.com/riddles

Braingle: http://www.braingle.com/Riddle.html

Fit Brains: http://www.fitbrains.com/blog/friday-fun-brain-teasers

Part III

Comics and
Cartoons

Wink, Wink, Nudge, Nudge: Examining Puns Through Corny Comic Characters

Clarissa Codrington and Trisha Dowling

Levels	*High-intermediate to advanced*
Aims	*Learn about different levels of semantic meanings in words*
	Understand U.S. comic strips
Class Time	*30–45 minutes*
Preparation Time	*20 minutes*
Resources	*Comic strips*

The corny character can be described as a trope, and the ability to recognize this can give students an immediate knowledge base to further understand U.S. humor through a deeper semantic understanding of language. But what is it that makes these characters corny? The answer is usually their use (or misuse) of the pun. Teaching students how to understand puns thus gives them two linguistic advantages: a deeper understanding of one type of humor and an ability to recognize the flexibility of the English language through wordplay. According to Monnot and Kite (1974), puns are meant to be recognized on sight, play with semantic features to create a surprise and a sense of wit, and are often funny. This activity is meant to address puns directly and can be adapted in several ways to be used throughout an entire semester.

PROCEDURE

1. Select several comic strips that provide examples of wordplay or puns. Many comic strips have running pun gags, including *Pearls Before Swine*, *Foxtrot*, *Garfield*, and *Dilbert*.

2. Preteach the meaning of puns, explaining how words can be changed to be interpreted in a different way, either through meaning or through sound.

3. The comic strip is viewed by the entire class. Students write the pun in the first column of their worksheet (see Appendix).

4. In pairs, students discuss their interpretation of the puns and fill out columns two and three of the worksheet.

5. Repeat Steps 2–4 multiple times, providing a decreasing amount of scaffolding each time.

6. After students become familiar with the use and meaning of puns, give students comic strips to look at and identify the use of puns on their own.

7. Students teach the rest of the class about their comic strip and explain its usage of puns.

CAVEATS AND OPTIONS

1. Students can determine how to clarify the sentence so that it has one clear meaning.

2. TV or movie clips can be used in conjunction with or in place of comic strips.

3. Comic books can be checked out from the library or found at library book sales for very cheap.

4. Although this lesson focuses on puns in comics, you can expand on this and teach students about the visual/aural cues that often accompany puns in other sources such as movies and TV shows (drum roll, groans, etc.).

5. Depending on class level, students can eventually work to make their own comic strips with puns.

REFERENCES AND FURTHER READING

Lucas, T. (2004). Deciphering the meaning of puns in learning English as a second language: A study of triadic interaction. Retrieved from http://diginole .lib.fsu.edu/islandora/object/fsu%3A175595

Monnot, M., & Kite, J. (1974). Pun and games: Paranomasia in the ESL classroom. *TESOL Quarterly, 8,* 65–71.

APPENDIX: *Puns in Comics Worksheet*

What was said . . .	Is it a play on words or a play on meaning?	What would the original words/meaning be?
(Sample) "Oh, Cey, can you see by the Don's Hurley light?" (Example from *Pearls Before Swine*, by Stephan Pastis)	Play on words	"O say can you see, by the dawn's early light?" (from *The Star-Spangled Banner*)

Creating Living Comics

Deirdre J. Derrick

Levels	*High beginner to advanced*
Contexts	*Young adult, university, intensive English program*
Aims	*Understand and use humor in English (includes pragmatic competence)*
	Develop reading competence in North American comics
	Practice creativity by using original humor
	Gain exposure to the target culture through comics
Class Time	*45–60 minutes*
Preparation Time	*10 minutes*
Resources	*Comic strips*
	Popsicle (or similar) sticks
	Cardboard paper
	Markers
	Scissors
	Tape/glue
	Camera

Comic strips often make use of a visual and cultural shorthand as a foundation on which their punch lines are based. This makes them difficult for English language learners to understand, but it also makes them valuable tools for teaching not only vocabulary and grammar, but also humor and culture. In this activity, comics are used as a basis on which students can exercise their creativity and practice using humor in English.

PROCEDURE

1. Find and copy four three-panel comic strips that are at or slightly below students' language level and align with their interests and developmental stage. Be aware that comics often assume shared cultural knowledge (i.e., they might reference a movie or a type of food). Be prepared to provide additional support to students (i.e., showing a clip from the movie or explaining the food) so that they can access the humor in the comic.

2. As a class, read one comic strip. Explain new vocabulary and visual shorthand (e.g., bold letters, asterisks or spirals for eyes, floating Zs around a character). Discuss how and why the comic is funny. This stage can continue as long as students are engaged and can include comparisons with comics in students' first language.

3. Divide students into small groups and distribute comic strips to groups. Have students read and discuss the comics as a group, then discuss them as a class. Provide support when and where needed, drawing students' attention to cultural knowledge and how it contributes to humor.

4. Explain to students that they will now make their own "living" comic strips. In groups, students write a three-panel comic based on a situation in class, in their lives, or in the comic strips they just read. Provide language support when and where needed.

5. Once students are finished, pass out Popsicle sticks, cardboard paper, markers, scissors, and tape/glue. Have students cut speech bubbles and write their dialogue inside, then attach the bubbles to the sticks so that they can hold them up. If students have additional language that is not dialogue but that provides context, have them write it on rectangular paper.

6. Have one group at a time come to the front of the class and pose for each panel of the comic strip holding their speech sticks. Students should hold rectangular paper with context at the base of the picture. Another student should take a picture of each "panel."

7. Combine the pictures into a single comic strip for each group. These can be e-mailed to students, put on a school website, printed and distributed to students, or printed and displayed in the classroom.

CAVEATS AND OPTIONS

1. A lot of humor in comic strips is culturally dependent. Because comic strips are by nature short and have limited space, a type of visual and cultural shorthand is often used. It is important to not assume that students know what certain symbols mean or have access to the background information and experiences that will allow them to understand punch lines. This is not necessarily a bad thing as it can provide a rich learning experience—much richer than might be assumed given the brevity of a comic strip. Students can gain a great sense of accomplishment when they "get" a joke in English and an even greater sense when they are able to make jokes in English.

2. Keep in mind that not all students feel comfortable when given complete creative freedom. For some students, this type of activity may be unfamiliar

and may make them uncomfortable. Provide students with as much explicit direction as they need. This spectrum of support can range from giving students specific situations to base their comics on (e.g., English students studying for or taking a test) to general suggestions (e.g., basing comics on love or school) to complete creative freedom.

3. Also, this is an easy activity to "level" by choosing comic strips that match students' abilities and interests. *Garfield* is better for lower levels and younger learners, whereas *Doonesbury* is best for highly advanced adults (who have an interest in U.S. politics). Comics like *Luann*, *Big Nate*, and *Baldo* generally contain topics that teenagers face, whereas comics like *Cathy* and *Dilbert* deal with working adults.

4. Finally, the comic strips mentioned in this activity are mostly from the United States. It is worth exploring English language comics from Kachru's outer circle (e.g., India, Nigeria) and expanding circle countries (e.g., Japan, Russia) and incorporating them into discussions of how culture is used in comic strips and how it influences humor.

A Discussion on Assessment: Is Equal Assessment Always Fair?

Nilufer Guler

Levels	*High-intermediate to advanced*
Aims	*Develop English speaking and writing skills by discussing the ideas in political cartoons*
	Practice supporting ideas in spoken and written language
	Practice refuting ideas in spoken and written language
Class Time	*30–35 minutes*
Preparation Time	*5 minutes*
Resources	*Political cartoons*
	Blackboard/whiteboard (or overhead projector)
	Notebooks
	Pencils

Research highlights that interaction is crucial for language learning, and English learners (ELs) need to practice their language skills through authentic tasks (Gibbons, 2014). Learning through speaking and writing occurs when both the language input and the language output are meaning-focused and when learners are focused on conveying their messages to their audience (Nation & Newton, 2009). Therefore, cartoons offer great potential in teaching ELs because learners can analyze the ideas in the cartoons and then focus on expressing their own thoughts on those ideas. In addition, cartoons are perfect ways to initiate discussions and writing prompts because "graphics or illustrations can reduce the cognitive load associated with complex reasoning tasks because they can present essential information more concisely than equivalent textual statements" (Liu, 2004, p. 237).

PROCEDURE

1. Students discuss the meanings of the terms *assessment, fair,* and *equal.* This information will help students comprehend the vocabulary items and support their background knowledge on these subjects (Avalos, Plasencia, Chavez, & Rascón, 2007). In addition, this information will be beneficial for students while discussing their ideas.

2. Introduce the political cartoon (Appendix A) by displaying it on the board, and ask students to analyze the cartoon for a few minutes.

3. Ask students to write down their ideas on the cartoon as outlines in their notebooks.

4. When students finish writing down their ideas, they then discuss the humor, irony, and ideas in the political cartoon. They discuss how equal may not be fair all the time and what can be done.

5. Ask some challenging questions such as these: If you use different tests or assessment methods for some students, do you think it will be fair to other students? How are you going to make sure the new test is fair?

6. Students discuss whether they have ever felt that how they were assessed was not fair.

7. Introduce students to the second cartoon (Appendix B) by displaying it on the board, and discuss the message in the cartoon.

8. Have students discuss how the ideas in both cartoons are related.

9. Ask students to write a short argumentative essay on equity and fairness, answering this question: Should assessment be fair or equal?

CAVEATS AND OPTIONS

1. Students may discuss their ideas in small groups first and then discuss them as a whole class. This provides opportunity for peer learning, yet may require sparing more classroom time for this activity.

2. You may print and give students a copy of the cartoons if it is not possible to display it on the board.

REFERENCES AND FURTHER READING

Avalos, M. A., Plasencia, A., Chavez, C., & Rascón, J. (2007). Modified guided reading: Gateway to English as a second language and literacy learning. *Reading Teacher, 61,* 318-329. doi:10.1598/RT.61.4.4

Bower, J. (2013, June 28). For the love of learning: Fair is not equal. *For the Love of Learning.* Retrieved from http://www.joebower.org/2013/06/fair-isnt-equal.html

Gibbons, P. (2014). *Scaffolding language, scaffolding learning* (2nd ed.). Portsmouth, NH: Heinemann.

Kajtar, E. (2014). Please climb that tree! Some thoughts on the obstacles that prevent members of "vulnerable groups" from entering the labor market. *Pravni Vjesnik, 14*(2), 15–38.

Liu, J. (2004). Effects of comic strips on L2 learners' reading comprehension. *TESOL Quarterly, 38*, 225–243. doi:10.2307/3588379

Nation, I. S. P., & Newton, J. (2009). *Teaching ESL/EFL listening and speaking.* New York, NY: Routledge.

APPENDIX A: *Political Cartoon by Edit Kajtar*

APPENDIX B: *Political Cartoon by Joe Bower*

Reading and Creating Comics Online

Louise Ohashi

Levels	All
Aims	*Develop an understanding of wordplay*
	Understand and enjoy humor in English
Class Time	*45–60 minutes*
Preparation Time	*20 minutes (allow more time if you want to make comic strips to use in your lesson)*
Resources	*Computers (or tablets) with Internet access to create comics*
	Comics generator (a free option that does not require registration is www.makebeliefscomix.com/Comix)

Comics often require an understanding of the nuances or multiple meanings of words in order to be understood. By studying comics, students gain a deeper understanding of English wordplay. Writing their own comics allows them to apply what they have learnt and gives them the opportunity to use English in a flexible, creative way.

PROCEDURE

Before Class (10–20 minutes the first time, 10 minutes after that)

1. Prepare some comics to introduce in the lesson. You can use well-known comics such as *Garfield* and *The Simpsons*, or create your own on sites such as www.makebeliefscomix.com/Comix. When selecting or creating comics, consider the level of the students, the complexity of the language used, and the cultural knowledge needed to understand the comic.

In Class (35–50 minutes)

1. Start by talking about famous comics and comic characters. Elicit the main purposes of comics and common strategies they use to make people laugh. For example, explain that puns and other forms of wordplay are common, and give some examples. This could be done with a joke about the literal and idiomatic meaning of "a piece of cake":

Student A: Why did the students eat their homework?

Student B: I don't know. That sounds crazy! Why?

Student A: Their teacher said it was a piece of cake.

This joke, or another like it, could be made into a comic before the lesson to serve as a model or could be used when demonstrating how to make comics online later in the lesson. It takes no more than a few minutes to create a short comic like this on www.makebeliefscomix.com/Comix. Although comics created on this site cannot be freely shared in books, they can be used in class handouts and shared online.

2. Show the class one of the comics you found/made, and ask students to discuss it in pairs. Elicit/explain why it is funny. Examine the language and cultural knowledge that readers need in order to understand it. Repeat with some more comics.

For example, if introducing *Garfield* comics, which have been around since the 1970s but may be unfamiliar to students, it would be useful to know that the main character is a lazy, overweight cat that uses sarcasm and pessimism to make readers laugh. He enjoys teasing the other characters in the comic. He hates diets, exercise, and Mondays. One of his funny one-liners is "I'm not overweight, I'm undertall."

3. Put students in pairs or small groups and direct them to www.makebeliefscomix.com/Comix. Demonstrate how to use the features required to make a short comic strip then instruct students to make one of their own.

4. Students print out their comics or share them electronically (via e-mail, blog, social networking sites, etc.). Please read the terms of use on the site for details of the attribution that is required when sharing the comics.

5. Students read each other's comics and try to understand why they are funny. The creators can explain their comics to the students who do not see the funny side.

CAVEATS AND OPTIONS

1. If there is no time to share the comics in class, students can share them online before the end of the lesson, then for homework they can read the comics and leave comments for the creators.

2. Instead of creating the comics, students can use premade strips that have nothing written in the speech bubbles. A wide selection can be found online with the search term "comics with blank speech bubbles."

Teaching Culture Through Comic Strips

Ildiko Porter-Szucs

Levels	Beginning to advanced, 10 years or older
Aims	Develop awareness of cultural conventions
	Recognize when cultural conventions are violated
	Create one's own comic strip illustrating a cultural topic (optional)
Class Time	20–60 minutes (depending on whether students act out their scenarios)
Preparation Time	5–10 minutes
Resources	Sample cartoon strips (see Appendices)
	Syndicated cartoon strips

As Bell (2009) asserts, humor can and should be used in the second language classroom not only because students enjoy it, but also because of the "potential of humor to facilitate language acquisition" (p. 249). While humor can be employed to teach various skills, it lends itself best to teaching culture. Culture is at the heart of humor, as humor is culturally situated. Humorous situations may often arise, for instance, when cultural conventions are misinterpreted by a visitor to the host culture.

Both cartoon strips in this lesson are based on real-life cross-cultural miscommunications. At the heart of one of the cartoons lies the North American ritual of saying "How are you" while performing an act of greeting. Very frequently, this expression is used as small talk, but it can easily be misinterpreted by someone from a country (such as Hungary) where "How are you?" is taken literally to be a request for information about the interlocutor's true well-being and is followed by a detailed and honest response. The second cartoon strip, titled "Trick or Treat," depicts a misunderstanding surrounding the Halloween tradition of trick-or-treating. An exchange student can easily misunderstand the direction in which the treating should occur and take the treat rather than give it.

PROCEDURE

1. Elicit from students information on customs or cultural situations in the target culture (such as the United States) that could lead to misunderstandings. Briefly discuss the source of misunderstandings.

2. Introduce a comic strip (such as from the Appendices) with the words in the speech bubbles covered up.

3. In small groups, have students fill in the missing text in the speech bubbles.

4. Distribute the comic strip with the text in the speech bubbles.

5. Elicit from students what cultural expectation lies at the heart of the situation depicted in the comic strip.

6. Discuss the various ways in which the utterances can be interpreted.

CAVEATS AND OPTIONS

1. Encourage students to act out their scenarios to their classmates (after Steps 3 and 6).

2. A possible homework activity based on Step 1 is to have students create their own cartoons on a cartoon-authoring website such as Pixton (www.pixton .com). Next, they can share their cartoons with the class.

3. Syndicated cartoons, such as the daily cartoon from *The New Yorker*, are likely to contain vocabulary, grammar, and concepts that are inaccessible to students with limited language proficiency.

REFERENCES AND FURTHER READING

Bell, N. D. (2009). Learning about and through humor in the second language classroom. *Language Teaching Research, 13*, 241–258.

Daily Cartoon: *The New Yorker*: Retrieved from http://www.newyorker.com /cartoons/daily-cartoon

Fun With Foreigners: Retrieved from http://funwithforeigners.wordpress.com/

GoComics: http://www.gocomics.com/features

Pixton Comic Maker: http://www.pixton.com

APPENDIX A: *Comic Strip "How Are You?"*

Created by author on www.pixton.com.

APPENDIX B: *Comic Strip "Trick or Treat"*

Created by author on www.pixton.com.

Comic Strip Collection

Christina Scally and Sally La Luzerne-Oi

Levels	Intermediate to advanced
Contexts	University
Aims	Read and analyze
	Orally present information about a particular genre of cultural humor
	Build understanding of stereotypical situations, characters, dialogue, and related vocabulary
Class Time	25 minutes for set up, variable for presentation practice
Preparation Time	4–5 hours for students
Resources	Newspapers or access to the Internet
	Poster board
	Tape/glue

Students can build complex reading and visual literacy skills by reading and studying comics. Comics require students to make inferences and are also a rich source of idiomatic expressions. By following the same comic strip for a week, students begin to connect with the strip, which makes it more likely they will continue reading it.

PROCEDURE

1. Ask students if they have ever read comic strips in their first language and/or other languages. Ask them if they can name any comic strips that regularly appear in newspapers.

2. Tell students to look at the comic strips in a daily newspaper or on the Internet to find one of particular interest to them. Examples of comic strips that work well are *Garfield*, *Calvin & Hobbes*, *Peanuts*, *Frazz*, and *Pickles*. In some cases, you might need to provide some background information on the strip.

3. Once they have done this, they should follow the comic strip for a week and select four representative examples of the strip. They should clip these examples and display them on poster board.

4. Give students these steps to follow to help them prepare a presentation on the strip. (We assign 10-minute presentations, but this can be adjusted depending on student level and class size.)

   a. Why does this comic strip interest you? Why did you select this one over others? (Possible answers include the message, the humor, the situations, the artwork.)

   b. Who is the likely audience/reader?

   c. What themes or stories does it deal with?

   d. What are the illustrations like? Are they simple, detailed, caricatures?

   e. What is the reader expected to enjoy or find funny? Does the strip use satire, puns, slapstick, or other obvious types of humor?

   f. Do the characters seem real like you or people you recognize?

   g. Are the situations and humor similar to what you might see in other countries, or do you think they are especially American? Explain.

5. Next, students should interview two Americans, asking them their reaction to the comic strip.

   a. Are they familiar with it? If not, ask the person to read the four representative examples you have chosen.

   b. Do they find it funny? Why or why not?

   c. Do they have any information about the comic strip that they could share with you?

6. Students should then do some research to find some interesting information about the creator of the comic strip and its history.

7. Students can deliver their study in a presentation to the class or in large groups.

CAVEATS AND OPTIONS

You can skip Step 5 if using this activity in a setting where it is difficult to find American informants.

Cartoon Character Convention: Casting Call!

Sean H. Toland and Daniel J. Mills

Levels	**High beginner +**
Contexts	**High school, university, new immigrants, job-experienced**
Aims	**Expand personal information vocabulary**
	Enhance awareness of authentic language
	Experience humor and excitement into the classroom
	Engage in cooperation
Class Time	**60 minutes**
Preparation Time	**15 minutes**
Resources	**Stopwatch**
	Lesson handouts
	Smartphones/tablets

Learning English is often perceived to be a challenging and tedious undertaking that requires students to be highly focused and constantly serious. A growing number of EFL educators in different parts of the globe are challenging this commonly held notion by incorporating humor into their lessons. One teaching strategy that can generate excitement and create opportunities to use authentic language in a classroom is role-playing activities. The lesson plan that follows requires learners to imagine that they are a cartoon character attending an animation convention with other characters. They have been selected to direct and star in a new animated movie. The learners must cast an interesting character to co-star in their film. The students create an original profile for their character and discuss this information in a "speed mingle" session. During the activity, students talk with nine different cartoon characters. Each meeting lasts 3 minutes. At the end of the activity, students select a suitable co-star for their upcoming movie and make a brief report to their classmates. This lesson not only injects humor into a lesson, it allows learners to use authentic language in a realistic context.

PROCEDURE

Before Class

1. Print out the lesson handouts from the appendices.

2. Search on the Internet (e.g., Google Images) for pictures of 10 funny-looking animation characters. Print each image on a separate piece of paper. These images will be used as examples and can be used by students who do not have a smartphone or tablet.

3. Reconfigure the desks in the classroom into a long line. Divide the students into group A or group B. Group A will sit on one side and group B on the other.

During Class

1. Brainstorm the term *speed mingling* with the class. This is similar to *speed dating*. Watch a video of a speed date in action (see Slow Dating, 2009). Explain that students must select a cartoon character and create an original character for the speed mingling part of the lesson. Show students the 10 characters you printed before class.

2. Provide students with a copy of the All-Star Gurl profile card (Appendix A). Select student volunteers to read items on the profile card. Review difficult vocabulary (e.g., *personality*) as well as examples of "funny things that happened to me in the last 3 months."

3. Give students a profile card template (Appendix B). They must search for a funny animation character on their mobile devices. Once they have made their selection, students have 20 minutes to complete their profile cards.

4. Provide the students with the Speed Mingle Activity Chart (Appendix C). This will help them remember the other characters and select a co-star when the activity is finished.

5. Explain the rules of the activity. Each meeting will last 3 minutes. Remind learners that they are the cartoon characters they created (and should use first person). Tell the participants that they must shake hands, introduce themselves, share the images from their mobile devices (or the printouts), as well as ask and answer questions. At exactly 3 minutes, you will signal that it's time to change. Group A will remain seated. Group B will stand up and go to the next character.

6. Before the activity commences, model a speed mingling session with a student volunteer. Emphasize that this a communicative role-play activity and not a reading exercise.

7. When the activity is finished, participants write on the board the name of the character they would like to co-star in their movie.

8. Ask each student her or his preferred choice so the class can see if any characters selected one another.

9. Learners meet in small groups and make a report about the character they would like to cast and the reasons behind their decision.

CAVEATS AND OPTIONS

1. This activity can be modified for different English proficiency levels. Lower level groups might need more time to create their profile. This task can be assigned for homework, and the speed mingling activity can take place during the next class.

2. The time for this activity can also be altered to fit into a shorter lesson. For example, the students can meet with five characters instead of nine.

3. More advanced learners can write a job offer email to the character they selected for their animated movie as a follow-up activity.

REFERENCES AND FURTHER READING

Slow Dating. (2009, July 28). *Good speed dating questions*. Retrieved from https://www.youtube.com/watch?v=Y584fdQldoI&list=TLRMA0LvAhbl8

APPENDIX A: *Cartoon Character Profile Card: All-Star Gurl*

Cartoon Character Profile Card	

A. **Cartoon character name:** All-Star Gurl
B. **Real name:** Sue Jones
C. **Age:** 17 years old
D. **Country:** Australia
E. **Nationality:** Australian
F. **Live:** Tokyo, Japan
G. **Education:** Tokyo University, first year (business administration)
H. **Likes:**
  • animals
  • pizza
  • sunsets and sunrises
I. **Dislikes:**
  • waking up early
  • math
  • spicy food
J. **Free time activities:**
  • yoga and playing volleyball
  • traveling to foreign countries
K. **Special talents:** singing and dancing; juggling fire
L. **Personality:** outgoing and kind
M. **Dream trip destination:** Cairo, Egypt
N. **A funny thing that happened to me in the last 3 months:** I made a chocolate cake for my friends. I used salt instead of sugar. The cake tasted awful!
	Insert image

APPENDIX B: *Cartoon Character Profile Card Template*

Cartoon Character Profile Card	(My cartoon character)
A. Cartoon character name:	
B. Real name:	
C. Age:	
D. Country:	
E. Nationality:	
F. Live:	
G. Education:	
H. Likes: • • •	
I. Dislikes: • • •	
J. Free time activities: • •	
K. Special talents:	
L. Personality:	
M. Dream trip destination:	
N. A funny thing that happened to me in the last 3 months:	

APPENDIX C: *Speed Mingle Activity Chart*

Name of Cartoon Character	Notes	Feelings			
1.		OK	Good!	Excellent!	Awesome!
2.		OK	Good!	Excellent!	Awesome!
3.		OK	Good!	Excellent!	Awesome!
4.		OK	Good!	Excellent!	Awesome!
5.		OK	Good!	Excellent!	Awesome!
6.		OK	Good!	Excellent!	Awesome!
7.		OK	Good!	Excellent!	Awesome!
8.		OK	Good!	Excellent!	Awesome!
9.		OK	Good!	Excellent!	Awesome!
10.		OK	Good!	Excellent!	Awesome!

Humor, Horror, and Halloween: Encountering and Negotiating Editorial Cartoons

Seth A. Streichler

Levels	*Advanced*
Contexts	*University ESL/EFL*
Aims	*Use visual material as a springboard for analysis, interpretation, and discussion*
	Understand attempts at humor related to current events, cultural topics, and social issues
	Understand various cultural, social, political, or ideological allusions in relation to humor
	Apply knowledge about humorous elements and techniques to analyze, explain, and interpret cartoons
	Enhance various communication skills, particularly expressing, supporting, and responding to opinions
Class Time	*40–45 minutes*
Preparation Time	*2–3 hours*
Resources	*Editorial cartoons*

This integrated-skills activity was originally designed for fully matriculated international graduate students taking an advanced-level course titled "Understanding American Humor." In the activity, Halloween-themed editorial cartoons function as a content-based vehicle for students to negotiate attempts at humor, learn cultural allusions, express and support opinions, and practice logical argumentation and rhetorical strategies. Visual material and compelling or controversial commentary stimulate analysis, interpretation, and discussion.

PROCEDURE

Provide sample cartoons to pairs or small groups of students. Websites or class sets of recent hard-copy publications (e.g., newspapers, magazines) may be used for this purpose. Referring to the cartoons provided, students discuss any or all of the following questions prior to a whole-class interchange:

1. Analyze and explain each of the cartoons provided. What conditions, events, and issues are the cartoonists alluding to? Describe and explain the subject matter and content of each image. What background information, if any, is necessary to understand and interpret the images?

2. Editorial cartoonists often depict the interplay among seasonal references (annual events, holidays, etc.) and current events, even if the references and the current events do not appear to be directly related to each other. Why do you think cartoonists use this technique? Why are the cartoonists using Halloween themes to express their points of view?

3. Examine the political perspectives or other opinions that the cartoonists appear to be expressing. What elements of the cartoons communicate these messages? Do you think that the cartoonists are being fair-minded? Why or why not?

4. Do the themes or messages of the cartoons appear to be timeless, or would you describe them as dated? What characteristics of the cartoons influence your response?

5. Explore how the cartoons produce a humorous effect. What comic techniques are the cartoonists exploiting (irony, improbable juxtapositions, fulfillment of expectations, violation of expectations, exaggeration and distortion, understatement, derision or mockery, etc.)?

6. Does the use of humorous techniques enhance the cartoonists' messages? If so, how? Conversely, is it possible that attempts at humor might actually inhibit or obscure the intended message?

7. Place yourself in the role of the cartoonists. Is there anything about the existing cartoons that you might alter to intensify their impact? In addition to explaining the reasons for such changes, attempt to convince the listener that your proposed modifications would significantly enhance the effect of the cartoons.

CAVEATS AND OPTIONS

1. Exercise discretion when using cartoons about controversial or sensitive topics. Although the use of controversial content is often seen as a way to stimulate discussion, it could also have the effect, however unintended, of inhibiting communication or creating a counterproductive classroom atmosphere.

2. You might wish to browse websites and other sources in order to select timely cartoons—that is, those published in October before Halloween—that

might appeal to your students or that might express opinions about other topics covered in class.

3. This activity can be adapted for other holiday-themed cartoons throughout the year. Examples of familiar topics include "out with the old in with the new" for New Year's Day (à la Baby New Year), love and romance for Valentine's Day, and abundance and gratitude for Thanksgiving. (It is worth noting that holiday symbolism can be multifaceted, despite these recognizable clichés, and is seldom restricted to a single motif per holiday.)

4. The Web and other sources offer an abundance of Halloween-themed cartoons with an immense range of topics and opinions. The following are among the many that may be useful for classroom purposes:

- Tom Toles produced a compelling example in October 2008, when it already seemed clear to many that Barack Obama would win the upcoming election. Toles's trademark George W. Bush caricature stands at the White House entrance under a "Welcome Barack" banner. Stereotypical Halloween imagery summarizes Toles's take on the Bush administration: The White House has been transformed into a haunted house. On the grounds, for example, a skeleton emerges from—or is about to seal itself inside—a coffin labeled "Health Care"; tombstones contain the inscriptions "Wages," "Environment," "RIP Global Economy," and "Here Lies Federal Budget"; and a witch stirs a cauldron labeled "Red Ink." By blending these and other classic Halloween images with unmistakable political commentary, the cartoon proclaims that the new president will enter a forbidding world of frightening conditions.

- In his take on media coverage of Hurricane Sandy in 2012, Walt Handelsman juxtaposes the disaster with Halloween clichés: Two trick-or-treaters, a witch and a monster, proclaim, "Now that's scary!!" as they welcome a third trick-or-treater, who is costumed as a television, its screen broadcasting the Weather Channel.

- In October 2013, Kevin Siers used the Headless Horseman (from Washington Irving's "The Legend of Sleepy Hollow") to comment on the Tea Party. The fearsome character holds a tea kettle in the form of a grinning jack-o-lantern; he also bears the famous Gadsden flag from the American Revolution, which depicts a coiled rattlesnake ready to strike along with the motto "Don't tread on me." Ominous and supernatural imagery complements allusions to current events and political history, thereby serving as a vehicle for social or political commentary.

REFERENCES AND FURTHER READING

Toles, T. (2008, October 19). Retrieved from http://www.gocomics.com/tomtoles /2008/10/19

Handelsman, W. (2012, October 28). Retrieved from http://www.gocomics.com /walthandelsman/2012/10/28

Siers, K. (2013, October 22). Retrieved from http://www.cagle.com/2013/10/the -headless-horseman

Part IV

Jokes and Joke Telling

IV

Bring It On

Solihin Agyl

Levels	Intermediate to advanced
Aims	*Express ideas through writing and speaking activities in a free and humorous way*
	Develop confidence in speaking in front of the class
Class Time	*60 minutes*
Preparation Time	*20 minutes*
Resources	*Jokes*

This activity is suggested for students in secondary school, language school, and even university showing a positive attitude toward collaborative learning. The opportunity to collaborate and share humorous stories has the potential to give the class a livelier atmosphere than with more traditional language learning activities. Students can engage in a range of speaking and writing activities in a serious but fun manner.

PROCEDURE

1. Put the students into groups of three or four.

2. Start the activity by providing students with one of your own original anecdotes (see Appendix for an example), and put it on the board or a PowerPoint slide that everybody can see easily.

3. Then, in groups, students have to create their own anecdote or take one from popular publications such as magazines or tabloids.

4. If taken from a publication, ask students to rewrite the story in their own words.

5. Once they have their completed stories, students practice retelling them to one another in their small groups. This way, as this is an anecdote, the re-teller can get some feedback from other members about his or her way of retelling the story, such as how well he or she tells it and how amusing it is.

6. Each group then nominates the best re-teller to represent the group by performing and retelling the anecdote in front of the class.

7. The whole class can then select the best re-teller/storyteller among the groups in the class. The one with the most hilarious anecdote or amusing way of retelling the story is the winner.

CAVEATS AND OPTIONS

1. This works best for a class of approximately 12–20 students.

2. For intermediate students—assumed as the lowest level in this activity—after displaying the example anecdote on the board/slide, provide each group with a different story so that they can work together to try to understand or even memorize it and then practice retelling it in their respective groups.

3. The next steps follow the ones mentioned in **Procedure** starting with Step 4 onward.

   • As another way of grouping the students, it can also be done as a jigsaw activity; each group member has to make one new group consisting of other members of each group—now called the "expert group" (Aronson, 1978).

   • In the new group, students tell one another about the story they created in the previous groups.

   • For the final step, after all students get back to the original group, provide quiz questions about all the stories. The group with the most correct answers is the winner.

REFERENCE AND FURTHER READING

Aronson, E. (1978). *The jigsaw classroom*. Beverly Hills, CA: Sage.

APPENDIX: *Sample Original Joke/Story*

The Aficionado

Maria Ulfa—my 4-year-old niece—was an aficionado of the legendary *Tom & Jerry* cartoon. One morning, in front of the TV set in the family room, she was watching the cartoon when her mother—while preparing breakfast—reminded her not to leave her sleeping baby brother unattended.

"Ulfa!' her mother yelled out from the kitchen, "Keep the mosquitoes away from your baby brother, honey! Swat them with the rolled-up newspaper nearby when they are flying around him." Being thrilled by the world's most-watched cartoon for kids and not wanting to miss a single scene of it, Ulfa responded, "OK, Mom, but please check on him first! When you see mosquitos buzzing around, just let me know!'

Knock Knock. Who's There? Pronunciation!

Alyssa Anders

Levels	Intermediate
Contexts	Grade 6 and up
Aims	*Produce pronunciation features of connected speech*
	Gain cultural understanding of U.S. humor through knock-knock jokes
Class Time	*10–15 minutes*
Preparation Time	*30 minutes*
Resources	*Knock-knock jokes that demonstrate connected speech in the punch line*

Knock-knock jokes are an iconic part of U.S. culture. Teaching ESL is also about teaching culture, and humor can be used as a bridge between English words and U.S. culture to improve students' intercultural competency (Forman, 2011; Wulf, 2010). Many knock-knock jokes are based on a play of sounds, where words with completely different meanings are substituted due to their similar pronunciation. With this in mind, knock-knock jokes can be a great way to teach students the types of connected speech, which are outlined by Celce-Murcia, Brinton, and Goodwin (2010), including linking, reductions, assimilation, dissimilation, deletion, and epenthesis. Teaching connected speech with knock-knock jokes gives students an excellent opportunity to first perceive pronunciation in connected speech and then produce the sounds themselves. The perception and production practice is based on meaning-focused input and output, two key factors in listening and speaking courses (Nation & Newton, 2009).

PROCEDURE

1. Select knock-knock jokes that demonstrate a previously taught pronunciation feature of connected speech (e.g., linking, specifically glide insertion: *Knock knock. Who's there? Canoe. Canoe who? Canoe help me with my homework?* see Appendix for more examples).

2. To practice perception, read one knock-knock joke out loud, modeling how the listener responds to the cues of the joke.

3. Students volunteer where they think the connected speech occurred.

4. Writes the punch line on the board, explaining new vocabulary as needed.

5. Students volunteer what is spelled incorrectly and how to correct it (e.g., *canoe = can you*).

6. Point out how connected speech is used in this joke (e.g., *canoe* sounds like *can you* because of the glide insertion).

7. The class discusses the meaning of this joke (e.g., Is it supposed to be serious? Silly? Why does it make someone laugh?)

8. To practice production, each student is given a knock-knock joke.

9. Students tell their jokes in pairs. They then discuss the meaning of the joke and where connected speech takes place, noting the difference in sound and spelling of the key words. Circulate throughout the class, monitoring for correct production of the connected speech and answering questions.

10. Students share their jokes with the class, emphasizing where connected speech occurs.

CAVEATS AND OPTIONS

More advanced students can write their own knock-knock jokes.

REFERENCES AND FURTHER READING

Celce-Murcia, M., Brinton, D., & Goodwin, J. (with Griner, B.). (2010). *Teaching pronunciation: A course book and reference guide*. New York, NY: Cambridge University Press.

Forman, R. (2011). Humorous language play in a Thai EFL classroom. *Applied Linguistics 32*, 541–565.

Nation, I., & Newton, J. (2009). *Teaching ESL/EFL listening and speaking*. New York, NY: Routledge.

Wulf, D. (2010). A humor competence curriculum. *TESOL Quarterly, 44*, 155–169.

APPENDIX: *Example Knock-Knock Jokes That Demonstrate Connected Speech*

Linking

Knock knock.
Who's there?
Canoe.
Canoe who?
Canoe help me with my homework?

Knock knock.
Who's there?
Justin.
Justin who?
Justin time for dinner.

Assimilation

Knock knock.
Who's there?
Dozen.
Dozen who?
Dozen anybody want to let me in?

Knock knock.
Who's there?
Roach.
Roach who?
Roach you a letter, did you get it?

Reductions

Knock knock
Who's there?
Iva.
Iva who?
Iva sore hand from knocking!

Knock knock
Who's there?
Alex.
Alex who?
Alex-plain later!

Ambiguity in Linguistic Jokes

Brita Banitz

Levels	**Advanced**
Aims	**Notice the double meaning of some typically well-known words**
	Develop awareness of the linguistic mechanisms language-based jokes are based on
Class Time	**50 minutes**
Preparation Time	**60 minutes**
Resources	**Worksheets (Appendices A and B)**

Humor, "a universal human trait" (Raskin, 1985, p. 2), is an essential component of communicative competence and, as such, should be taught in the language classroom since being able to handle humor in another language bears many advantages for the language learner, for example, to create and maintain group solidarity and to criticize others in socially acceptable ways (Yarwood, 1995), to reduce anxiety and tension and to increase mood and motivation (Banitz, 2005), and to stimulate intellectual creativity (Holmes, 2007). However, to successfully integrate humor in language teaching, the students' proficiency levels and personal backgrounds need to be considered. To that end, Schmitz (2002, p. 89) suggests a categorization of three types: universal or reality-based humor, culture-based humor, and linguistic or word-based humor. The latter, the most sophisticated of the three because of its play with language, is the topic of this lesson.

PROCEDURE

1. Ask students to try to think of some jokes in English. In pairs, have them write down their favorite ones or search for some on the Internet (see References and Further Reading for suggestions). (Select language-based jokes to be used for later analysis.)

2. Give students a worksheet (Appendix A) with sentences that are based on semantic ambiguity to be answered individually. Compare and discuss answers and explain that linguistic jokes work with ambiguity. This can be based on meaning (semantics), structure (syntax), and/or pronunciation (phonetics).

3. Give students another worksheet (Appendix B) with two or three linguistic jokes. Students read the jokes in pairs and search for the trigger. They underline the trigger, determine the mechanism on which the joke is based (semantic, syntactic, and/or phonetic), and explain the joke.

4. Students analyze and explain another pair's jokes from Step 1. (Prepare additional jokes in case students did not write down more linguistic jokes.)

CAVEATS AND OPTIONS

1. Separate worksheets focusing on each of the linguistic mechanisms can be elaborated for very advanced learners, who have to deduce the different strategies (semantic, syntactic, and/or phonetic) that each set of jokes is based on.

2. For upper intermediate learners, focus on knock-knock jokes, a particular language-based type of humor common in the United States, and the role of pronunciation in these jokes (e.g., Knock knock! Who's there? Doris. Doris who? Door is locked, that's why I had to knock!). More adventurous students could even create their own knock-knock jokes and perform them in front of the class, thus practicing pronunciation.

REFERENCES AND FURTHER READING

Banitz, B. (2005). Humor in the language classroom: Challenges and advantages. *INTESOL Journal*, *2*(1), 73–85.

Holmes, J. (2007). Making humor work: Creativity on the job. *Applied Linguistics* *28*, 518–537.

Raskin, V. (1985). *Semantic mechanisms of humor.* Dordrecht, Netherlands: Reidel.

Schmitz, J. R. (2002). Humor as a pedagogical tool in foreign language and translation courses. *Humor*, *15*(1), 89–113.

Yarwood, D. L. (1995). Humor and administration: A serious inquiry into unofficial organizational communication. *Public Administration Review*, *55*(1), 81–90.

Joke Sites on the Internet

http://jokes.cc.com

http://www.laughfactory.com/jokes

http://www.rd.com/jokes

http://iteslj.org/c/jokes-short.html

http://www.jokesgallery.com/jokes

APPENDIX A: *Student Worksheet*

Explain the semantic ambiguity of the following sentences. Underline the word that seems to carry the ambiguity, and provide two (or more) sentences that paraphrase the multiple meanings.

Example: She can't bear children.

    a.   She can't give birth to children.

    b.   She can't tolerate children.

Other examples:

1. Joan waited for him by the bank.

    a.   John waited by the financial institution.

    b.   John waited by the lake shore (or river side).

2. Is he really that kind?

    a.   Is he really that nice?

    b.   Is he really like one of them (comparing him to other people who share a specific characteristic)?

APPENDIX B: *Sample Jokes and Linguistic Categories*

Joke 1 (Semantic)

Man in restaurant: "I'll have two lamb chops, and make them lean, please."

Waiter: "To which side, sir?"

Explanation: *lean*$_1$: no fat; *lean*$_2$: tilted to one side

Source: Seewoester, S. (2009). *Linguistic ambiguity in language-based jokes* (Master's thesis). De Paul University, Chicago, IL. Retrieved from http://via.library.depaul.edu/cmnt/3

Joke 2 (Syntactic/Pragmatic)

A man spoke frantically into the phone: "My wife is pregnant and her contractions are only two minutes apart!"

"Is this her first child?" the emergency operator asked.

"No, you idiot!" the man shouted. "This is her husband!"

Explanation: *Is this X?*$_1$: refers to whoever the caller is talking about (in this case, the child his wife is having); *Is this Y?*$_2$: refers to who is calling (in this case, the husband who is making the phone call)

Source: http://www.jokes2go.com/jokes/8027.html

Joke 3 (Syntactic)

A man goes into a restaurant dragging a 10-foot alligator. He manages to get the alligator stuffed under a table. When the waitress approaches, he asks her if they serve senior citizens here.

"Of course," she says.

"Good," he answers. "Give my alligator a senior citizen, and I'll have a cheeseburger."

Explanation: *to serve X*$_1$: to supply food; *to serve Y*$_2$: to attend to someone

Source: Nilsen, D., & Nilsen, A. (2015). *Ambiguity, puns and visual ambivalence.* Retrieved from http://www.public.asu.edu/~dnilsen/documents/ambiguity.ppt

Joke 4 (Phonetic/Knock-Knock)

Knock knock!
Who's there?
Police.
Police who?
Police hurry up; it's chilly outside.

Explanation: police; please

Source: http://www.funology.com/knock-knock-jokes-page-3

Joke 5 (Bilingual)

What if soy milk is just regular milk introducing itself in Spanish?

Explanation: *soy milk* (a type of milk); *soy* (Spanish for "I am")

Source: http://littlefun.org/posts/what-if-soy-milk-is-just-regular-milk-introducing-itself-in-spanish

How Do You Get to (*Somewhere Other Than Carnegie Hall*)?

Richard Hodson

Levels	*Low-intermediate +*
Contexts	*University, young adult, or adult*
Aims	*Create an original joke by rewriting the cultural elements of a well-known English joke*
	Understand cultural symbols of one's own culture
Class Time	*30 minutes*
Preparation Time	*10 minutes*
Resources	*Whiteboard, presentation, or handout to explain the original joke*
	Handout or paper for student joke writing

Creating an original joke from scratch is a task that can prove daunting not just for learners, but even for some native speakers of a language. However, jokes exist to be told and retold, and the task of retelling an existing joke by modifying certain cultural elements allows learners to create an original, appealing, and personal humorous text. The simple structure and clear relationships between cultural and linguistic elements in the Carnegie Hall joke make it particularly suitable for modification by language learners.

PROCEDURE

1. Introduce the original Carnegie Hall joke in a form suitable for classroom use, for example:

   A tourist in New York realizes that he's lost and asks a passer-by, "How do you get to Carnegie Hall?" The passer-by replies, "Practice, practice, practice!"

2. Explain or elicit the main structural elements of the joke:

   - Location: New York

   - Destination: Carnegie Hall

   - Punch line: Practice, practice, practice!

3. Explain or elicit the relationship between the destination and the punch line, and the double meaning of the phrase *get to*. Students should understand that the destination is both a geographical place and an institution with demanding admission standards.

4. Have students rewrite the joke, replacing the location and destination with elements from their own personal experience or cultural context and writing an appropriate punch line.

5. Have students tell their jokes to classmates, in pairs, groups, or as a whole class. Students who finish quickly can be encouraged to produce multiple variations of the joke.

CAVEATS AND OPTIONS

1. Some students may need individual assistance in coming up with original destinations. A few hints about relevant cultural, educational, or sporting institutions in their own contexts may help them.

2. Depending on students' level and the time available, you can give students free rein to rewrite any or all of the joke text from scratch or instruct them explicitly to replace the location, destination, and punch line. Alternatively, you can give them prepared worksheets containing the joke text with blanks to be filled in.

3. The original joke text can be constructed in any number of ways to incorporate target language or vocabulary appropriate to the class. The text given here has a simple, repetitive punch line, but this does not need to be the case, and students can be encouraged to construct the punch line in any way that they choose.

REFERENCES AND FURTHER READING

There are various explanations of the origin and history of the Carnegie Hall joke, and there are numerous variations of the joke text itself. The following two references give further information on the joke.

Carnegie Hall. (2016). History of the hall. Retrieved from http://www.carnegie hall.org/History/History-FAQ

Cerf, B. (1956). *The life of the party: A new collection of stories and anecdotes*. New York, NY: Doubleday.

APPENDIX: *Three Sample Jokes*

Learner retellings vary in ambition and complexity, as the following three examples created by students at a univeristy in Japan show:

A tourist in Hyogo Prefecture realizes that he's lost, and asks a passer-by, "How do you get to Koshien Stadium?" The passer-by replies, "Practice, practice, practice!"

> In this, the simplest possible variation of the joke, the writer has replaced only the location and destination: Koshien Stadium is a baseball stadium in Hygo Prefecture, in western Japan. It is home to the Hanshin Tigers professional baseball team as well as a venue for hugely popular national high school baseball tournaments. High school baseball players practice rigorously year-round in the hopes that their school will qualify for these tournaments.

A tourist in Tokyo realizes that he's lost, and asks a passer-by, "How do you get to Tokyo University?" The passer-by replies, "Study, study, study!"

> A slightly more complex variation, in which the punch line verb also has been changed to accompany the educational theme of the new destination. Tokyo University is the most prestigious university in Japan.

A tourist in Akihabara realizes that he's lost, and asks a passer-by, "How do you get to AKB Theater?" The passer-by replies: "Cosmetic surgery!"

> This variation has abandoned the triple repetition of the punch line entirely. AKB48 is a popular Japanese idol girl group with its own theater in the Akihabara area of Tokyo.

Humor Contest

Sally La Luzerne-Oi

Levels	*High-beginning to advanced*
Contexts	*University*
Aims	*Practice public speaking*
	Practice storytelling
	Build English program dynamics
Class Time	*10–20 minutes over several class periods*
Preparation Time	*Varies*

A humor contest is a public speaking event for students that is less formal than a traditional speech contest. Students who participate say the contest helped them gain confidence and courage to speak in front of a group. They feel their English improved by repeatedly practicing the timing, stress, and gestures needed to make their jokes interesting and comprehensible. Both participants and audience report the contest is fun and has a wonderful atmosphere.

PROCEDURE

Before the Contest

1. Decide on a location and date to hold the contest, and announce at least 1 month ahead of time. Make all necessary arrangements.

2. Determine guidelines for participants' entries. For example, prepare to tell a funny story or joke. It must tell a story in the past tense, have a surprising or humorous ending, and be inoffensive.

3. Brainstorm ways to encourage student participation (see Appendix A).

4. Ask two or three faculty members to be judges, perhaps those colleagues who have a reputation for being funny.

5. Ask the program director or another faculty member to be the MC. This person should have a repertoire of jokes.

6. Solicit prizes.

7. Publicize the event.

8. Have students submit entry cards (see Appendix B). Order the cards and number them. One way to order them is according to the students' levels, with lower levels going first.

9. If possible, arrange to record the contest. You can then use the recording to publicize future contests and give future participants an idea of what the humor contest is like.

On the Day of the Contest

1. The MC welcomes everyone, introduces the judges, and starts off the contest with a few jokes.

2. The MC uses the entry cards to call up contestants one by one.

3. When all contestants have finished telling their jokes or stories, the judges leave the room and deliberate on the awards (see Appendix C). Awards can be given by categories. Sometimes these categories need to be made up on the spot. During this time, the MC tells more jokes.

4. Once the judges have decided, students are called up to receive prizes. Larger prizes for outstanding contestants and token prizes for all others works well.

After the Contest

1. Send out thank-you notes to all who helped so that they will help again!

2. Publish/post the names of the winners/contestants.

APPENDIX A: *Encouraging Students to Participate in a Humor Contest*

The success of the humor contest depends for the most part on how much classroom teachers encourage their students to participate. It is good to designate specific classes in an English language program (e.g., speaking classes) as the place where teachers will explain the contest, answer questions, help students prepare, and collect entry cards. Here are some ways to encourage students to participate.

1. Give information about the humor contest and reasons it would be good for students to participate.

2. Do a unit on humor if time permits. At a minimum, spend some time talking with students about humor and what they find humorous. Give examples of funny English anecdotes, jokes, puns, and riddles.

3. Model telling the kind of story or joke that follows the humor contest guidelines. Explain the importance of timing, stress, and body language. Discuss what kinds of jokes and stories are acceptable for the humor contest.

4. Ask students to prepare a story or joke in one of the following ways: translate a joke from their native language to English, write a narrative about something funny that happened to them or someone they know, ask a native speaker of English to tell them a joke. After doing one or all of these, they should practice telling the story or joke. Give feedback on grammar if necessary and suggestions for gestures, stress, and pauses. During a class period, give students time to mingle and tell their jokes. Give them the lead-in "Have you heard any good jokes lately?" and "Have you heard the one about . . . ?"

5. Ask how many people would like to volunteer to represent the class in the program-wide humor contest. As an alternative, have an in-class humor contest. Ask each student to vote on the three entries they thought were the funniest. Ask the winners to represent the class, and ask their classmates to cheer them on.

APPENDIX B: *Sample Entry Card*

EFP 1300	
(Student's Level)	(Speaker's Number)
Chuang I-Fen	Sally La Luzerne-Oi
(Student's Name)	(Teacher's Name)
The Mushroom	
(Title of Joke)	

Acknowledgment: Thanks to Rob Wilson for this idea.

IV

APPENDIX C: *Joke Checklist for Judges*

Speaker No. _____

Possible Category _____

(Rate each component from 1 to 10, with 10 being the highest.)

1. Oral Delivery

    spoke clearly _____

    stressed key words and paused at appropriate places _____

    spoke naturally _____

    spoke loudly _____

2. Physical Delivery

    maintained eye contact with audience _____

    used gestures _____

3. Joke Quality

    appropriate for the audience _____

    humorous _____

 Total _____

Possible Category _____

Example Prize Categories

   Best Overall Joke

   Best Gestures

   Best Visual Aids

   Best Rapport With Audience

   Best Play on Words

   Best Joke Involving Culture

   Best Animal Joke

   Clearest Joke

Acknowledgment: This checklist is based on one made by humor contest judge Hari Harrison.

Can You Ruin a Good Joke?

Michelle Lam

Levels	*Intermediate to advanced*
Contexts	*English-speaking country*
Aims	*Develop observational skills*
	Develop joke-telling social skills
	Learn differences between joke-telling in the home country and in the English-speaking country
Class Time	*45–60 minutes*
Preparation Time	*15 minutes*
Resources	*Short video of a standup comedian*
	Worksheet (see Appendix)

Telling a good joke is more than the words used. Having students observe a standup comedian for social cues teaches both the social cues as well as the importance of observing them in the first place. By switching the goal from trying to be humorous to instead trying to ruin a good joke with poor social cues, this activity removes the anxiety involved on the part of the learner.

PROCEDURE

1. Invite several students to tell a joke from their own language translated into English. Discuss as a class what makes these jokes funny (or not). Try to introduce nonlinguistic elements into this discussion. For example, is it funnier if the joke teller is using his or her body in some way?

2. Watch a video clip of a standup comedian doing a comedy bit about only one topic (e.g., Seinfeld on airplanes; many examples can be found on YouTube). Have students practice telling the joke using the same words.

3. In pairs, have students tell the same joke but intentionally try to make it not funny.

4. Discuss as a class what types of social cues (body language, chuckling during a line, etc.) make jokes funnier (or less funny).

CAVEATS AND OPTIONS

1. For lower level students, providing a transcript of the video clip or using subtitles during the clip might be useful.

2. Encourage students to build this practice into their regular lives. If students can learn that communication is more than just words, this observational practice will help them become more adept in their new language.

3. For beginning or intermediate students, having a worksheet (see Appendix) might be helpful.

APPENDIX: *Can You Ruin a Good Joke?*

Sort these statements into the two categories below:

- My partner is looking at my face.

- My partner is looking at the floor.

- My partner is smiling.

- My partner is very serious.

- My partner starts laughing when he or she is talking.

- My partner moves his or her hands a lot.

- My partner does not move.

- My partner speaks very loudly.

- My partner speaks very softly.

- My partner speaks quickly.

- My partner speaks slowly.

Makes Me Laugh More

_____

_____

_____

_____

_____

Makes Me Laugh Less

_____

_____

_____

_____

_____

What other things help make a joke funny? _____

_____

_____

_____

Humor as a Key to Culture: Interviewing a Local Comedian Project

Betty Litsinger

Levels	*Advanced*
Contexts	*College seminar on U.S. culture (can be modified to fit a range of contexts)*
Aims	*Learn to analyze text through a conceptual or cultural lens*
	Identify commonalities and differences in humor among cultures
	Expand ability to participate in classroom discussion and informal conversations in English
Class Time	*Three 80-minute sessions*
Preparation Time	*30 minutes*
Resources	*YouTube clip of a stand-up comic (My students interviewed local comedian Chanel Ali, featured in* Inherently Funny: *www.youtube.com/watch?v=2N2TPjUui98. If you are able to get access to a local comedian for your students to interview, show a video of the comedian to help students get familiar with the person's work.)*
	Articles providing taxonomy and analysis of jokes (see References and Further Reading)

ESL students are often hesitant to speak in spontaneous classroom discussions. Scaffolded activities that allow them to prepare for and control the direction of the academic conversation help to build fluency and confidence. Outside the classroom, international students sometimes feel excluded from informal conversations that rely heavily on humor, one of the most complex and deeply cultural aspects of language competency. By applying structural analysis to a joke and interviewing fellow students and (hopefully) a professional comedian, students participate in both critical inquiry involving primary (jokes) and secondary (research articles) sources and in authentic academic and social interactions with Americans.

PROCEDURE

My class project was divided over 3 days. If your teaching context is different, you can also just do the Day 1 activity (see Caveats and Options for more information).

Day 1

1. Students bring to class a joke that they find particularly funny or incomprehensible. I suggest that they ask their roommates or an American friend to tell them a joke.

2. Students tell their jokes. The class discusses whether the joke is understood, whether it is funny, and whether a similar joke is told in any of the students' cultures. Through discussion students are able to clarify misunderstandings in interpretation and are often surprised to find that a particular joke is funnier than they thought or that the reason they found a joke funny was the result of misinterpretation and actually not part of the joke teller's intention.

Day 2

1. *Before class:* Students read two articles (see References and Further Reading) and attempt to apply the principles and models to their joke.

2. *In class:* Discuss the usefulness of the ideas in the readings to explain humor. Students generate and apply criteria for evaluating the strength of a theory. As a class, view a video clip of the comedian who will visit during the next class session.

Day 3

1. *Before class:* Students each prepare at least three interview questions for the stand-up comedian. Encourage them to ask follow-up questions for clarification.

2. *In class:* Students address their questions to the guest speaker. This activity allows students to examine the relationship between theory and practice and to learn about the process of writing and performing jokes.

CAVEATS AND OPTIONS

1. Since the focus of my class is writing, I follow this lesson with an essay assignment in which students analyze a video clip of a stand-up performance. There are many on Comedy Central's website (www.cc.com) and YouTube. This activity provides an opportunity to apply and evaluate ideas

from the readings and the interview. It also gives students practice in citing material from class discussion, interviews, and journal articles.

2. Depending on students' ages and cultural backgrounds, it is important to choose the stand-up comic with care. I was fortunate in finding a delightful and informative speaker whose views reinforced the value of a liberal arts education, the importance of library research, and the need for smart career planning.

3. Days 2 and 3 probably wouldn't be appropriate for less advanced learners, but the Day 1 activity, which requires students to determine the meaning of a joke and decide if and why it is funny, could work well in an intermediate-level class as well. Of course, not everyone will be lucky enough to have access to a local professional comedian. However, the Day 1 activity itself is a useful start in helping ESL students understand the humor of the target culture and gain the confidence to take part in spontaneous conversations outside of the classroom.

REFERENCES AND FURTHER READING

Davies, C. (2008). The comparative study of jokes. *Society*, *47*, 38–41. doi:10.1007/s12115-009-9279-5

Earleywine, M. (2010). Models and mechanisms—Funny in theory. In *Humor 101* (pp. 1–35). New York, NY: Springer.

APPENDIX: *Sample Discussion and Interview Questions*

Sample Questions for Day 2 Discussion

1. Is there a group in your culture about whom people tell "blonde jokes"? What social conditions or cultural beliefs account for this characterization?

2. What are some consequences of the use of humor as a way to assess commonality?

3. Is it possible to develop what Earleywine calls a "grand theory of humor"?

4. How useful is Earleywine's incongruity-resolution theory in accounting for the structure of the jokes we have discussed and in predicting whether a joke is funny?

5. Earleywine points out several problems with studying humor in the laboratory. Can you think of other difficulties the researcher might encounter?

Sample Question Frames for Interviewing the Guest Speaker

1. (Author of article) says (summary of an argument from the article). What do you think about that?

2. Can you tell us how you (verb + noun related to the process of writing a joke)?

3. How do you change your act if the audience is (adjective describing the audience)?

4. Are there topics that you consider to be too (adjective)?

Listen and Complete: Understanding One-Liners

Theresa McGarry

Levels	*High intermediate to advanced*
Aims	*Develop pronunciation and fluency in listening*
	Learn about cultural topics and references in English humor
Class Time	*10–20 minutes*
Preparation Time	*15–30 minutes the first time, 10 minutes thereafter*
Resources	*Internet*
	Photocopier

According to Nation and Newton (2009, p. 151), "learners demonstrate fluency when they take part in meaning-focused activity and do it with speed and ease without holding up the flow of talk." This activity serves as a scaffolding task for students to heighten fluency, focusing on listening. In a controlled task with clear outcomes, students process idiomatic language at an advanced level similar to that required for natural conversation. This activity requires learners to focus on the meaning of the utterances, since sophisticated messages must be understood in order to complete the sentences. At the same time, learners are motivated to pronounce clearly for their partners and to process the utterances in order to appreciate the humor, which then relieves the tension of working with natural, colloquial language. The activity can be particularly helpful to learners living in an ESL context because the utterances reference aspects of culture such as proverbs, familiar jokes, and common practices and topics of conversation.

PROCEDURE

1. To prepare the activity, find about 10–15 short funny utterances. (To find them on the Internet, you can use search terms such as "one-liners" or "anti-proverbs.") Divide the utterances into two equal groups, then divide each utterance at a natural breaking point. Prepare a Worksheet A that contains the first half of each utterance in the first group and the second half of each one in the second group, in scrambled order, and a Worksheet B that contains the second half of each utterance in the first group and the first half

of each one in the second group, scrambled. Make enough copies so that half of the students have Worksheet A and the other half have Worksheet B. (See Appendix for the worksheets.)

2. Arrange students in pairs, with the members of each pair facing each other. Hand out the worksheets so that in each pair one partner has A and the other has B. Tell them to read the sheet they're given but not show it to their partner.

3. The A partner reads the utterance beginnings one by one, and the B partner scans the list of endings to find the one that fits, then reads it to A so they can both appreciate the full utterance. If B has trouble with any item, the pair can skip that one temporarily and come back to it after eliminating some other choices.

4. When the first half of the utterances have been matched, it's B's turn to read the first half of the utterances in the second group and let A give the completions.

CAVEATS AND OPTIONS

1. If the activity is done with material that references well-known sayings or quotations (e.g., "If life gives you limes, make gin and tonics," "I don't think much, therefore I might not be"), it might be desirable to let the class read the standard versions of the sayings first to make sure they're familiar with them. Also, a potential follow-up activity to working with these kinds of utterances is a class discussion on ideas and situations that the sayings evoke and how they compare to sayings, beliefs, or situations in the learners' home cultures.

2. Materials to make the worksheets are plentiful on the Internet (e.g., http://cfcl.com/vlb/Cuute/Quotes/oneliners.txt). Search terms useful for finding material include "one-liners," "anti-proverbs," and "funny quotes." It is also useful to search the names of comedians who are known for one-liners, such as Steven Wright and Demetri Martin.

REFERENCES AND FURTHER READING

Nation, I. S. P., & Newton, N. (2009). *Teaching ESL/EFL listening and speaking.* New York, NY: Routledge.

APPENDIX: *Sample Worksheet Pair*

Worksheet A

He who laughs last . . .

People who live in glass houses . . .

Give a man a fish and you feed him for a day. Teach a man to fish . . .

If at first you don't succeed, . . .

Don't criticize someone until you've walked a mile in their shoes. . . .

The early bird gets the worm, . . .

gets most of the covers.

the movie version.

safer than one overhead.

but three lefts do.

but it takes longer to load.

ask for salt and tequila.

Worksheet B

but the second mouse gets the cheese.

and he'll sit in a boat and drink beer all day.

might as well answer the door.

didn't really get the joke.

skydiving's not for you.

That way, if they get mad, you're a mile away and you have their shoes.

A bird in the hand is . . .

If life gives you lemons, . . .

Don't judge a book by . . .

A picture is worth a thousand words, . . .

One good turn . . .

Two wrongs don't make a right, . . .

Changing a Light Bulb to Turn On Nonverbal Communication

Gloria Munson

Levels	*Varies with choice of jokes*
Aims	*Develop ability to use nonverbal communication to enhance verbal communication*
Class Time	*20–25 minutes plus 1–2 minutes per student for presentations*
Preparation Time	*Varies*
Resources	*Videos of one or two stand-up comics*
	Level-appropriate light bulb jokes

Cultural differences and fear of mistakes may make language learners reluctant to use gestures while speaking a foreign language. However, facial expressions and body movements can help improve their listener's comprehension of a story or joke. Using gestures while telling jokes gives students the opportunity to experiment with different types of body language, improve oral communication, and laugh at themselves.

PROCEDURE

1. Search YouTube for clips of stand-up comics who use a variety of facial expressions and/or gestures. The videos of young Robin Williams, Gilda Radner, Steve Martin, and Jim Carrey demonstrate strong facial expressions and body movements. Select one or two. Don't worry about the language on the audio; you will mute the sound. However, you should avoid clips with inappropriate gestures.

2. Introduce the activity by playing Simon Says. Choose prompts that reflect the movements that students will see in the video clips. Add mimicking screwing in a light bulb.

3. Play a section of the comic video (with the sound off). The first time, students watch without movement. The second time, instruct them to mimic the movements of the comedian.

4. Explain stereotypes and then demonstrate a few light bulb jokes. Stress that the stereotypes used in light bulb jokes give people a chance to laugh at themselves. Do one light bulb joke without gestures followed by the same one with exaggerated gestures. Repeat with other jokes as needed.

5. Divide the class into pairs. Give each pair a set of light bulb jokes. (These can easily be found on the Internet.) Consider a set of jokes that three people could split in case you have an odd number of students in your class. Students work together to prepare telling a designated number of jokes with as many gestures as possible.

6. Students take turns telling the jokes to the class. (See the Appendix for the structure of light bulb jokes.)

CAVEATS AND OPTIONS

1. Encourage students to record their joke presentations on their cell phones. The clips can be uploaded to a class website.

2. Because light bulb jokes are intended to make light-hearted fun of particular groups of people (professions, countries, universities), warn students that stereotypes should not be used to hurt other people and they should be careful how they use stereotypes when joking. Encourage students to restructure the jokes to make fun of their own characteristics or interests, not others in the classroom. To help students, ask them to google "how many ____ does it take to change a light bulb?" For example, if you have an engineering student, he or she might put "engineers" in the blank.

3. Other types of jokes could be substituted for light bulb jokes (knock-knock jokes, puns, riddles).

4. Allow students to be creative and change the original jokes as appropriate.

5. Provide a box of props that encourages the use of gestures.

6. After students finish preparing their joke presentations, show the muted clip again then add another minute of rehearsal time.

7. If the Internet is unavailable, you may spend more time demonstrating gestures and facial expressions. For example, you may make an expression or movements and students guess the emotion or action.

REFERENCES AND FURTHER READING

To find jokes, use keywords *light bulb jokes for ESL* or *light bulb jokes for kids*.

APPENDIX: *Anatomy of a Light Bulb Joke*

Question: How many of a certain • culture • profession • group of people	does it take to	• change • replace • screw in	a light bulb?	**Answer:** (Shows stereotype.)

Joke of the Day

David R. M. Saavedra

Levels	Intermediate to advanced
Contexts	Middle and secondary
Aims	Build close reading skills
	Analyze language features
Class Time	8–10 minutes
Preparation Time	5 minutes
Resources	Student double-entry journals (each page is divided into two columns)
	Board, projector, or chart paper to display the joke

Jokes often use puns, plays on words, and homophones to create humor. This activity is a great way to expose students to these uses of language. Additionally, the skill of close reading is necessary for truly engaging with text and is being emphasized more and more with the adoption of the Common Core State Standards. This opening routine gives students a daily opportunity to read closely while examining the language of humor. The routine builds both skills over time. Students read a small amount of text deeply, thinking about its meaning and how language is used to make its meaning.

PROCEDURE

1. Buy or check out a joke book, or find a website with hundreds of jokes (see References and Further Reading for suggestions).

2. Each day, choose one joke and write it on the board or on chart paper. Under the joke, write one to three focus questions that get students thinking about the situation and/or the language of the joke. Below is an example from *Jokelopedia: The Biggest, Best, Silliest, Dumbest Joke Book Ever* (Weitzman, Blank, Benjamin, Green, & Sparks, 2013, p. 78).

Sample Joke

Why was Susan's Dad kicking the computer?

He was trying to boot it up.

Sample Focus Questions

Which word in the answer connects with the work *kicking*?

What does *boot it up* mean?

Why is this joke funny? (Hint: What does Susan's father *not* understand?)

3. This is the opening routine for class. Students enter and read the joke. In the left-hand column of their journal, they write the questions. In the right-hand column they write their thoughts (see Appendix for a sample).

4. If time permits, share some thoughts about the joke as a whole class.

CAVEATS AND OPTIONS

1. When possible, create questions that focus student attention on language structures or vocabulary they are in the process of acquiring. Or create questions on structures/vocabulary that you will introduce in that lesson. It can be a fun way to reinforce learning.

2. As students become comfortable with the routine and their close reading skills improve, provide fewer questions. Encourage them to create their own questions about the joke that they can discuss with others.

3. This routine can be used with straight quotations as well. Quotations can be from texts being read in class or famous quotes you want students to ponder.

REFERENCES AND FURTHER READING

Double Entry Journals

García, O. (2009). *Bilingual education in the 21st century: A global perspective.* Malden, MA: Wiley/Blackwell.

Sandbox Networks. (2000–2016). Double entry journals. Retrieved from https://www.teachervision.com/writing/letters-and-journals/48536.html

Joke Books

Elliott, R. (2010). *Laugh-out-loud jokes for kids.* Grand Rapids, MI: Spire.

Just joking: 300 hilarious jokes, tricky tongue twisters, and ridiculous riddles. (2012). Washington, DC: National Geographic.

Weitzman, I., Blank, E., Benjamin, A., Green, R., & Sparks, L. (2013). *Jokelopedia: The biggest, best, silliest, dumbest joke book ever* (3rd ed.). New York, NY: Workman.

Joke Websites

http://www.ajokeaday.com

http://www.greatcleanjokes.com

http://www.kidsjokesoftheday.com

APPENDIX: *Double Entry Journal Sample*

Prompt	Student response/student thinking

TALL Tales

John Schmidt

Levels	*High-beginning to advanced*
Contexts	*Secondary, university, intensive English program*
Aims	*Enjoy a humorous and entertaining context for the development of aural skills and oral fluency*
	Enhance creative, imaginative, and semi-extemporaneous communication in English
	Enjoy language use, as students express themselves whimsically
	Foster a lively and engaging classroom atmosphere
Class Time	*20–30 minutes (but could be abridged)*
Preparation Time	*Less than 5 minutes*
Resources	*Small piece of paper for each student*
	Board
	Time piece (e.g., mobile phone with timer)
	Green, yellow, red "timing cards" (pieces of paper) for each student pair (optional)

TALL Tales is adapted from Toastmasters International Tall Tales district speech contests held worldwide. TALL Tales sparks ESL/EFL students' desire to create humorous, outlandish tales, transporting classmates to other lands or worlds, along with renowned celebrities. Lively TALL Tales storytelling engages listeners to catch the details of exciting, imaginative, and magical adventures. Surprising, fantastical, and zany stories bring lots of laughter to the classroom.

PROCEDURE

1. Elicit the following from students, choosing and writing on the board items from each category:

    • a city or other specific place on earth—or elsewhere (in the universe)

    • a famous TV or movie actor (known to everyone present)

- a famous musician, political leader, or athlete (known to everyone present)

- a superhuman, superpower, supernatural feat, skill, or ability (or an extraordinary vehicle or machine)

2. Having pre-trained a student as timekeeper, extemporaneously tell students about your wild weekend (or vacation), incorporating the items on the board into a TALL Tale full of excitement, exaggeration, and unbelievable, impossible, and sometimes heroic situations.

3. After 2 minutes the timekeeper shows the green light (timing card). Wrap up the story or continue.

4. After 3 minutes, the yellow light. End or prepare to end within 30 seconds.

5. By 3½ minutes (red light), you must finish the story.

6. Erase the board, and pass out paper to students. Restate the prompts (from Step 1), and have students write responses.

7. Students are paired up with a set of timing cards. Standing up and around the classroom, a member of each pair starts telling the partner a TALL Tale. Half of the students are talking at the same time, making for a loud but orally productive classroom. Listeners try to remember as much as they can about the story and don't interrupt, converse, or ask questions while their partner tells the tale.

CAVEATS AND OPTIONS

1. Abridge or extend the speaking time frame, depending on student proficiency and experience speaking extemporaneously.

2. The challenging, supernatural ability or aspect may be substituted at the outset by another celebrity or an animal. Regardless, tales will involve fantasy and whimsy!

3. Hopefully, times permits to expand the activity with two pairs of students meeting up. The listener from each pair tells the others an abridged version of the tale heard. Time permitting, each foursome chooses one of the four TALL Tales to be told to the whole class. The class could vote on the best TALL Tale.

4. Humor, whimsy, and laughter, along with classmate curiosity, elevate when the TALL Tale is told in the third person about a classmate. Thus after Step 6 above, give each student a secret slip of paper with the name of a classmate. The TALL Tale story is extemporaneously told in the third person about that student, not about oneself. This is ideal for group expansion (Caveat 3).

5. Record TALL Tales.

6. Conduct a TALL Tale speech contest in the semi-extemporaneous format above. Alternately, it could be totally extemporaneous: Contestants leave the room with the audience and then return individually to hear the same set of prompts and compete. Toastmasters International Tall Tales contests allow participants to fully prepare their tales in advance for 3- to 5-minute presentations.

7. Listen to TALL Tales on the Internet from Toastmasters contests or other sources. (See References and Further Reading for suggested sources.)

8. Storytelling tends to involve the past tense, but you could build other grammatical points or sets of lexical items into the lesson.

9. Students could write TALL Tales as a homework assignment before or after delivering a TALL Tale, including one for a contest.

10. Extend TALL Tales to reading and discussion activities involving historic and contemporary, real or fictional heroes from TALL Tale and related comic book legends in English-language frontier culture folk literature (e.g., Americans Calamity Jane and Paul Bunyan, Canadian Big Joe Mufferaw, Australian Crooked Mick).

11. Students could introduce TALL Tales and legendary characters from their cultures.

REFERENCES AND FURTHER READING

Wikipedia describes traditional tall tales and provides examples from U.S., Canadian, Australian, and European cultures: https://en.wikipedia.org/wiki/Tall_tale

An extensive list of simplified tall tales from U.S. folklore: http://americanfolklore.net/folklore/tall-tales/

A Toastmasters International district in Texas offers extensive information on Tall Tales: http://www.d25toastmasters.org/education/talltale.html

A Toastmasters International club in Colorado describes Tall Tales and related contests: http://georgesuttontoastmasters.com/blog/anatomy-of-a-winning-tall-tales-toastmasters-contest.html

"I Get No Respect": Opening Your Presentation With a Dialogue

James Carpenter and Linxiao Wang

Levels	*Intermediate to advanced*
Contexts	*English for academic purposes*
Aims	*Learn how to begin a presentation in a humorous way using a dialogue*
Class Time	*20–30 minutes*
Preparation Time	*5–10 minutes*
Resources	*Copies of Appendices A and B (Appendix A can be adapted into a PowerPoint presentation)*

While international conferences have become common in the professional community, such conferences are usually conducted in English (Ventola, 2002). Therefore, it is necessary in English for academic purposes (EAP) contexts to teach students presentation skills. In general, a successful presentation in English will be less formal and more audience-friendly than in other language contexts (Reershemius, 2011). To achieve this, EAP students should be taught a basic understanding of English humor as it applies to presentations conducted in English.

A natural place to apply humor in an English presentation is at the beginning. This activity guides students through the process of creating a humorous dialogue. A humorous dialogue is a good way to begin a presentation and is a useful convention for grabbing the audience's attention and building rapport with them. This activity assumes that students have already chosen a topic and completed an outline for a class presentation.

PROCEDURE

1. Put the students into pairs and have them discuss the question: What makes a good presentation?

2. Solicit answers from students, and direct them to the concept of humor as a presentation tool.

3. Distribute the humorous dialogue example (Appendix A) and walk through it with students.

4. Check students' comprehension of each section of the example.

5. Distribute the humorous dialogue worksheet (Appendix B), and have students complete it.

6. Have students rehearse their dialogues for about 5 minutes.

7. Ask a few students to come to the front of the room and try their dialogue in front of the class.

CAVEATS AND OPTIONS

1. Encourage students to relax and feel free to experiment with their humor as it develops. For example, it is not a bad thing if other students in the class do not find their dialogue funny the first time they try it.

2. It is helpful for students to use themselves as one of the characters in the dialogue.

3. The second person in the dialogue should resemble the intended audience for the students' presentation. For example, if the audience is a group of people from Shanghai, the dialogue should consist of the student talking to someone from China.

4. Ideally, a dialogue should have only one to two exchanges between characters.

REFERENCES AND FURTHER READING

Reershemius, G. (2011). Research cultures and the pragmatic functions of humor in academic research presentations: A corpus-assisted analysis. *Journal of Pragmatics*, *44*, 863–875.

Ventola, E. (2002). Why and what kind of focus on conference presentations? In E. Ventola, C. Shalom, & S. Thompson (Eds.), *The language of conferencing* (pp. 15–49). Frankfurt am Main, Germany: Peter Lang.

APPENDIX A: *Humorous Dialogue Example*

1. Topic of your presentation: *Flow theory*

2. Audience's background

    a. Where: *Tokyo, Japan*

    b. Who: *Business people struggling to learn English*

IV

3. Write down some basic ideas about your topic:

   a. *How to be happy*

   b. *Concentration*

   c. *Enjoy your work*

   d. *Time flies*

   e. *Balance challenge with skill*

4. Write down the opposite of those basic ideas:

   a. *How to be miserable*

   b. *Absent minded*

   c. *Hate your work*

   d. *Time goes by slowly*

   e. *It's way too difficult/way too easy for me*

5. Give your audience some background information for your dialogue:

   a. Place: *Tokyo*

   b. Your relationship to the other character: *Friend who is trying to study English*

   c. Opening sentence: *So I was with a friend of mine last night who is trying to learn English at a conversation school.*

6. Let's continue your dialogue:

   Step 1: The "other character" asks you about your topic.

   He said to me, "What are you teaching your students?"

   Step 2: You give the basic idea about your topic.

   I said, "I'm teaching them about flow theory. It can help you concentrate better at your job."

   Step 3: The "other character" says the opposite of that basic idea.

   He said, "Wait? What did you say?"

7. Finally, simply transition from the dialogue to the beginning of your presentation and you are done!

Note: Connect the "other character's" perspective to the audience.

Well, I hope after this presentation today you can concentrate a little better than my friend did.

APPENDIX B: *Humorous Dialogue Worksheet*

1. Topic of your presentation _____

2. Audience's background

   a. Where _____

   b. Who _____

3. Write down some basic ideas about your topic:

   _____

   _____

   _____

4. Write down the opposite of those basic ideas:

   _____

   _____

   _____

5. Give your audience some background information for your dialogue:

   a. Place _____

   b. Your relationship to the other character _____

   c. Opening sentence _____

6. Next, let's continue your dialogue:

   Step 1: The "other character" asks you about your topic.

   ⬇

   Step 2: You give the basic idea about your topic.

   ⬇

   Step 3: The "other character" says the opposite of that basic idea.

7. Finally, simply transition from the dialogue to the beginning of your presentation and you are done!

Note: Connect the "other character's" perspective to the audience.

Part V

Sitcoms and Movies

Monty Python Teaches Euphemisms and Black Humor

Jean L. Arnold

Levels	Advanced
Contexts	Language school, young adult, university
Aims	Learn about the use of euphemisms for death
	Gain exposure to British humor
	Explore cultural differences about death
Class Time	40 + minutes
Preparation Time	5 minutes
Resources	Newspaper obituary column
	Worksheet with various euphemisms for death (see Appendix)
	Video of Monty Python's "Dead Parrot Sketch"

Language learners are often unsure how to broach sensitive topics such as death. By having an opportunity to focus on euphemisms specifically and compare them to expressions in their own language, the threat of having these expressions be taboo is lifted. Rabab'ah and Al-Qarni (2012) carried out a study among university students of both genders about euphemisms related to death, lying, and bodily functions. Their results suggest "that increasing second/foreign language learners' awareness of euphemism is essential for intercultural communication" (p. 730).

PROCEDURE

1. Introduce the idea of black humor—a way of laughing at the inevitable. The following joke will likely work well as an introduction to the topic:

   The elementary school children had all been photographed, and the teacher was trying to persuade them each to buy a copy of the group picture. She said, "Just think how nice it will be to look at it when you are all grown up and say, 'There's Jennifer; she's a lawyer,' or 'That's Michael; he's a doctor.'" A small voice at the back of the room rang out, "And there's the teacher; she's dead."

2. Ask students if people in their culture can easily talk about death or if it's taboo in different situations. Ask if there are figurative ways to talk about death (e.g., euphemisms).

3. If you teach in an ESL setting, have students read through the obituaries in the local newspaper. In an EFL setting, online obituaries or a handout can be used. Examine the various ways to say that someone has died, and determine which expressions are the most common (e.g., *died*, *passed away*, *gone to heaven*).

4. Give students the handout in the Appendix. As a class, watch the Monty Python "Dead Parrot Sketch" (which can be found easily online), and have students circle on their handout the expressions for death that they hear. Because of the difficult nature of the clip, you may want to play it more than once.

5. Discuss the meaning of the expressions on the handout. After talking about the meaning and usage, students can rank the expressions according to how socially acceptable they think they are, how humorous, and so on, or determine which expression they'd want in their obituary. Alternatively, students could write a serious and then a humorous version of their own or someone else's obituary.

CAVEATS AND OPTIONS

If students are curious about how far is too far to go with black humor, you can play the Monty Python "Undertaker's Sketch" (also easily found online). You may need to print out the dialogue, as they speak rather quickly. This will undoubtedly provide fodder for a good discussion.

REFERENCES AND FURTHER READING

Pound, L. (1936). American euphemisms for dying, death, and burial. *American Speech, 11*(3), 195–202.

Rabab'ah, G., & Al-Qarni, A. M. (2012). Euphemism in Saudi Arabic and British English. *Journal of Pragmatics, 44*, 730–743.

APPENDIX: *Euphemisms for Death*

a stiff	is resting in peace
bit the dust	is six feet under
bought the farm	is stone dead
ceased to be	joined the choir invisible
checked out	kicked the bucket
croaked	laid down his/her burden
died	passed away
expired	passed on
gave up the ghost	ran down the curtain
his/her number's up	shuffled off his/her mortal coil
is an ex-_____ (noun)	the late _____ (noun)
is deceased	took a permanent vacation
is demised	was called home
is knockin' on heaven's door	was laid to rest
is no longer with us	went to be with the Lord
is no more	went to his/her just reward
is pushing up the daisies	went to meet his/her maker
is resting	went to the other side

Are there any funny expressions for dying or death in your culture?

How would you translate them to English?

V

Finish the Story

Timothy Buthod

Levels	**Beginner to intermediate**
Contexts	**Junior high school to early university, better for large classes**
Aims	**Develop practical application of grammar and vocabulary by focusing on expressing original ideas**
Class Time	**1 hour**
Preparation Time	**About 1 hour**
Resources	**DVD player or computer**
	Projector
	Short comical sketch

Drama has been shown to be an effective learning tool, but writing or performing full productions is a long drawn-out process that often offers relatively little time for active target language use. This activity addresses that by calling on the learners to produce only the key final scene. What is more, deliberately choosing a silly or outlandish base story can help diminish learners' hesitancy to be creative and take chances. The base story sends the signal that it's OK to go a little crazy.

PROCEDURE

1. Choose a TV program or short film on video. It should be short, 10 minutes maximum, and a little bit silly with twists and turns. Halloween specials from *The Simpsons* work well because of all the outrageous plot twists, or you could use something older like *The Three Stooges*, *Benny Hill*, or a Bugs Bunny cartoon. (See Caveats and Options for further information.)

2. Show the video to the class, but suddenly stop it about 80% of the way through. Tell students they have to finish the story and perform it for the class.

3. Break the class into groups of three or four, and let them work for 5–10 minutes. Then show them the video again, being careful to stop it at the same point.

4. Let the groups work for another 10 minutes or so, monitoring and answering their questions as they go.

5. Call each group up to perform their skit for the class. Depending on the class, you can even record their performance on video.

6. When everyone has finished, you can show them the "real" ending.

CAVEATS AND OPTIONS

1. The most important job for you in this activity is choosing a story. The more ridiculous, the better. Of course, there should be natural suspense at the stopping point so people wonder what might happen next. A somewhat complicated story with several characters is ideal so the climax is not too obvious.

2. If you are teaching schoolchildren, you can record their performances and post them on your school's website for their parents to see. Parents love to see their little darlings are actually doing something at school all day, especially if they're paying a lot of tuition.

3. If you have no access to video technology, you can set up the story simply by reading to students.

4. Some notes about finding and choosing a clip: *The Simpsons* is not generally available on YouTube, but DVDs are commercially available. One Halloween short that has worked well is "Dial 'Z' for Zombies" from the season 4 Halloween special. You can find Bugs Bunny or Daffy Duck by searching for *Looney Tunes* on YouTube. You might try "Wackiki Wabbit." *Benny Hill* can be a little risqué, and some of the sketches don't have dialogue, but you might try "The Police Raid in Waterloo Station." *The Three Stooges* episodes are available on YouTube, but their videos tend to be a little longer, ranging from 15 to 20 minutes.

Why's Everyone Laughing? A Sitcom-Based Speaking and Listening Activity

Clarissa Codrington, Trisha Dowling, and Zuzana Tomaš

Levels	***Intermediate to advanced***
Contexts	***Young adults and adults, academic and nonacademic***
Aims	***Enhance cultural understanding of humor through the use of popular TV sitcoms***
	Practice speaking and listening skills
Class Time	***20–40 minutes***
Preparation Time	***10–60 minutes***
Resources	***Sitcom excerpts***
	Graphic organizer

Humor is an inherently cultural aspect of language and, as such, is difficult for even advanced language learners to understand and appreciate. At the same time, humor is considered an excellent vehicle for language learning. As Hu and Jiang (2008) point out, "by watching and listening to engrossing materials, students are greatly motivated to learn their target language" (p. 238). This activity is designed to provide a structured opportunity for students to deepen their understanding of cultural references while practicing listening and speaking skills. The medium at the center of this activity is a humorous situational comedy (sitcom), ideally accompanied with a laugh track. The advantage of having the laugh track is a cue to students to join in on the laughter or else to further investigate what made the audience laugh.

PROCEDURE

1. Select a 3- to 8-minute segment from a sitcom appropriate for the age, level, and interest of your students. (Note: YouTube includes many sitcom samples with laugh tracks. Examples that we have successfully used are *Home Improvement*, *Friends*, *That '70s Show*, and *Seinfeld*. Alternatively, use DVDs.)

2. Introduce the selected sitcom and explain the instructions for the activity.

3. Provide students with a graphic organizer (see Appendix) and explain how to complete it.

4. Play a short clip from a popular sitcom.

5. Pause the video after a joke has been delivered and the audience begins laughing.

6. Using the graphic organizer, students write a brief explanation of why the segment is funny.

7. Repeat Steps 4, 5, and 6 several times.

8. Ask students to compare notes in small groups.

9. Lead a discussion on humor in those segments that were difficult for students to explain. Elicit from students the extent to which the humor in the sitcom is similar to humor encountered in the students' cultures.

10. For additional speaking practice and with any extra class time, you can ask students to role-play a possible follow-up segment form the sitcom. Students can vote for their favorite segments.

CAVEATS AND OPTIONS

1. Allow students to make suggestions for the sitcoms.

2. Provide students with written scripts when video is not available.

3. For written practice, ask students to reflect on the humor and culture in the target segment or write a script for a segment that may follow the scenes students have watched.

REFERENCES AND FURTHER READING

Hu, X., & Jiang, X. (2008). Using film to teach EFL students English language skills. *Changing English: Studies in Culture and Education, 15*, 234–240.

APPENDIX: *Explaining Humor Graphic Organizer*

Video title	Explanation for humor in the segment
(Sample) *Home Improvement* Season 1, Episode 1: Pilot	(Sample) The audience laughs because the size of the drill is unnecessarily large for the job; Tim always tries to use too much power for each job.

Using *The Office* to Explore Business Culture

Henri de Jongste

Levels	Advanced
Contexts	EFL/ESL students in business programs
Aims	Develop understanding of the notion of (leadership) roles as an aspect of business culture in different cultures
Class Time	1–2 hours
Preparation Time	Minimal
Resources	DVD of The Office (UK)

Although there are obvious overlaps, the role of managers is defined differently across cultures. People in some cultures prefer an egalitarian, context-dependent style of leadership and distribution of power. In such cultures, power is based on the manager's role and confined to specific work-related situations. These are cultures with low power distance (Hofstede, 1980; Hofstede, Hofstede, & Minkov, 2010). People in other cultures share a preference for an autocratic, context-independent style of leadership. In these cultures, power is ascribed to the manager as a person who has high status across a wide range of situations, both work-related and not work-related. These are cultures with high power distance.

To demonstrate that the United Kingdom is a low-power-distance culture and to illustrate what this means for people's expectations concerning power distribution in a work context, this activity uses a fragment from *The Office*. In series 1, episode 4, the manager of a small UK company, David Brent, has organized a training session for his staff and Brent himself takes part in the session. In the context of the training, which is new for Brent, he turns from a manager into a training participant and is expected to yield his power to the trainer, Rowan.

In a high-power-distance culture, such a change in status would be unacceptable to both managers and their subordinates, and managers would typically prefer not to participate. In such cultures, with a context-independent distribution of power, power must be visible in all contexts. In contrast, a temporary shift of power is normal in a culture with low power distance such as the United Kingdom. Since power is context-dependent in such cultures, a change of context can lead to a new distribution of power, limited to the context in question. Temporarily giving up his authority should therefore not be a problem to Brent, and his subordinates should understand that this is not a threat to his status.

However, instead of acting in accordance with the rules in British culture, Brent holds on to a position of authority over Rowan, thereby sabotaging the training. If Brent chooses to participate in the training, he must take on the same role as his subordinates in the training context. When subsequently Brent does not really yield his power to the trainer, things go wrong and this creates a humorous effect. A British viewer must recognize Brent's behavior as inappropriate, which demonstrates that a context-dependent notion of power distribution, or low power distance, is prevalent in the United Kingdom.

PROCEDURE

1. Teach students about national cultural differences in notions of power distribution and leadership, for instance, by studying Hofstede's dimension of power distance (Hofstede, 1980; Hofstede et al., 2010).

2. Students discuss the consequences for a manager who participates in a staff training program together with her or his subordinates. What does this mean in terms of the manager's authority in the training context and in the long run? What differences might there be in different cultures related to the desirability of managers joining their staff in a training program? What are these differences based on? Where do the notions we have in such matters come from?

3. Students watch the video (with captions) and discuss whether and why they find this scene funny. Do they expect that people in their culture would generally find this funny? What is the humor in the video based on?

4. Students discuss British assumptions on the nature of authority.

CAVEATS AND OPTIONS

1. As a follow-up assignment, students can think of other situations in which notions of power distance might manifest themselves differently in various cultures.

2. Students try to assess what notions of power distribution are prevalent in their own culture. Do they share the prevalent view in their culture? What kind of manager would they like to be themselves? What do they expect from their subordinates?

3. Students gather information about preferred management styles in various cultures and reflect on the consequences for interaction between managers and subordinates.

4. As an expansion, students could also watch scenes from the U.S. version of *The Office*. This is an opportunity to compare leadership roles in the two countries as well as British and American English.

REFERENCES AND FURTHER READING

Hofstede, G. H. (1980). *Culture's consequences: International differences in work-related values.* Beverly Hills, CA: Sage.

Hofstede, G. H., Hofstede, G. J., & Minkov, M. (2010). *Cultures and organizations: Software of the mind: Intercultural cooperation and its importance for survival* (3rd ed.). New York, NY: McGraw-Hill.

http://worldbusinessculture.com is a good resource for students to collect information about business culture in different countries.

Applying Humor Theory to Sitcoms: *Modern Family and Beyond*

Mark Firth

Levels	*Intermediate +*
Contexts	*University*
Aims	*Develop skills in analyzing humor using humor theory*
	Decide whether stereotypes are being reproduced or resisted in a situational comedy
Class Time	*90–120 minutes*
Preparation Time	*10 minutes*
Resources	*DVD of* **Modern Family***, Season 1, Episode 1*
	Handout (see Appendix)

Sitcoms offer students an abundant source of material for learning about how to deconstruct humor. To gain a deeper understanding of language and culture, students can learn and apply humor theory (tendentious vs. innocuous, superiority theory, incongruity theory) to obtain a more critical perspective on what they may or may not find humorous. By analyzing the stereotypes that are being exploited in a comedy, students should be able to discern whether stereotypes are being resisted or reproduced.

PROCEDURE

1. Engage students by having them call out some of their favorite sitcoms, and write them on the board. Talk about why they find these shows funny, and ask if they can explain any of the humor using humor theory terms.

2. If needed, choose one of the sitcoms the students are aware of, and quickly write an analysis as an example. The following is an example using the sitcom *Fawlty Towers*:

Fawlty Towers is a very *tendentious* kind of humor. It *mocks* foreign people who come and stay at the hotel. It also *mocks* the foreign waiter, Manuel, who wants to learn English and live and work in England. Basil's behavior is *incongruent* because we don't expect him to act so stupidly all the time. This program *reproduces the stereotypes* that people have toward those from different countries because we laugh even though we know it is difficult for foreigners to work abroad. On the other hand, if we consider Basil's behavior to be *self-depreciative* as a *parody* of white middle-class attitudes, then we can say that Fawlty Towers *resists stereotypes*. None of the humor in this program can be said to be *innocuous* because there is always a victim, or a target, of the humor.

3. Hand out the worksheet in the Appendix and work through it as prescribed.

CAVEATS AND OPTIONS

1. Students need to already have some understanding of humor theory. A good place to start learning about humor theory is with Quock (2007) and the references listed therein. Alternatively, this activity could be expanded into a major unit of work to actually teach the theory.

2. A follow-up activity might also involve having students analyze and present on a different sitcom each. Short video clips can often be found online for students to use to help present their analyses. Having the students transcribe 3- to 5-minute clips helps them notice the cross-cultural and linguistic nuances that they might not be aware of with normal viewing.

REFERENCES AND FURTHER READING

Quock, T. H. (2007). Laughing matters: On the theory and teaching of Western humor, and how it can be utilized in the EFL/ESL classroom. In K. Bradford-Watts (Ed.), *JALT 2006 Conference Proceedings*. Tokyo, Japan: JALT.

APPENDIX: *Humor Theory Review: A Sitcom—Modern Family*

Before Viewing

With a partner, discuss the family tree. Talk about the relationships and try to guess each character's personality. You can use the Internet to supply students with pictures of these characters.

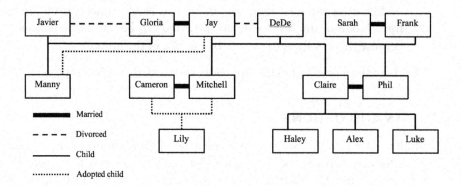

Tasks

1. In groups of four to six, each person chooses a different character to focus on while watching *Modern Family*. Choose Jay, Gloria, Cameron, Mitchell, Claire, Phil, or Haley.

2. Watch the first 10–15 minutes of *Modern Family* and take notes on your character, but also try to describe the other people and their relationships, anything surprising, questions, and so on.

3. Share your notes and feedback with the group. Talk about how the theories of humor (tendentious vs. innocuous, superiority theory, incongruity theory, intention vs. perception) are used to explain *Modern Family*.

4. Continue watching and taking notes as time allows.

Writing Assignment Topics

1. This mockumentary is a parody on the stereotypes of a current-day, middle-class American family. Discuss and give examples of some of the stereotypes it is poking fun at. Include some of the comments that came out of your group discussion using humor theory in Questions 2 and 3 above.

2. Do you think *Modern Family* is a funny sitcom? Why or why not?

3. Whose family would you fit into best? Give reasons for your answer.

   • Mitchell and Cam

   • Claire and Phil

   • Jay and Gloria

   • None of the above

4. If a new version of this sitcom were created in your culture, what kinds of family roles would it use? Describe the characters and relationships.

Fish-Out-of-Water Scenes

Scott Gardner

Levels	**Intermediate +**
Aims	**Gain listening practice**
	Appreciate how certain forms of humor work
	Learn from communication failures
Class Time	**45–60 minutes**
Preparation Time	**5–30 minutes (to prepare scripts, if needed)**
Resources	**Humorous scenes from movies or TV shows that portray characters in alien or "fish out of water" situations, such as Back to the Future (1985), Johnny English (2003), The Devil Wears Prada (2006) (choice of movies may depend on age of learners)**

Movie scenes are commonly used to expose language students to native-like input. But the right choice of scenes can also serve other functions. Students trying to use a new language, perhaps in a new culture, are "fish out of water" in a sense. They may have difficulty processing common idiomatic phrases used by native speakers. Movie and TV scenes portraying characters stumbling through novel situations as outsiders—often with humorous results—not only give students useful language input, but can resonate with students' own linguistic and cultural inadequacies in a humorous way that perhaps lessens some of their anxieties.

EXAMPLES

1. A scene in *Crocodile Dundee* puts the hero, Mick, in a bar in New York when a local man tries to engage in conversation with him. Mick is from the Australian outback, and his version of English does not click with the African American English of his interlocutor:

   Man: Hey, my man, what's happenin'?

   Mick: Where?

   Man: What's goin' down, bro?

   Mick: "Goin' down"? Oh, yeah, [*indicates beer in his hand*] just blowing the froth off a couple.

2. A scene in *Enchanted* shows fairy-tale princess Giselle's struggles to interpret the actions and words of people in "real world" New York. She is in a restaurant with Robert, the man who found her and has been trying to look after her. Robert already has a girlfriend, so he tries to hide his interest in the strange "princess":

Giselle: This is a very nice place.

Robert: Yeah?

Giselle: And we're eating dinner.

Robert: Yeah.

Giselle: [*thinking*] . . . This is a date!

Robert: Yeah! . . . No, no! No, no, no, we're just, uh, we're just friends.

3. A scene in the animated film *Home* depicts an alien (a "Boov") named Oh who is helping the earthling Tip find her mother during a space invasion, but they often struggle to understand each other:

Tip: You know, when I'm stressed out, my mom tells me jokes.

Oh: Boov do not do telling jokes.

Tip: It's not that hard. I'll teach you. Knock knock.

[*Oh says nothing*]

Tip: You would say, "Who's there?"

Oh: *You* are there.

Tip: No, just ask me.

Oh: Who is there?

Tip: Now I say, "The interrupting cow." Now you say, "The interrupting cow who?" Let's just do it. Knock knock.

Oh: Who is there?

Tip: The interrupting cow.

Oh: The interrupting c—.

Tip: Mooooo! Hahaha!

Oh: You did not let me finish my response. I was to say, "The interr—"

Tip: Mooooo!

Oh: There, you did it again. Oh! That is the joke!

PROCEDURE

1. Warm up students to listen and watch the scene as you would do with any video. Anticipate vocabulary or grammar issues with handouts or help on the blackboard.

2. Remind students that what they will watch is an example of a struggle to communicate. Tell them to listen carefully for words or ideas that are misinterpreted or not understood. (The careful listening step could be saved for a second viewing of the scene.)

3. After one or two viewings (or more), get feedback from students on what the characters' difficulty was in communicating with each other. If after several viewings the students still don't understand the intended message(s) in the scene, they can start from what they did hear, and you can help fill in blanks as needed. If the scene is short enough, you can write dialogue on the board as students remember it, but if the scene is lengthy, a prepared script on a handout might be more feasible. Throughout the discussion, it helps to remind students that although the characters seem to be speaking English fluently, they still at some point fail to understand each other.

CAVEATS AND OPTIONS

1. If learners find the scenes amusing enough, they can act out the scenes to each other as pairs, in groups, or in front of the class.

2. The scene from *Home* above involves intercultural difficulty with humor. A relevant activity might be to ask learners to bring to class examples of jokes they've heard that were difficult to understand, which could then be analyzed or deconstructed by the class. You needn't worry about ruining the humor of the jokes, since the jokes already failed once with students. (See Evans Davies, 2015, on second language classroom analysis of student-provided jokes.)

3. Regardless of the overall humor of the scenes, it stands to reason that "learners in the alien world of a foreign language" (Illés, 2009, p. 150) can to some extent identify with these "fish out of water" scenes. You can prompt learners to consider examples of their own "fails" at second language communication. If they are willing to share these experiences—to discuss what went wrong and to "laugh it off" as a group—it may be an important motivational step for them.

REFERENCES AND FURTHER READING

Cornell, J. (Producer), & Faiman, P. (Director). (1986). *Crocodile Dundee*. Australia: Rimfire Films.

Evans Davies, C. (2015). Humor in intercultural interaction as both content and process in the classroom. *Humor, 28*, 375–395.

Illés, É. (2009). What makes a coursebook series stand the test of time? *ELT Journal, 63*(2), 145–153.

Josephson, B., Sonnenfeld, B. (Producers), & Lima, K. (Director). (2007). *Enchanted*. United States: Walt Disney Pictures.

Soria, M., Jenkins, C., Buirgy, S. (Producers), & Johnson, T. (Director). (2015). *Home*. United States: DreamWorks Animation.

Using Comedic Movie Posters to Learn and Practice English

Scott Henderson

Levels	*High beginner and above*
Contexts	*High school and above*
Aims	*Learn new vocabulary and expressions*
	Use the images and language on movie posters to predict the plot of movies
	Practice giving opinion and stating preferences
Class Time	*50–100 minutes*
Preparation Time	*30–60 minutes*
Resources	*Internet access*
	Examples of various movie posters and plot summaries

This lesson aims to introduce commonly overlooked elements of the movie-making process: movie posters and taglines. Movie posters are useful lesson materials because they often depict people and situations that are humorous regardless of language used in the poster. Thus, students might find the humor in the image even if they do not understand the meaning of the language. Additionally, if students only partially understand the language used in the poster, they may be able to infer the meaning of the text with the images they see.

Taglines are short statements that quickly highlight a plot element and help influence theater goers to watch the movie. Taglines are useful for English lessons as they generally are short, are easy to understand, and rely on humor and wit.

As there are numerous movie posters available online, teachers can customize this lesson and choose posters they find appropriate for the students they teach and the cultures they live in. Also, this lesson has many steps and variations, so it can be broken down into several lessons, or some steps can be assigned as homework.

PROCEDURE

1. Lead a warm-up discussion by giving students questions about a sample movie poster. A good example is from the movie *Office Space*, which shows a worker covered in Post-it notes. The visual can be found by searching for "*Office Space* movie poster" on Google Images.

Warm-Up/Discussion
a. What is happening in the picture?
Why do you think the man is covered in Post-it notes?
What do you think the movie is about?
What is your opinion of the movie poster?
b. Choose one of the following taglines that matches the picture.
Work sucks.
He's stuck at work.
He always brings his work home with him.
c. (Optional: Create your own tagline)

2. Show students movie posters from the following comedies with the taglines hidden or removed. Ask them to match the tagline to the movie. Again, these movie posters can be found by doing a search on Google Images.

Taglines	Movie
1. For Harry and Lloyd, every day is a no-brainer.	A. *Tommy Boy*
2. A romantic comedy. With zombies.	B. *The Hangover*
3. A tale of murder, lust, greed, revenge, and seafood.	C. *A Fish Called Wanda*
4. If at first you don't succeed, lower your standards.	D. *Shaun of the Dead*
5. Some guys just can't handle Vegas.	E. *Dumb and Dumber*

3. After you reveal the answers, students gather in small groups and choose their favorite and least favorite tagline and poster combination. They must give reasons why they made their choices.

4. Using only the posters and taglines, students predict the plot summaries of the movies.

5. Students present their plot summaries to the class or to other groups.

6. Give students the original plots summaries. (These can be found on Wikipedia, www.wikipedia.org, or the Internet Movie Database, www.imdb.com.) Students must compare and contrast their summaries with the original plots. As an additional option, after reading the plot summaries, students create their own tagline for one or two of the posters of their choice.

7. Provide short plot summaries to different movies not already discussed. Using the plot summaries, students become the actors and create a movie poster using their cell phone cameras. Then they create a tagline to use with their movie posters. (Optional: Students create a poster on paper instead of using themselves and a camera.)

8. After preparing, students read their plot summaries and present their posters and taglines to the class or other groups.

9. Students vote for the best poster and tagline combination. They must give two or more reasons for their number-one choice. Count all of the first-place votes to determine the most popular combination.

10. Show students the original movie posters and taglines. Compare and contrast the students' taglines and movie posters with the original movie posters and taglines.

CAVEATS AND OPTIONS

1. Students use the language or grammar they are currently studying to create taglines and plot summaries.

2. Watch the movie trailers. Do they match the movie posters? Why or why not?

3. Students are given only the movie posters. They must create original taglines.

Make 'Em Laugh, Make 'Em Think: Using Sitcoms to Teach Critical Thinking Skills

Susan Kelly

Levels	**Intermediate to advanced**
Contexts	**High school or university**
Aims	**Develop critical thinking skills while reinforcing listening and writing skills**
Class Time	**40–50 minutes**
Preparation Time	**20–25 minutes**
Resources	**DVD or ability to stream sitcoms from the Internet**
	Handouts (see Appendices)

In recent years critical thinking has been emphasized in reform efforts in school systems throughout the world (Mason, 2009). Thus, teachers in all subjects, including English language classes, are required to embed reasoning skills into their courses. Fortunately, comedy often highlights characters' mistakes due to poor critical thinking, providing clear examples for study in an engaging way.

This activity can be adapted, depending on how you would like students to analyze the respective sitcom(s). Sitcoms I have used in my classes are given as examples, but you can also modify the lesson using sitcoms chosen by you or your students.

PROCEDURE

Cause-Effect Analysis

1. Briefly introduce to students the respective sitcom (*Leave it to Beaver* in this case). If some students have seen the series, ask them to summarize its premise. Ask students to focus on what problems occur and how the characters try to solve the problems.

2. Watch the episode and pause if necessary to summarize the important plot points.

3. After viewing the episode, distribute a blank version of the handout in Appendix A and put students into pairs or small groups.

4. Students discuss and record what caused the episode's main problem and what effects arose. Students may also add arrows or boxes to show how multiple causes create a problem and how a problem may have several effects.

Compare-Contrast Analysis

1. Choose two sitcoms with similar themes or structures, such as two family sitcoms or two workplace sitcoms. The programs should have some noticeable similarities and differences. For example, both *Leave It To Beaver* and *Outnumbered* capture family life, but the former shows a fairly ordered life in the early 1960s, while the latter shows chaotic life in the Internet era.

2. After viewing both sitcoms, students work individually or in pairs to complete a Venn diagram (see example in Appendix B) that shows the similarities and differences between the two programs.

Point of View Analysis

1. Select a sitcom, like *The Wonder Years*, with stories told from one character's point of view.

2. Introduce the program and explain who narrates the story. Instruct students to concentrate on this character's personality, interests, and biases.

3. Students work with partners or in small groups to discuss their opinions of the show and the narrator.

4. Explain and define point of view. Elicit the ways in which Kevin in *The Wonder Years* expresses his point of view throughout the story.

5. Distribute the handout in Appendix C. Ask students to consider how the story would differ if told from the point of view of the mother, the older brother Wayne, or another character.

6. Ask students to share their ideas with the class or with another pair of students.

CAVEATS AND OPTIONS

1. Students can watch the episodes as homework or conduct their discussions online. For students to master each critical thinking skill, they may need to repeat these activities; handouts may not be necessary, as students can record their ideas in notebooks.

2. You may also ask students to suggest programs to view and analyze.

REFERENCES AND FURTHER READING

Emihani, M. (2012). Critical thinking and the language factor: The case for the English language learner. *Arab World English Journal, 3*(3), 4–17.

Mason, M. (2009). *Critical thinking and learning.* Hoboken, NJ: Wiley-Blackwell.

Tanriverdi, B., & Apak, O. (2008, September). *Culture and language through media.* Paper presented at the WCCI13th World Conference in Education, "Creating a Global Culture of Peace: Strategies for Curriculum Development and Implementation," Antalya, Turkey. (ERIC Document Reproduction Service No. ED504866)

APPENDIX A: *Cause and Effect Analysis of Leave It to Beaver, Season 1, Episode 15 "Party Invitation"*

Main Problem: Beaver is invited to a party and doesn't want to go because he'll be the only boy.

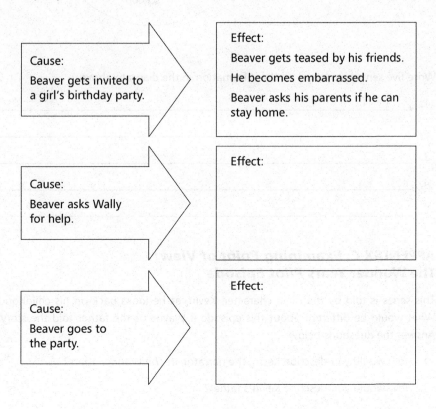

APPENDIX B: *Compare and Contrast*
Two Family Sitcoms

Make a Venn diagram comparing and contrasting *Leave It to Beaver* and *Outnumbered*.

How are they similar? How do they differ?

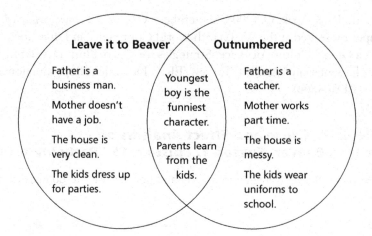

Leave it to Beaver

Father is a business man.

Mother doesn't have a job.

The house is very clean.

The kids dress up for parties.

Youngest boy is the funniest character.

Parents learn from the kids.

Outnumbered

Father is a teacher.

Mother works part time.

The house is messy.

The kids wear uniforms to school.

Write five sentences based on the information in the diagram above.

1. _____

2. _____

3. _____

4. _____

5. _____

APPENDIX C: *Examining Point of View:*
The Wonder Years *Pilot Episode*

This series is told by the main character, Kevin, as he looks back on his childhood. What would be different about this episode if Wayne or the father told the story? Answer the questions below.

1. How would you describe Kevin, the narrator, in *The Wonder Years*?

2. How would you describe Kevin's father?

3. How would you describe Kevin's brother, Wayne?

4. Imagine the story told from Wayne's point of view. What would be different? Complete the chart.

Kevin says . . .	But Wayne would say . . .

5. Imagine the story told from the father's point of view. What would be different? Complete the chart.

Kevin says . . .	But his father would say . . .

What effects does point of view have for the audience of the show?

We All Love Lucy: Using *I Love Lucy* to Teach English Language and U.S. Culture

Margaret V. Layton

Levels	*Intermediate*
Aims	*Improve English pronunciation*
	Develop awareness of participial adjectives
Class Time	*1 hour for each lesson*
Preparation Time	*10–20 minutes each*
Resources	*"Lucy Does a Television Commercial" and "Job Switching" episodes of* I Love Lucy
	Script for Lucy's television commercial
	Handouts (Appendices A and B)

U.S. situation comedies welcome students into U.S. culture. These comedies are effective language teaching tools because they use authentic language in often-repeated situations with quickly familiar characters in predictably humorous situations. *I Love Lucy* is particularly good because its humor is universal and easily comprehensible. This lesson shows how two episodes can be exploited to provide practice on different language learning points.

PROCEDURE

1. Introduce *I Love Lucy* and its characters, with one theme being Lucy's desire to work in show business.

2. Watch the episode "Lucy Does a Television Commercial." Distribute the script (readily available through a web search) and discuss the linking rule by which English speakers join words that end in a consonant to the next word when it begins with a vowel. Work with students to indicate the phrases in the script that will link. Practice with students. Divide the class into pairs to practice more. Encourage them to use "bright, peppy" intonation. Promote home practice.

3. In the next class, students audition for the part. Their classmates use a feedback form (Appendix A) to judge each person's performance. The student who gets the highest score gets the "part." (I also grade my students' efforts, marking both their linking and their intonation.)

4. Watch "Job Switching." Teach the use and meanings of the past (*-ed*) participial adjective. Distribute a grammar exercise (first part of Appendix B) that focuses on these adjectives and have students complete it.

5. In the next class, teach students about use of the present participial adjective ending in *-ing*. Distribute the second grammar exercise for review (second part of Appendix B).

6. Watch "Lucy Does a Television Commercial" again. Give students a list of appropriate verbs, and let them write sentences with both present and past participial adjectives. They can work in groups.

CAVEATS AND OPTIONS

Because *I Love Lucy*'s humor is physical and easily comprehensible, the show is adaptable to other grammar lessons and levels. The "Lucy Does a Television Commercial" script exhibits other kinds of linking as well. The past participial exercise could become a pronunciation lesson on the three pronunciation variants of the *-ed* ending on the past participles of regular verbs. After viewing "Job Switching," students could be encouraged to discuss gender role differences in the 1950s and today or gender roles in their own cultures. There are endless possibilities if you become as active in viewing as students will need to be in order to complete these activities.

REFERENCES AND FURTHER READING

Oppenheimer, J., Pugh, M., Carroll, B., Jr. (Writers), & Asher, W. (Director). (1952). Job switching [Television series episode]. In D. Arnaz (Executive Producer), *I love Lucy*. Los Angeles, CA: Columbia Broadcasting System.

Oppenheimer, J., Pugh, M., Carroll, B., Jr. (Writers), & Daniels, M. (Director). (1952). Lucy does a TV commercial [Television series episode]. In D. Arnaz (Executive Producer), *I love Lucy*. Los Angeles, CA: Columbia Broadcasting System.

Washburn, G. N. (2001). Using situation comedies for pragmatic language teaching and learning. *TESOL Journal, 10*(4), 21–26.

APPENDIX A: *"Lucy Does a Television Commercial"* *Audience Feedback Form*

Listen as your classmates audition for the part of the Vitameatavegamin girl or boy. Give feedback by filling in the chart below. Check the features of each reader's version, and indicate the type of intonation used with a number. The first has been completed as an example. All the charts will be tallied to determine who gets the "part."

Student Name	Accurate Reading	Fluent Reading	Intonation 2 points = bright and breezy (like Lucy the first time) 1 point = ordinary, everyday intonation 0 points = monotone
Example: Smith	✓	✓	1

APPENDIX B: *"Job Switching"* *Participles Practice*

Day 1

Write the past participle form of the verb in parentheses in the blank in each sentence below.

1. (infuriate) _____, Ricky comes home from the bank where he has just learned that Lucy's checking account is overdrawn again.

2. (convince) Lucy and Ethel are _____ that they can get good jobs despite the fact that they have no real job experience.

3. (scorch) Ricky thought he could present the _____ blouse as a new and different pattern.

4. (confuse) The _____ man in the employment office didn't understand why Lucy kept asking him what kind of jobs he had.

5. (frighten) _____ as the woman yelled at them, Lucy and Ethel jumped.

6. (dip) The _____ chocolates were going by on the conveyor belt at much too quick a speed.

7. (unwrap) The _____ chocolates slipped past Lucy and Ethel into the room for boxing the chocolates.

8. (sicken) A _____ Lucy and Ethel came home to a dirty house.

Day 2

Write the present participle form of the verb in parentheses in the blank in each sentence below.

1. (infuriate) Ricky gets angry about Lucy's _____ spending habits.

2. (confuse) The man in the employment office makes mistakes because of Lucy and Ethel's _____ answers.

3. (dip) The chocolate-_____ woman did not pay any attention to Lucy until Lucy slapped the fly off her face.

4. (explode) The _____ pot ejected chicken onto the ceiling of the kitchen when Ricky was cooking chicken and rice.

5. (overflow) The _____ rice gushed all over the kitchen floor as Ricky and Fred tried to clean it up.

6. (frighten) The _____ boss surely fired Lucy and Ethel from their jobs in the chocolate factory. She was really scary.

7. (sicken) Lucy and Ethel fell on the couch when they thought about eating five _____ pounds of chocolate each.

Homework

Write ten sentences of your own using participial adjectives. Five of your adjectives should be past participles, and five should be present participles.

V

Defining Types of Humor Through Sitcoms and Cartoons

Robert McGuire

Levels	Beginning to intermediate
Contexts	ESL or EFL
Aims	Develop basic vocabulary related to kinds of humor (visual, physical, and situational)
	Practice critical thinking skills (organizing by type and giving reasons for decisions and opinions)
	Create a simple presentation or dialogue
Class Time	One or two 90-minute classes
Preparation Time	1 hour
Resources	DVDs of sitcoms or cartoons (see References and Further Reading for a list of suggested titles)
	Worksheet (see Appendices)

Students often find that one of the biggest hurdles they face in discussing humorous media is their lack of vocabulary and a simple framework to talk about what they have seen and why they find it funny. This activity helps students learn the basics of talking about three types of humor: visual, physical, and situational. This basic introduction can later aid students as the teacher introduces more humorous material into the lessons.

PROCEDURE

1. Define these three types of humor on the board:

   Visual: something that looks funny

   Physical: a funny action

   Situational: something that is funny because of when and where it happens

2. Distribute the worksheet in Appendix A or B (depending on the level of your students) or a similar one. Go over the directions and example sentence on the worksheet with the students. Note: Appendix A is designed for creating a short conversation about the humor they have viewed, while Appendix B is designed for creating a presentation. Less proficient students could start with the former.

3. Model the vocabulary and sentences using an example scene from a sitcom or cartoon. For example, the launderette vignette from *Mr. Bean* contains examples of visual humor (Mr. Bean's facial expressions), physical humor (his actions in the launderette), and situational humor (what he washes in the laundry machine and how he prepares his washing). (The clip can be found on YouTube: www.youtube.com/watch?v=E1k_THq622E).

4. Show students a simple scene from a sitcom or cartoon as a way for them to practice the vocabulary and sentences. Students can present their sentences individually if the class is small or in groups if the class is large.

5. Students watch a complete episode of a sitcom or cartoon and then make a short presentation about it. The presentation should include examples of the types of humor that were taught earlier and the reason why the student thought their examples were this kind of humor. The presentation may be lengthened or shortened depending on the ability of the students.

CAVEATS AND OPTIONS

1. Presentations may be modified into short conversations between students, with them asking each other what kinds of humor they saw in the examples and why they thought it was this kind of humor.

2. Different kinds of humor may be added to the list depending on the students' level and language ability.

3. Some of the suggested shows in the References and Further Reading contain no spoken language. You may wish to use material with spoken English with higher level students.

4. Cartoons and drawings can be found in many different places, such as newspapers, magazines, and the Internet. Be sure to find resources that are appropriate for your class with respect to level and content.

REFERENCES AND FURTHER READING

Suggested Sitcoms and Cartoons

> *Mr. Bean*
>
> *The Big Bang Theory*
>
> *Loony Tunes*
>
> *Shaun the Sheep*
>
> *Seinfeld*
>
> *The Simpsons*

APPENDIX A: *Worksheet for Creating a Conversation About the Humor in a Sitcom or Cartoon*

Name _____

Kinds of Humor

Visual: something that looks funny

Physical: a funny action

Situational: something that is funny because of when and where it happens

Helpful Phrases for Talking About Humor

Your opinion

> I think this is funny because _____
>
> I don't think this is funny because _____
>
> I like/don't like visual, physical, situational humor.
>
> My favorite/least favorite part/joke was _____

Asking for other people's opinion

> What do you think (about it)?
>
> What part did you like/not like? Why?
>
> What kind of humor do you like? For example?
>
> Why do you think this is funny/not funny?

APPENDIX B: *Worksheet for Creating a Presentation About the Humor in a Video or Cartoon*

Name _____

Kinds of Humor

Visual: something that looks funny

Physical: a funny action

Situational: something that is funny because of when or where it happens

Helpful Phrases for Talking About Humor

Your opinion

I think this is funny because _____

I don't think this is funny because _____

I like/don't like visual, physical, situational humor.

My favorite/least favorite part/joke was _____

Find at least three examples of each kind of humor, describe each one in one or two sentences, and tell us which one was your favorite and why.

Visual

Physical

Situational

Funny Sitcom and Movie Scenes as a Springboard for Student-Generated Role-Plays

Maria Petkova

Levels	*Intermediate to advanced*
Contexts	*Teenagers to adults*
Aims	*Develop better cross-cultural understanding of and competence with humor*
	Practiced humor in role play situations
Class Time	*1 hour*
Preparation Time	*20 minutes*
Resources	*Movie scenes that show examples of American or British conversational humor*
	Humor vocabulary cards (Appendix A)
	Role-play situations (Appendix B)
	Evaluation rubrics (Appendix C)

Humor in another language or culture is difficult to master, yet subtly important in social interaction and even professional negotiations. This activity draws students' attention to different types of humor presented in humorous movie clips and invites students to produce their own humorous remarks in the "safe" classroom environment, where they can get feedback from the teacher as to how funny and appropriate they were.

PROCEDURE

1. Find several examples of appropriate conversational humor from your favorite comedies. Many are available free of charge on YouTube or from your DVD collection, resource center, and library. Some titles that have worked well in my classes are the sitcoms *Friends* and *The Big Bang Theory* and the movie *It's Complicated*.

2. Choose and cut out the vocabulary cards (Appendix A) corresponding to the type of humor demonstrated in your video clips (e.g., irony, sarcasm).

3. Explain and give verbal examples of each type of humor. Try to relate your examples to your classroom situation or your students' lives so they can understand the humor.

4. Distribute copies of the cards to small groups of students to match the vocabulary, for example, *irony*, to its meaning and later write down which TV or movie scene showed irony.

5. Show the video clips you chose. Make sure the humor and scenes are appropriate for your t students and teaching situation.

6. In small groups, students discuss the clips and decide which type of humor each one demonstrated. Circulate and help as needed, and finally check answers with the whole class.

7. Ask the class to think of the functions of the humorous remarks they just watched. Point out that humor can be used to ease tensions, bring people together or exclude someone, hint at something, and indirectly communicate important information.

8. Tell students that now they get to perform and come up with a funny remark in a delicate situation in their host country.

9. Distribute copies of the role-play cards (Appendix B) to students. Give them a few minutes to think of what to say and discuss it with their small groups before they share with the whole class.

10. Give feedback on how funny and appropriate students' remarks were (use the rubrics in Appendix C, if desired).

11. As a class, compare humor types and perceptions in the shows they watch in class to those of students' native cultures'.

CAVEATS AND OPTIONS

1. You can give each group a different role-play card or use the same situation for everyone and then compare the different responses. Use another role-play card in another lesson, and so on.

2. It would be ideal for teachers and students to create their own role-play cards, based on real-life needs and experiences. Students can recall situations they have been in, when they wanted to say something funny but didn't have the time, language skills, or cultural competence to come up with humor.

3. You can also invite native English speakers of different ages, genders, and backgrounds to the classroom to give feedback to students or videotape the role-play and evaluate it later.

REFERENCES AND FURTHER READING

Petkova, M. (2013). *Effects and perceptions of a humor competence curriculum in an intensive English program in Southern California* (Doctoral dissertation). Available from ProQuest Dissertation and Theses Database. (UMI No. 3552234)

APPENDIX A: *Humor Vocabulary* (adapted from Petkova, 2013)

Type of Humor	Definition	Example Scene	Functions of Humor
Humorous narrative	Funny story		
Satire	Using wit for social criticism		
Parody	Funny imitation		
Amusing observation	Making jokes about what you see		
Creation of alternative realities	Fantasy scenarios		
Play with phonology	Making jokes using the sounds of the words		
New voice and persona	Jokingly speaking as if you were someone else		
Wordplay	Using similar or related words to a funny effect		
Irony and sarcasm	Jokingly saying the opposite of what you actually mean.		
Semantic ambiguity	Playing with words that may mean several different things—one obvious and normal and the other funny		

Self-deprecating humor	Making fun of yourself		
Humorous insult	Jokingly calling someone names		
Tease	Playfully annoying someone		
Puns	Play on words		
Hyperbole	Exaggeration		
Allusion	Indirect reference, making fun of something without naming it, but expecting the listener to know it		
Indirect negation	Yeah, right		

APPENDIX B: *Role-Play Situations (Petkova, 2013)*

1. You are working in an office and must spend a lot of time at your desk. A coworker whose desk is right next to yours keeps a lot of smelly food on his desk and constantly eats there. Can you jokingly say something to show him that you do not like this, but still want to keep a pleasant tone and a good relationship?

2. You are an American college professor. Some of your students are constantly late to class and this irritates you. How can you lightheartedly let them know you do not like this, but still like the students and want them to enjoy your class?

3. You are an international student living with an American host family. Their dog loves to get into your room, play with your shoes and clothes, jump on you, and lovingly lick your hands and face. How can you jokingly let them know you do not like this, but still like their dog and the family?

4. You are an American parent hosting an international student in your house. The student sometimes cooks for himself, but never cleans the stove after he spills and burns something. You have to scrub the stove yourself, and you do not like it. How can you tell your student to clean up the stove after cooking without making him feel bad?

5. You are an international student talking with some American students. They are laughing about something you don't understand. How can you take part in the conversation and join the fun?

6. You are the boss at an office where some employees are unhappy that they have to work late the afternoon before a major holiday. What could you say to lighten up the mood, show you understand them, and still get all the work done?

APPENDIX C: *Role-Play Scoring Rubrics (Petkova, 2013)*

How funny is this response?

5	Very funny	"That's a good one!" Sharp wit; you would laugh in response in this situation.
4	Funny	The speaker is clearly using humor. You would at least smile in this situation and be amused to some extent.
3	Not very funny	Some attempt at humor, but not really successful. You would not laugh or smile in this situation and may be puzzled.
2	Not funny at all	The student is not even attempting to use humor; speaking seriously.
1	Unintelligible	The response is audible, but you cannot understand the student's accent. Pronunciation, wrong vocabulary, and/ or foreign intonation obscure the meaning.
0	No response	The student is present and attempts the task, but cannot come up with anything to say about this situation.

How appropriate is this response?

5	Very appropriate	Such a response is likely to accomplish all of the speaker's multilayered goals as described in each situation.
4	Appropriate	Such a response is likely to accomplish some but not all of the speaker's multilayered goals as described in each situation. It will definitely not offend the listener.
3	Inappropriate	May offend or puzzle the listener. Serious questions will probably be asked to clarify the student's intended meaning.
2	Insulting	The comment may cause a fight or end a relationship. Apology will definitely be needed.
1	Unintelligible	The response is audible, but you cannot understand the student's accent. Pronunciation, wrong vocabulary, and/ or foreign intonation obscure the meaning.
0	No response	The student is present and attempts the task, but cannot come up with anything to say about this situation.

Using Comedy for Cross-Cultural Analysis

Andrew Reimann

Levels	*Intermediate +*
Aims	*Interpret and understand the nuances and elements of humor across cultures*
	Develop awareness of individual differences and an understanding of the requirements for a sense of humor
Class Time	*20–45 minutes*
Preparation Time	*15 minutes*
Resources	*Worksheets (see Appendices)*

Humor is a cross-cultural phenomenon; however, the elements that make it understood or enjoyable are culture-specific. In cross-cultural communication, humor is often used as a powerful speech act for breaking the ice, building relationships, or diffusing a difficult situation. However universal, the idea of "funny" is rarely translatable and is highly personal as well as context- and culture-specific. As a result, many jokes and sarcastic or ironic remarks, which may be deeply tied to culture, are often unperceived, misunderstood, or even offensive. The activity described here uses examples of humor in context and describes ways in which they may be applied to communication and cultural understanding. The goal is to try to use humor to bridge cultures and work as a mutual communication strategy. Skills and strategies developed through this activity include flexibility, creativity, and multilevel awareness of individual and cultural differences in communication styles.

The first task provides input from various mediums and styles of humor. In the case of English, examples from the United Kingdom, Canada, Australia, and the United States are efficient and accessible. It is also interesting and useful to compare these with examples from other English-speaking countries on the periphery, such as India, Malaysia, and Hong Kong, to experience firsthand how cultural differences affect language and communication.

The final task requires students to consider their own perceptions of "funny" by analyzing and ranking the examples of humor. In conclusion, the factors affecting the success or failure of humor in interpersonal and intercultural settings should be considered and discussed. The purpose of the activity is to promote open-mindedness and flexibility toward interaction while exposing students to real-life language and situations. By considering humor in context, students are able to reflect on how it is used and form their own conclusions. Cross-cultural examples of humor can also provide a sense of curiosity to motivate and facilitate inquiry and interest beyond the classroom.

PROCEDURE

1. *Screening:* Show students examples of humor from different cultures or languages. (Some examples that are both representative of different comedy styles and readily accessible are Mr. Bean, *Saturday Night Live*, Monty Python, Russell Peters, *Jackass*, and Charlie Chaplin.) See Reimann (2010) for an extensive list, along with student reactions. These should be short and simple examples and be representative of the target language or culture.

2. *Evaluation:* Students should evaluate each example giving it a rank on a scale of 1–5 (see Appendix A). They should also determine the level of funniness, their level of understanding, and the elements that made it funny or not. Following this they can analyze the examples of humor by applying simple questions (see Appendix B). Who is involved? What happened? Where did the situation take place? When? What exactly was funny? What was the intended purpose? What was the pattern? Could I recognize the surprise, twist, or deviation from logic? Was there a resolution? To develop a complete understanding, learners should compile their own list of key words and key questions about the examples (see Appendix B).

3. *Discussion:* Explain the key elements of the examples of humor. Students can then compare interpretations and opinions with each other. Which examples were most popular and least popular? What are some common elements in determining the success or failure of humor? What sort of individual differences are there in the class?

4. *Reflection and interpretation:* Finally, students deconstruct the examples considering social, cultural, and linguistic perspectives. Use questions like those in Appendix B to form a basic understanding of the social or communicative elements connected to the examples of humor. Encourage students to try to understand the values and perspective behind each example of humor. Why was it funny? How can the humor be understood? Learners should also write down their own interpretations, which can be shared and discussed.

CAVEATS AND OPTIONS

1. This lesson can be modified for different levels of English proficiency by using visual humor or humor with very simple language (Charlie Chaplin, Mr. Bean, *Jackass*, Monty Python).

2. In larger classes this activity can be conducted as pair or group work.

3. If learners find it difficult to understand humor, use a simple example and focus on identifying patterns, stereotypes, or deviations in logic or expectations.

4. Tell students to keep an open mind and pay close attention to all details.

5. As some humor can cross boundaries and taboos, carefully consider the background and values of all students in the class to avoid using any examples that may be inappropriate.

REFERENCES AND FURTHER READING

Byram, M. (1997). *Teaching and assessing intercultural communicative competence.* Clevedon, England: Multilingual Matters.

Reimann, A. (2010). Intercultural communication and the essence of humour. *Journal of International Studies* (Utsunomiya University), *29*(1), 23–34.

Reimann, A. (2015). *Culture in context: Critical incidents for raising cultural awareness.* Tokyo, Japan: Intergraphica Press.

APPENDIX A: *Humor Analysis Worksheet*

Indicate how funny each example of humor is on the chart below.

Example	Not funny			Very funny		Reason
1.	1	2	3	4	5	
2.	1	2	3	4	5	
3.	1	2	3	4	5	
4.	1	2	3	4	5	
5.	1	2	3	4	5	

APPENDIX B: *Interpretation and Analysis Worksheet*

Analyze the examples of humor. Consider the criteria listed below.

Background knowledge					
Keywords					
Expectations/ assumptions					
Turning point/ surprise					
Punch line					
Resolution					
Difficulties					
Language-specific information					
Culture-specific information					

Key Questions
Which examples of humor were easiest to understand? Why?
What was the purpose of the humor?
What was necessary to understand the examples of humor?
How might the humor be communicated across cultures?
How can humor be applied to intercultural communication?

Captioned Comedy With Charlie Chaplin's *Modern Times*

Gregory Strong

Levels	*Lower intermediate*
Contexts	*Young adult, university, English language school*
Aims	*See how humor can arise through visual repetition, anticipation, and surprise*
	Develop appreciation of classic silent comedy films and their use of captions
	Learn about the rich comic repertoire of Charlie Chaplin
	Expand writing ability
Class Time	*1–2 classes*
Preparation Time	*About 2 hours*
Resources	*Modern Times on DVD or access to YouTube to view scenes from it*
	DVD player or Internet access, an overhead projector, and screen

This activity explains concepts in humor such as exaggeration, repetition, anticipation, surprise, comic persona, and visual gags. These are best understood when students view scenes from Charlie Chaplin's silent film *Modern Times* that employ these concepts and create captions for them.

PROCEDURE

1. Describe Charlie Chaplin's "Little Tramp" as a comic persona with his stubby moustache, oversize clothes and shoes, and comical walk.

2. As in his earlier silent films, the captions remain central to the audience understanding of plot developments. Among the film's captions is a scene very late in the film. A teen runaway, played by Pauline Goddard, who has gotten a job as a dancer at a restaurant, tries to help Chaplin prepare a song for the crowd. "Let's rehearse your song," reads her caption. We see Chaplin do a comic dance and start to sing. But he keeps halting. "I forget the words." The girl suggests, "I'll write them on your cuff." As she writes them on his shirt cuff, we read the song lyrics. Chaplin rehearses them. The manager

calls him onto the stage. During his elaborate dance steps, the shirt cuff with the song lyrics flies off his wrist. Desperately, he looks toward the girl. "Sing! Never mind the words," she says. So Chaplin sings in a nonsense language with strange, elaborate gestures and becomes a huge hit.

Show this sequence to students, pausing the video at points such as where Chaplin stops his dance and asks Goddard for help and later when he loses the shirt cuff with the lyrics. Then, working individually or in groups, students brainstorm potential captions. The students' lyrics should be compared with each other and with those that actually appear in the movie.

3. Challenge students with a sequence in the film where there are fewer captions and more scope for their creativity. Earlier in the film, there is a famous sequence where Chaplin becomes the unwitting guinea pig in a test of "the Billows Automated Feeding Machine," designed to eliminate long lunch breaks for workers; they can be fed while remaining on the assembly line.

This sequence has some wonderful sight gags such as the machine feeding Chaplin a corn cob on a revolving spit. The machine goes haywire and the spit spins like a lawnmower against Chaplin's teeth. Although the gag has no captions, students can create one for the scientists trying to repair their machine. At another point, a repair technician accidentally puts two steel nuts on a dessert plate. Pause the film here and ask students what will happen next. This is a great example of anticipation in comedy. The machine will force Chaplin to swallow the nuts. Although there is no caption about him eating the nuts, you could ask students what the technician might say.

Finally, a pie is advanced toward Chaplin on the machine's turntable. Stop the film here, and ask students what will happen next. The machine hits Chaplin in the face with a pie, a twist on the silent comedy cliché of pie throwing. Again, students should write what might be spoken by a technician watching. These captions should be shared with the class.

Because there are few captions in this entire scene, it's a good opportunity for students to create their own. Finally, at the scene's end, Chaplin's boss has a remark that is captioned. Again, pause the video and have students write their own. The boss remarks of the machine, "It's not practical." Point out to students this fine example of irony: The boss rejects the machine because it breaks down too much, not because of the distress it caused Chaplin.

CAVEATS AND OPTIONS

In more advanced classes, students can work in groups to create captioned cell phone stories. Each group is given a maximum of 20 photographs to establish a comic persona, a situation where the character is in trouble, and the ending in which the conflict is resolved. The cell phone story should involve exaggeration, visual gags, and the other comic aspects described earlier, and it should provide some captions. These stories can be shared with the class by laying each phone under the overhead camera and projecting the images onto the viewing screen.

REFERENCES AND FURTHER READING

Chaplin, C. (1936). *Modern Times*. DVD Release Date: November 16, 2010. Criterion Collection.

Kamin, D. (2011). *The comedy of Charlie Chaplin: Artistry in motion*. Lanham, MD: Scarecrow Press.

Robinson, D. (2004). Filming Modern Times. Retrieved from http://www.charlie chaplin.com/en/biography/articles/6-Modern-Times

Cultural Aspects of Humor in Sitcoms

Jules Winchester

Levels	Intermediate and above
Aims	Notice social and cultural cues to better understand humor in short comedy clips
Class Time	30–40 minutes
Preparation Time	20 minutes
Resources	Humorous clips from movies or sitcoms
	Graphic organizer (Appendix)

It is often social and cultural cues, not the language, that make humorous exchanges difficult to understand. By watching humorous clips, students can get a deeper understanding of the cultural contents of humor.

PROCEDURE

1. In small groups, students discuss any occasions (e.g., watching films, engaging in conversation) during which they have had difficulties either communicating or understanding humor. As a class, discuss what students think contributed to their difficulties, if any, and what can make understanding humor difficult in another language and/or cultural context.

2. Show students a short humorous clip (e.g., "I Know Nothing!" clip from *Fawlty Towers*: www.youtube.com/watch?v=s6EaoPMANQM) and ask them if they find it funny, and if not, why not. As a class, identify (a) unknown vocabulary, (b) relevant social and cultural references, and (c) interactional norms that contribute to the humor, and discuss the meanings and/or significance of the language, references, and interactional norms. Students can take notes on the graphic organizer (Appendix).

3. Discuss with the class the importance of developing social and cultural knowledge, as well as linguistic knowledge, in order to increase their understanding of humor.

4. Show students a second clip (e.g., "Ricky Gervais in The Dragons Den" from *Extras*: www.youtube.com/watch?v=zDAtTxSaVN8&feature=player

_detailpage). After watching, ask students to watch it again and note down language, cultural and social references, social interactional norms, and body language that they think contributed to the humor of the clip or text.

Examples of cultural references in "The Dragons Den" clip include *Extras* (a British sitcom), Globes (Golden Globe Awards for achievements in film and television), and Emmys (Emmy Awards for achievements in the television industry). Students may not understand the reference to "Dragons" (the panel are "Dragons" who decide whether to invest in a business idea brought before them in the "den") or their associated catchphrase "I'm out!" (spoken when the Dragons state that they are uninterested in investing in the proposition set before them). Furthermore, students may be surprised by the apparent rudeness of the Dragons, who are in fact playing up to their stereotyped roles in order to create a humorous effect in this clip.

5. As a follow-up, encourage students to translate a joke or humorous exchange into English from another language and explain the social and cultural references that are necessary to know in order to understand the humor.

APPENDIX: *Graphic Organizer for Watching Humorous Clips*

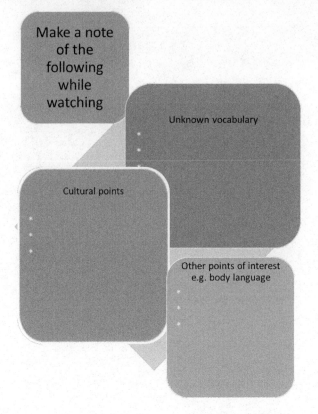

Part VI

Internet Resources and Digital Literacy

Driving Dogs

Bryan Corbin

Levels	Intermediate to advanced
Aims	Develop critical thinking, presentation, and writing skills
Class Time	1 hour
Preparation Time	5 Minutes
Resources	Computer with overhead projector, speakers, and Internet access
	For students, personal laptops or access to computers

Stories that are unusual or funny are a great resource to captivate students' minds. The goal of this activity is to encourage students to think critically outside of their normal parameters and, in the process, improve their presentation and writing skills.

This activity helps students think critically about the need for many dogs to be adopted into loving homes. Students can learn the important lesson that using humor is a terrific way to gain the attention of an audience and to disseminate worthwhile information. After all, students learn more with humor and by doing activities (Huss, 2008).

PROCEDURE

1. Show students the 2-minute video titled "Meet Porter: The World's First Driving Dog," which can be found on YouTube (www.youtube.com /watch?v=BWAK0J8Uhzk). This video highlights a campaign geared toward encouraging New Zealanders to adopt dogs from their local animal shelters.

2. After showing students the video, have them discuss the following questions in class for approximately 10 minutes. This step can be completed in groups or together as a class.

   - Will this new advertising campaign encourage people to adopt a dog from their local animal shelters?

   - Could the money spent on teaching dogs to learn how to drive have been better spent elsewhere? If so, where should it have been spent?

- What did you enjoy about the video?

- Is there anything you did not enjoy about the video?

- Do you think Westerners are too obsessed with taking care of their animals? Why or why not?

- Would this idea work with other animals? Why or why not?

- Did the music in the video add or detract from the message?

3. After discussing the above questions, have students answer the following question in groups and prepare a 5-minute group presentation to give later in the week:

> If you were in charge of creating a campaign to raise awareness of animal needs, what would you do? Be as innovative as possible, and please remember that humor adds to the creativity and persuasiveness of a message. Also, don't worry too much about financial constraints. In order to keep your focus narrow, consider discussing one type of animal to help.

CAVEATS AND OPTIONS

1. Students could create presentations individually rather than in a group.

2. Students could also write an essay in response to the question in addition to, or instead of, giving a presentation.

3. Additionally, this could be a semester-long project that students work on in groups or independently, with the length of the presentation to be determined by you based on students' skill and age level.

REFERENCES AND FURTHER READING

Huss, J. A. (2008). Getting serious about humor: Attitudes of secondary teachers toward the use of humor as a teaching strategy. *Journal of Ethnographic & Qualitative Research, 3*(1), 28–36.

Discussing and Debating Elements of Humor in Media

Susan Goldstein and Lan Ngo

Levels	*Intermediate +*
Contexts	*High school +*
Aims	*Learn and practice vocabulary words to describe humor*
	Recognize elements of humor in media
	Use oral language to communicate elements of humor and to debate and persuade
	Write a summary about the main elements of humor used in media
Class Time	*60 minutes*
Preparation Time	*45 minutes*
Resources	*Video projection device*
	Graphic organizer (Appendix A)
	Handout with the lesson's key vocabulary words with definitions
	Exit ticket (Appendix B)

English language learners (ELLs) must be able to draw conclusions and convey information persuasively regarding any subject (Short, 2002). In lessons on persuasion through speech, establishing structures for classroom talk (e.g., debates) helps to evenly allocate speaking opportunities (Duff, 2001; Olivo, 2003). Through organized speaking activities, the teacher can create a classroom environment that cultivates learners' willingness to communicate (Cao, 2014).

To provide a platform on which ELLs may collaboratively participate in intellectual engagement, we adapted Johnson and Johnson's (2007) framework on creative controversy in developing the lesson's debate structure. After speaking and rebutting on behalf of their position, students end the debate by seeking a synthesis that considers both perspectives, thereby learning to cooperate and solve problems from different viewpoints (Johnson & Johnson, 2007).

Lastly, analyzing media aligns with conceptualizations of literacy that incorporate negotiating multiple discourses (McKay & Wong, 1996) nested within various technologies (Gee, 2007). In addition to fostering the ability to read traditional texts, we should also support ELLs in their reading of media and images to prepare them to navigate meaning and information presented in different modalities.

PROCEDURE

1. *Introduction/motivation:* Make sure the following "Do Now" question is on the board as students enter the room: What makes something funny? (A "Do Now" is an introductory activity intended to focus students' attention on the topic that will be addressed in the lesson.)

2. *Presentation:* Show an example of a funny TV commercial to build students' background knowledge (see Appendix A for some sample commercials). Engage students in a discussion about why the commercial is funny. To model, present the elements of humor and guide students in completing a graphic organizer about the commercial (see Appendix B).

3. *Practice and application:* Show two different funny TV commercials to the class. Assign students to work in groups of four. Two students from the group will represent Commercial A, while the other two students will represent Commercial B. Each partnership prepares a graphic organizer to identify the elements of humor in their assigned commercial and show why their commercial is funnier. Debate begins:

   - Partner 1 in Team A speaks.

   - Partner 1 in Team B speaks/rebuts.

   - Partner 2 in Team A speaks.

   - Partner 2 in Team B speaks/rebuts.

4. *Review and assessment:* Each group of students collaboratively summarizes the elements of humor in each commercial in an exit ticket (see Appendix C). (An exit ticket is an informal assessment of students' learning. You can analyze students' progress to inform future instruction.)

CAVEATS AND OPTIONS

1. Ask students to switch positions and complete another round of the debate.

2. During the group-work portion of the lesson, students may choose their own groups, depending on the class dynamics.

3. More advanced students could find their own commercials.

4. Use print media such as ads or political cartoons.

5. Sentence prompts may be needed during the debate.

6. Adapt the lesson to use commercials in English or with English subtitles from different countries.

REFERENCES AND FURTHER READING

Cao, Y. (2014). A sociolinguistic perspective on second language classroom willingness to communicate. *TESOL Quarterly, 48*, 789–814. doi:10.1002/tesq.155

Duff, P. A. (2001). Language, literacy, content, and (pop) culture: Challenges for ESL students in mainstream courses. *Canadian Modern Language Review, 58*(1), 103–132. doi:10.3138/cmlr.58.1.103

Gee, J. (2007). *What video games have to teach us about learning and literacy* (2nd ed.). New York, NY: Palgrave Macmillan.

Johnson, D. W., & Johnson, R. T. (2007). *Creative controversy: Intellectual challenge in the classroom* (4th ed.). Minneapolis, MN: Interaction Book.

McKay, S. L., & Wong, S. L. C. (1996). Multiple discourses, multiple identities: Investment and agency in second-language learning among Chinese adolescent immigrant students. *Harvard Educational Review, 66*, 577–609.

Olivo, W. (2003). "Quit talking and learn English!": Conflicting language ideologies in an ESL classroom. *Anthropology & Education Quarterly, 34*(1), 50–71.

Short, D. J. (2002). Language learning in sheltered social studies classes. *TESOL Journal, 11*(1), 18–24. doi:10.1002/j.1949-3533.2002.tb00062.x

APPENDIX A: *Sample Commercials*

Below are sample commercials that have been used in the lesson. If links are no longer current, do a YouTube search for the key words.

Doritos: "When Pigs Fly"

https://www.youtube.com/watch?v=YQo0TfuueaY

Real California Milk

https://www.youtube.com/watch?v=qw8Py97OjX8

Snickers: "Football: You Are Not You When You Are Hungry"

https://www.youtube.com/watch?v=dbpFpjLVabA

VI

Sour Patch Kids: "Promposal"

https://www.youtube.com/watch?v=YufmFvUGo2M

Volkswagen: Sales Event: What About a Deal"

https://www.youtube.com/watch?v=jYxkDiMZbuw

APPENDIX B: *Elements of Humor Graphic Organizer*

Name _____ Date _____

Commercial Topic _____

Element of Humor	Evidence From the Commercial
Words and phrases	
Physical actions	
Acting style	
Voice and tone	
Unexpected elements	
Visuals	

APPENDIX C: *Exit Ticket*

Name _____ Date _____

Commercial A is funny for these two main reasons:

1. _____

_____

2. _____

_____

Commercial B is funny for these two main reasons:

1. _____

_____

2. _____

_____

Internet Memes to Learn and Practice English

Scott Henderson

Levels	*High beginner and above*
Contexts	*High school students and above*
Aims	*Learn the concept of Internet memes*
	Learn and use new vocabulary and grammar
	Learn about joke set-ups and punch lines
	Learn and use appropriate format for creating memes
	Use own experiences to create memes
Class Time	*50–100 minutes*
Preparation Time	*30–60 minutes*
Resources	*Internet access*
	Examples of various Internet memes
	Worksheet for matching and understanding memes

Using memes may help students become knowledgeable about current popular trends on the Internet in other cultures. The use of images can also help students comprehend the meaning and message of the text. The format of the memes' text (a situation or condition on top, the outcome on the bottom) can help students relate to other forms of humor, such as common spoken jokes in which there is a set-up to the joke and then a punch line.

PROCEDURE

1. Students match the picture to the meme name.

Bad Luck Brian Success Kid First-World Problems			

2. Explain vocabulary and meaning as necessary (e.g., *first world*, *bad luck*, *success*).

3. Use the examples below of the three famous memes, or search the Internet and select other examples. Students can choose examples they like and give reasons for their choices, or they can explain which meme is their favorite.

4. Match the memes to the examples below, or find other examples on the Internet. (Note: These are original examples that I created to fit the pattern. Numerous examples can easily be found online.)

Bad Luck Brian	My new winter jacket . . . is too warm.
Success Kid	My neighborhood . . . has so many good places to eat, and I can't choose one.
First-World Problems	My Facebook account . . . has too many friends.
	I just bought the newest iPhone . . . the next model comes out next month.
	Gets to school without being late . . . it's Saturday, and he has no classes.
	Writes a long essay for English class . . . leaves it at home.
	Rides brand new bike to school . . . gets two flat tires.
	I didn't know the answer on a test, so I guessed . . . I got the right answer.
	I forgot to bring lunch to work . . . our boss bought us all lunch.
	I didn't do my homework . . . my teacher forgot to collect it.

5. Students brainstorm in groups about their own first-world problems. Write all of the group ideas on the board. Students use these ideas to make a meme individually or as groups.

6. For homework, students think of their own lives and make memes about their own bad luck or success stories.

CAVEATS AND OPTIONS

1. Give students short paragraphs with different situations to read. Have them turn the situations into memes.

2. Students watch short videos and then make them into a meme. ("Fail" videos in which people commit humorous bloopers work well for bad luck memes.)

3. Students create memes but they must use specific grammar structures, vocabulary, or topics being studied in class.

4. Students find pictures on the Internet and create their own memes. Here are two websites they can use: http://memegenerator.net and www.meme creator.org. Numerous cell phone applications for creating memes are also available for free.

5. Students use their own pictures from their cell phones to create their own memes.

Cause and Effect With DirecTV

Jolene Jaquays and Sara Okello

Levels	*Intermediate to advanced*
Contexts	*University, adult*
Aims	*Learn about the concept of cause and effect as well as the logical fallacy of slippery slope through the use of humorous online commercials*
Class Time	*20 minutes*
Preparation Time	*20 minutes*
Resources	*YouTube videos of DirecTV commercials*

Humor is crucial in learning and understanding a second language (Bell, 2005). Using verbal humor in second language classrooms offers opportunities for students to increase their linguistic and cultural knowledge by observing and participating in humorous exchanges (Ziyaeemehr & Kumar, 2014). Since humor is inextricably tied to culture, it is imperative to expose students to various examples of cultural humor. In this activity, students watch humorous commercials and examine the cause-effect relationship between the events in the commercials as well as the logical fallacy of slippery slope. The focus of the DirecTV commercials is to encourage viewers to avoid the hassles of cable TV by providing ridiculous scenarios. The humorous commercials create a lighthearted atmosphere in the classroom while encouraging students to evaluate cause-effect relationships using the necessary grammar and vocabulary. The cause and effect presented is ridiculous and exaggerates what can happen if someone doesn't have DirecTV. It is an example of the logical fallacy device slippery slope.

PROCEDURE

1. Introduce or review the basic concept of cause and effect and the words that relate to it (e.g., *because, due to, since, as a result*).

2. Preview vocabulary in the video you are about to show. (See Appendix A for sample and Appendix B for template.)

VI

3. Show students a DirecTV commercial (see References and Further Reading for list of videos).

4. After playing it through once, replay scene by scene and have students complete the cause-and-effect chart. (See Appendix C for sample and Appendix D for template.) Stop the video after each step in the cause and effect.

5. Discuss how one event leads to the next.

6. Show another clip. Repeat the process.

7. Have students work with a partner to create their own example of slippery slope.

   Example: Did homework → doorbell rang, so left paper on table → cat jumped on table and pushed paper off table → assignment fell into dog's food bowl → dog ate homework → no homework to turn in

   (Students can also use Appendix D to create their own examples.)

8. Discuss other logical situations with cause and effect.

   Example: Bad weather → poor road conditions → difficulty controlling vehicle → car accident

9. Explain why slippery slope should be avoided in cause-and-effect speeches and papers (see Logical Fallacies, 2009).

CAVEATS AND OPTIONS

1. Be ready to stop each commercial before the next one begins.

2. Choose other commercials that have cause and effect

3. Use magazine pictures or advertisements that show cause and effect.

4. Search for DirecTV commercial parodies for more options.

5. Use www.viewpure.com to remove the advertisements surrounding the commercials.

6. Use screenshots from the commercial or a source such as Google Images to find pictures to represent each step.

7 Have students write and create their own DirecTV commercials.

REFERENCES AND FURTHER READING

Bell, N. (2005). Exploring L2 language play as an aid to SLL: A case study of humor in NS NNS interaction. *Applied Linguistics*, 26(2), 192–218. doi:10.1093/applin/amh043

Logical Fallacies. (2009). Slippery slope fallacy. Retrieved from http://www.logical fallacies.info/presumption/slippery-slope

Ziyaeemehr, A., & Kumar, V. (2014). The role of verbal humor in second language education. *International Journal of Research Studies in Education*, 3(2), 3–13. doi:10.5861/ijrse.2013.474

DirecTV Videos to Use in Lesson

"Get Rid of Cable" (chasing butterflies): http://viewpure.com/GdhlRtMGEp8?start=0&end=0

"Get Rid of Cable" compilation minus accompanying ads: http://viewpure.com/NZ80SVOHKoo

"Get Rid of Cable" compilation: http://viewpure.com/u9vbXpMKz6I?start=0&end=0

APPENDIX A: *Sample Cards for Vocabulary Introduction of DirecTV Commercials*

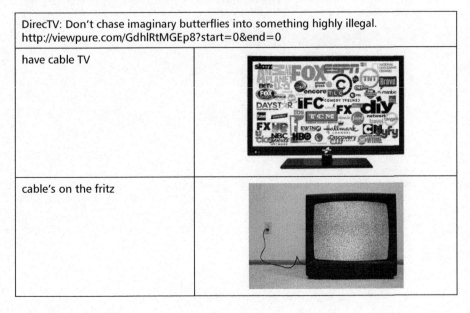

DirecTV: Don't chase imaginary butterflies into something highly illegal. http://viewpure.com/GdhlRtMGEp8?start=0&end=0	
have cable TV	
cable's on the fritz	

VI

one thing leads to another	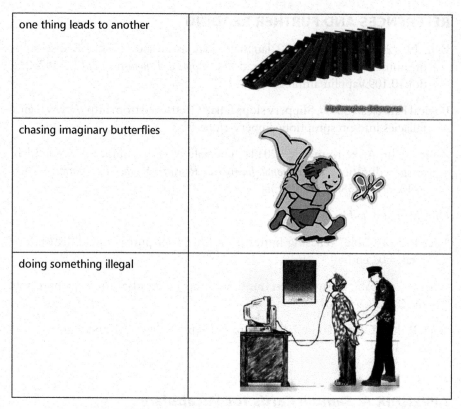
chasing imaginary butterflies	
doing something illegal	

Images from Google Images.

APPENDIX B: *Template for Creating Vocabulary Cards*

Line From Commercial	Image to Illustrate the Line

VI

APPENDIX C: *Cause and Effect Example*

Cable goes out	Get stressed	Need to get away

Exotic	Get bitten by something exotic	Things swell up

Can't go home	Become a local fisherman they call "fatty face"

APPENDIX D: *Cause and Effect Blank Template*

Lie Like a Dog: Humorous Memes and Grammar Mistakes

Jolene Jaquays and Sara Okello

Levels	*Intermediate to advanced*
Contexts	*University, young adult*
Aims	*Learn/review grammar points, vocabulary, writing concepts, and/or spelling through the use of humorous Internet memes*
Class Time	*10–15 minutes*
Preparation Time	*10–15 minutes*
Resources	*Internet to access*

Memes have been described as "the product of every teenager's desire for self-expression, sarcasm, and humor, combined with the pervasiveness of technology and this generation's unique, slightly quirky culture, stemming from the fact that geeks are becoming slightly more mainstream" (Bruder, 2013, p. 1). Capitalizing on students' interest in "all things Internet," using memes is a natural way to spark students' attention. As memes are created for their humorous perspective, many either unintentionally have grammatical errors or make fun of grammatical errors. Internet-savvy students who are digital natives have already been exposed to popular and current memes. Holwerda (2012) emphasizes the importance of using the Internet in class: "To better prepare our students for their digital citizenship, access to and understanding of internet culture is imperative" (para. 1). Allowing students to combine their own originality with grammar and memes, teachers can expand beyond the textbook.

PROCEDURE

1. Explain what a meme is: Internet memes are images that are spread online that often have a humorous or creative message.

2. Show students a meme that showcases a particular grammar point, vocabulary word, writing concept, or spelling issue. Most memes actually have misuses of these.

3. Examples of memes can be found at many sites, such as www.someecards .com, www.pinterest.com, and www.memes.com. Once at the website, type "grammar memes" into the search box.

4. Ask students what misuse is being highlighted or unintentionally used.

5. Ask students why they think the meme is supposed to be funny.

6. Introduce correct use of terms or grammar.

CAVEATS AND OPTIONS

1. Have students bring memes they have found to class to share and explain.

2. Have students work with a partner to create their own memes.

3. Screen memes for classroom appropriateness.

4. Use memes to show class rules.

5. Many websites and apps exist for creating original memes. (We have used http://memegenerator.net/create/instance and the app mematic.)

REFERENCES AND FURTHER READING

Bruder, P. (2013, February). Ermahgerd: Memes in the classroom? *NJEA Review*. Retrieved from https://www.njea.org/news-and-publications/njea-review

Holwerda, L. (2012, March 4). Steps to Web 2.0. Retrieved from http:// stepstoweb2.blogspot.com/2012/03/memes-in-classroom.html

APPENDIX A: *Sample Created Meme*

Created using mematic.

Humor in TED Talks

Lisa Leopold

Levels	**Advanced**
Contexts	**University**
Aims	**Develop public speaking, pragmatic, and intercultural communication skills**
Class Time	**About 40 minutes**
Preparation Time	**10 minutes**
Resources	**Internet access**
	Handouts

Learners may have many opportunities to present to audiences from diverse cultural and linguistic backgrounds in their future professions when pitching a business proposal, delivering a conference presentation, making a ceremonial toast, and so on. If they incorporate humor effectively into their speeches, it can make the audience more joyful, calm, and receptive (Dlugan, 2013). And if the joke makes the audience laugh, it is considered one of the best indicators of the speaker's pragmatic competence. This lesson is designed to help learners uncover the pragmatics of humor for a U.S. audience: students analyze humorous excerpts from TED speeches, identify what makes them funny (for a U.S. audience), create their own quip, and gather feedback from native and non-native English speakers.

PROCEDURE

1. Ask learners why humor is important for public presentations: it makes the speaker memorable and likeable, provides emotional release, and minimizes the distance between the speaker and the audience (Dlugan, 2010; Donovan, 2014).

2. Tell learners that humor is welcome in most public speaking contexts in the United States. Although humor may be used frequently in light-hearted speeches (e.g., wedding speeches), it can also be used occasionally in professional presentations (e.g., conference and business presentations) and even sparingly in somber speeches (e.g., eulogies). Tell students they will learn principles of effective humor for a U.S. audience.

3. Invite students to watch humorous excerpts from TED Talks (Appendix A) and identify what made these excerpts funny: surprise or unexpectedness, self-deprecation (Donovan, 2014), exaggeration, understatement, verbal irony (Jackson, 2012).

4. Have students think about a speech they might deliver in their future careers in which humor might be appropriate and develop a quip for that speech.

5. In teams of four, have students give and receive peer feedback to make the quip more humorous.

6. For homework, assign students to seek feedback from at least three native English speakers: Did they find the quip funny? Why or why not? What might make it funnier?

7. Have students report back to the class what they learned and whether they noticed any cultural differences in the feedback from their peers and the native English speakers.

8. For homework, have students revise their quip and either deliver it live in class or video-record it at home for instructor feedback.

CAVEATS AND OPTIONS

1. Learners can compete to develop the most humorous quip as judged by you and their classmates (or a panel of native speakers).

2. By selecting culturally relevant excerpts from the repertoire of TED Talks available online, you can adapt the activity for learners in other English-speaking countries. Although a joke may not be universally funny, the above-mentioned techniques such as exaggeration, understatement, and verbal irony are universally appreciated aspects of humor (Jackson, 2012).

REFERENCES AND FURTHER READING

Dlugan, A. (2010, March 15). 18 paths to pathos: How to connect with your audience. Retrieved from http://sixminutes.dlugan.com/pathos-examples-speaking

Donovan, J. (2014). *How to deliver a TED talk.* Chicago, IL: McGraw-Hill.

Jackson, S. (2012, May 18). What's funny? *Psychology Today.* Retrieved from https://www.psychologytoday.com

APPENDIX A: *Humorous TED Excerpts*

1. Chris Downey: Design With the Blind in Mind

   http://www.ted.com/talks/chris_downey_design_with_the_blind_in_mind

   9:11–9:21

   > "In fact, I've heard it said in the disability community that there are really only two types of people: There are those with disabilities, and there are those that haven't quite found theirs yet."

   Humorous strategies: **Parody**, to mimic the famous saying of Mark Twain who once said, "There are two types of speakers: Those who get nervous and those who are liars." **Surprise**, as most people don't think of themselves as not having discovered their disability yet.

2. Chris Downey: Design with the Blind in Mind

   http://www.ted.com/talks/chris_downey_design_with_the_blind_in_mind

   10:31–10:41

   > "In fact, cars, who needs them? If you're blind, you don't drive. They don't like it when you drive."

   Humorous strategies: **Understatement**, as it's certainly not just that it isn't preferred that the blind do not drive, it's actually prohibited.

3. Ken Robinson: Bring on the Learning Revolution!

   http://www.ted.com/talks/sir_ken_robinson_bring_on_the_revolution?language=en

   5:48–5:54

   > "We don't teach American history in Britain. We suppress it. You know, this is our policy."

   Humorous strategies: **Exaggeration**, as it's not likely that American history is entirely suppressed in Britain.

4. Ken Robinson: Bring on the Learning Revolution!

   http://www.ted.com/talks/sir_ken_robinson_bring_on_the_revolution?language=en

   13:24–13:43

   > "I worked out recently that I was given a guitar as a kid at about the same time that Eric Clapton got his first guitar. It worked out for Eric, that's all

I'm saying. In a way—it did not for me. I could not get this thing to work no matter how often or how hard I blew into it."

Humorous strategies: **Self-deprecation** to reveal how he was not as successful as the famous musician Eric Clapton and that he did not understand how to correctly play the guitar. **Verbal irony**, as one does not expect anyone to play a guitar by blowing into it.

Humorous Wedding Speeches

Lisa Leopold

Levels	Advanced
Contexts	University
Aims	Develop public speaking and intercultural communication skills
Class Time	Varies depending on class size
Preparation Time	10 minutes
Resources	Internet access
	Handouts (see Appendices A and B)

One way to make a presentation memorable is to use humor (Donovan, 2014). While important for most presentation genres, humor is particularly well suited for wedding speeches in which the goals are to commemorate the couple and to entertain the audience. However, it is well known that humor varies cross-culturally: What is funny in one culture may not be funny in another (Jackson, 2012). This lesson equips learners with the skills they need to understand and apply effective strategies for entertaining a U.S. audience when delivering a wedding speech. Even though not every student might have such an opportunity, this lesson still provides students with helpful insight into how humor is used in different cultural and situational contexts.

PROCEDURE

1. Discuss with learners the goals of wedding speeches (to commemorate the couple, reveal why they are an excellent match, and entertain the audience—primarily through humor).

2. Ask learners whether wedding speeches are common in their cultures and, if so, whether they serve similar functions.

3. Tell learners they will learn strategies for making a wedding speech humorous to a U.S. audience and that these techniques are also helpful for adding humor to other speech genres.

4. Invite learners to watch humorous video excerpts of wedding speeches and optionally follow along with a transcript (see Appendix A).

5. Have learners analyze what made those excerpts funny: surprise or unexpectedness, self-deprecation (Donovan, 2014), exaggeration, understatement, verbal irony (Jackson, 2012).

6. Using the above-mentioned techniques or the questions in Appendix B as a guide, have learners imagine they are either the best man or maid of honor in a close family member or friend's wedding in the United States, and invite them to deliver a witty remark for it.

7. Invite learners to deliver their anecdotes to the class and to solicit feedback from peers and you to make them more humorous.

CAVEATS AND OPTIONS

1. Learners can compete to develop the most humorous quip as judged by you and their classmates.

2. Learners can explain how they would modify their quip for an audience in the United States and in their home country.

REFERENCES AND FURTHER READING

Atkinson, M. (2004). *Lend me your ears.* New York, NY: Oxford University Press.

Donovan, J. (2014). *How to deliver a TED talk.* Chicago, IL: McGraw-Hill.

Jackson, S. (2012, May 18). What's funny? *Psychology Today.* Retrieved from https://www.psychologytoday.com

APPENDIX A: *Humorous Wedding Speech Excerpts*

1. Best Man's Speech

   https://www.youtube.com/watch?v=QRxcc_7didA

   0:00–0:33

   > "There comes a time in everyone's life when they meet their one true love: their soul mate, the person that's going to know and love them for the rest of their life. That moment came for George 25 years ago when he met me."

   > *Techniques*: Unexpectedness and exaggeration. With his serious delivery, the listeners expect the best man is talking about George's wife, not about him—George's younger brother.

2. Best Man's Speech

https://www.youtube.com/watch?v=7YWMVXh-wFs

1:36–1:56

> "I'm slightly bothered with the title of being a best man. If I'm the best man, then why is Kim marrying Simon? So I'm just happy to say that I'm a pretty good man. And today Simon is the best man."

> *Techniques*: Verbal irony, surprise, and self-deprecation. The speaker plays on the literal definition of the word *best*, using the irony to indirectly compliment the bride. He also uses self-deprecation to show the groom is really the "best man."

3. Maid of Honor Speech

https://www.youtube.com/watch?v=AtKzhXJ6Jp0

0:10–0:22

> "So when I first started to prepare what I wanted to say for my maid of honor speech, I remember thinking to myself: I can't believe that my sister is getting married in a half an hour."

> *Techniques*: Surprise and exaggeration. It is surprising that the speaker started to prepare her speech only half an hour before the wedding, also likely an exaggeration.

APPENDIX B: *Finding Funny Wedding Speech Material (adapted from Atkinson, 2004)*

1. Are there any embarrassing or funny stories you could tell about the couple's early dating experiences?

2. Could you make a joke about any changes in the person's behavior when she or he fell in love?

3. Is there a contrasting strength and weakness in the person that you can poke fun at?

4. Is there a humorous current events story that relates to the person's job or hobbies?

5. Can you draw a humorous comparison with any famous occurrences that happened on the person's birthdate?

VI

6. Does the individual's first name mean something at odds with the person's character?

7. Can you draw any funny comparisons with the person's astrological or Chinese zodiac sign?

8. Can you make any humorous predictions based on that day's or year's horoscopes?

Humor and Digital Literacy: Teaching Cohesion Through *Tonight Show* Hashtags

Michael Madson

Levels	High-intermediate to advanced
Contexts	English language school, high school, university
Aims	Acquire cohesion strategies
	Gain cross-cultural competence
Class Time	15–20 minutes on Day 1; 30 minutes or more on Day 2
Preparation Time	10–20 minutes
Resources	Computer with Internet connection and speakers
	Twitter accounts

Social media language learning, such as through Twitter, has proven effective in developing both communicative and cross-cultural competence (Borau, Ullrich, Feng, & Shen, 2009). This is, in part, because social media language learning provides authentic input and encourages meaningful output (Chartrand, 2012).

PROCEDURE

Before Class

1. As necessary, familiarize yourself with Twitter (www.twitter.com,) a social media service. The posts, all 140 characters in length or less, are called "tweets" and organized under "hashtags."

2. Review clips online of the hashtags segment on the *Tonight Show Starring Jimmy Fallon*. Each week, Fallon starts a humorous hashtag, such as #ThatWasStupid or #MyWeirdFamily, and shares his favorite tweets that result. You can find these clips on YouTube, Hulu, or NBC.com.

3. Find a clip that is appropriate for your class, and determine ways to scaffold. For example, one hashtag on the *Tonight Show* was #ThanksgivingFail. Students may be unfamiliar with the Thanksgiving holiday in the United

States. They might also be unfamiliar with the clipped, vernacular English of the Internet, such as using *-fail* as a suffix. For scaffolding, students might research U.S. Thanksgiving traditions or how the *-fail* suffix has been used online. Since *cohesion* may be a new term, students might also study cohesion strategies in advance.

In Class, Day 1

1. Play the *Tonight Show* clip that you have chosen, and have students identify cohesion strategies. These strategies might include transitional phrases, repeated key words, clear introductions and conclusions, or the Twitter hashtag itself.

2. Assign students to start a humorous hashtag on Twitter and prepare a brief, cohesive presentation on their favorite tweets that result. The dialogue format between Jimmy Fallon and the audience can serve as a model.

3. For language practice, encourage students to tweet using each other's hashtags.

After Class

1. Have students create a Twitter account (if they are not already Twitter users). Once they create their account, they can start their hashtag.

2. Allow two or three days for students to collect tweets and prepare their presentations, offering assistance as necessary.

In Class, Day 2

1. Have students present their hashtag and favorite tweets. The funnier, the better!

2. Divide the class into small groups, and ask them to discuss the cohesion strategies they used (as a presenter) or noticed (as an audience member). Have them set goals to develop their cohesion strategies further.

CAVEATS AND OPTIONS

1. Consider dividing the class into groups of two or three earlier in the process and having them work together. That way, the presentations will take less time in class.

2. Use hashtags to teach written cohesion as well. A hashtag is essentially a topic sentence, and the tweet message is much like a supporting sentence. Thus, students might combine several tweets into a cohesive paragraph.

3. Students can read several tweets with the hashtag removed. They can then formulate their own hashtag and, in small groups, explain why they feel theirs is a good choice.

4. Instead of clips, consider presenting *Tonight Show* hashtags on a handout. Doing so will help tailor the activity for lower proficiency levels.

REFERENCES AND FURTHER READING

Atenos-Conforti, E. (2009). Microblogging on Twitter: Social networking in intermediate Italian classes. In L. Lomicka & G. Lord (Eds.), *Next generation: Social networking and online collaboration in foreign language learning* (pp. 59–90). San Marco, TX: Calico.

Borau, K., Ullrich, C., Feng, J., & Shen, R. (2009). Microblogging for language learning: Using Twitter to train communicative and cultural competence. In *Advances in Web Based Learning—ICWL 2009* (pp. 78–87). Berlin, Germany: Springer.

Chartrand, R. (2012). Social networking for language learners: Creating meaningful output with Web 2.0 tools. *Knowledge Management & E-Learning, 4,* 97–101.

Gibson, R. O. (2012, April 10). Using social media as a language learning tool. *The Guardian*. Retrieved from http://www.theguardian.com

VI

Exploring Gender Stereotypes Through Advertising

Germain Mesureur

Levels	*Low-intermediate and above*
Contexts	*High school and above (students should be mature enough to understand basic gender issues)*
Aims	*Learn about common gender stereotypes*
	Develop awareness of the regional and cultural variations of gender stereotypes
	Develop understanding of different cultures through their use of stereotypes in advertising
Class Time	*60–90 minutes*
Preparation Time	*30 minutes*
Resources	*Computer with large monitor or projector and audio playback*
	Ability to either play Internet videos directly in the class or download video files for offline viewing

Gender stereotyping is far less politically correct nowadays than it may have been in the 1950s, but it is still nonetheless very present in a large number of commercials, which is a clear illustration of the pervasiveness of the issue in modern society. The way these stereotypes have been used has changed over time, just as humor preferences may be changing as society changes. This is particularly true of issues related to gender (Gulas & Weinberger, 2006).

Stereotypes remain high on the list of humorous devices used in advertising, although "there has recently been a tendency, in some countries, for advertisements to reverse traditional stereotypes, portraying women as dominant, resourceful and capable and men as foolish, immature and inept" (EASA, 2004). It is thus possible to find humorous commercials that poke fun at both genders, making it easier to approach an otherwise sensitive issue. Utilizing such adverts in the classroom is useful, in terms of both fostering awareness of gender issues and providing ample room for discussion and debate.

PROCEDURE

1. Divide the class into groups of three to five students, preferably separating them by gender.

2. Show a couple of humorous commercials that use gender stereotypes (see Appendix). Choose commercials that have a level of language appropriate to your class.

3. Students discuss whether they find the commercials funny, and why, and report the main points of their discussion to be written on the board.

4. Show a couple more commercials, have students draw a list of the way each gender is represented in the commercials, and add their list to the board.

5. Students select one of the commercials and recreate it for the opposite gender. This can be done in written or drawn form, or by playacting.

CAVEATS AND OPTIONS

1. As it is possible to find commercials that use levels of English understandable by learners of every proficiency level, it is possible to adapt this activity to lower level classes.

2. If you are not able to play videos directly from the Internet in the classroom, download the files first. A range of options are available for this, including free add-ons for web browsers and the use of websites that specialize in providing direct download links from YouTube and other video sites.

3. An exciting extension task is to ask students to search for commercials in their own language. They prepare a short presentation for a later class, explaining the humor of the commercial and any cultural difference in the stereotype that can be observed.

4. When using this activity in a college or university setting, a number of additional questions can be raised, drawing on students' background knowledge. For example, business and marketing majors could pursue a discussion about the efficiency of the advertising strategy used in the commercials and its applicability to their own culture; sociology and psychology students could focus on the schemas used to define each gender in the typical 30- to 90-second duration of most commercials.

VI

REFERENCES AND FURTHER READING

European Advertising Standards Alliance. (2004). *Gender stereotyping and the portrayal of women and men*. Brussels, Belgium: Author.

Gulas, C., & Weinberger, M. (2006). *Humor in advertising: A comprehensive analysis*. Armonk, NY: M. E. Sharpe.

APPENDIX: *Sample Commercials*

Below is a selection of commercials featuring clear gender stereotypes used in a humorous setting. All of these are rather famous and widely available on a number of video websites. Keywords and titles are included in case the URL provided is no longer current.

Castro Dog Food:

https://www.youtube.com/watch?v=9c2Ss7aoUHc

Keystone Light "Always Smooth":

http://www.youtube.com/watch?v=PfJb1E3fnHs

Kia Optima "A Dream Car for Real Life":

http://www.youtube.com/watch?v=9RI6OGXq11Y

Sealect Low Fat Tuna "Thai Elevator":

http://www.youtube.com/watch?v=jFyiIL2p9sA

Mercedes Benz "Beauty Is Nothing Without Brains":

http://www.youtube.com/watch?v=GHX2mvFVQMs

Mercedes Benz "CLS Blue Efficiency":

http://www.youtube.com/watch?v=nCXczVl_18I

What's Funny About That?

Daniel J. Mills and Sean H. Toland

Levels	*Intermediate+*
Contexts	*High school, university, business*
Aims	*Improve ability to seek information, cooperate with classmates, communicate in the target language, present new information, and make humor from another culture more accessible*
Class Time	*30 minutes*
Preparation Time	*5 minutes*
Resources	*Computer with Internet access*
	Blackboard or whiteboard
	Projector
	Speakers
	Students' personal mobile devices

In many cases, humor presented in authentic contexts can be difficult for language learners to comprehend, not because of the difficulty of the language used, but because of a lack of cultural knowledge. However, mobile devices and information-seeking skills can help make humor in the target language more accessible. In this activity, students watch a humorous commercial by the U.S. athletic shoe company Foot Locker, which features five sports celebrities who are well known in the United States: Mike Tyson, Evander Holyfield, Dennis Rodman, Craig Sager, and Brett Favre. In the four scenarios presented in the commercial, knowledge of the background of these individuals is essential to understanding why it is humorous. This lesson provides students with an opportunity to practice their ability to research a topic and present that information to their peers, while also improving their communicative abilities in a cooperative environment.

PROCEDURE

1. Lead a brainstorming session with the entire class on the meaning of humor and examples of humorous incidents. Take notes on the board as students give their examples. Here are some warm-up questions that could be

included to get students talking: Who is your funniest friend? Why is she or he funny? Can you tell us about a funny story involving this friend?

2. Divide the class into groups (four groups is ideal for this activity because that is the number of situations featured in the commercial).

3. Students discuss what they find humorous both in their own culture and in the target language culture. Are there any movies, TV shows, or comedians that they think are funny? What makes them funny?

4. Tell students that they will watch a commercial for an athletic shoe store that presents some humorous situations related to sports events and figures. Remind students that while they may not understand why this commercial is funny at first, they will be given the opportunity to find out.

5. Write the names of the sports personalities featured in the video on the board: Mike Tyson, Evander Holyfield, Dennis Rodman, Craig Sager, Brett Favre. Assign each group one situation featured in the video. (Note: Tyson bit off part of Holyfield's ear during a boxing match on June 28, 1997. Rodman is a former professional basketball player who visited North Korea twice in 2014; these visits created a lot of controversy. Sager is a sports commentator who always wears outrageous suits. Favre is a former U.S. football player; he was indecisive about retirement and subsequently retired on three separate occasions.)

6. Play the YouTube video titled *Footlocker's Week of Greatness 2013: All Is Right* (www.youtube.com/watch?v=9KMUnqB_NiU).

7. Instruct students to work in groups for approximately 5 minutes. They will use their mobile devices to discover the humor in the situation assigned to their group.

8. Check that students were able to find information on their situation. If they are struggling, provide the following hints on the board next to the names of the sports figures, and give them an additional 5 minutes to research their subject: Mike Tyson and Evander Holyfield—ear; Dennis Rodman—North Korea; Craig Sager—outrageous suits; Brett Favre—retirement.

9. Students create a short explanation describing the person(s) featured in their situation and why the depiction of that person(s) in the commercial is humorous.

10. Students present their description to the class and answer any questions that other students have.

11. Play the video a second time for the class, and explain additional details of the video and answer questions.

CAVEATS AND OPTIONS

1. This activity can be extended to 60 minutes by including one or more of the following activities:

   - Extend the discussions in Step 3 by rotating students between groups to provide more communicative opportunities.

   - Following the activity, students can work in groups to find other humorous commercials that they will present to the class with an explanation of why they found them humorous.

2. Possible homework assignments:

   - Students can participate in an online discussion where they present videos of humorous commercials with an explanation. Students must comment on a minimum number of posts as decided by you.

   - Students can create a storyboard of a humorous commercial that they can present in the following class.

3. In classes where only a few students own a mobile device, evenly distribute these students between the groups to ensure access, or let students without devices use your mobile device or one that belongs to the school.

VI

Sharing Laughs and Increasing Cross-cultural Understanding With Memes

Louise Ohashi

Levels	*All*
Aims	*Develop cross-cultural understanding*
	Understand and enjoy humor in English
Class Time	*45–60 minutes*
Preparation Time	*10–15 minutes*
Resources	*Web-capable device and a way to share images (e.g., a projector); ideally, students would also have Internet access*

All materials (memes) for this lesson can be found on the Internet. Three particular memes are focused on here, and additional ones can be easily accessed online. While memes can be found through an image search with the keyword "meme," this will display some images/words that are inappropriate, so care should be taken if directing students to access memes themselves. "Clean" memes, which do not contain the profanity that is often found in a meme search, can be found on sites such as Clean Memes (www.cleanmemes.com). Images from popular memes can be found at https://imgflip.com/memetemplates; this site can be used to generate new captions for photos on the site or the students' own photographs.

Studying memes allows students to gain insight into the way humor is understood and enjoyed in different cultures while simultaneously working on their English skills. Writing their own captions allows students to use English creatively to make use of their newly gained cross-cultural knowledge or, if translating memes from their own language, to share their own culture in an amusing way in English.

PROCEDURE

Before Class

1. Search online for the following three memes: Grumpy Cat, The Most Interesting Man in the World, and Bad Luck Brian.

2. Find other suitable memes online and think about what students need to know in order to understand why they are funny.

In Class

1. Start by explaining or eliciting what a meme is. Oxford Dictionaries defines a meme as "an image, video, piece of text, etc., typically humorous in nature, that is copied and spread rapidly by Internet users, often with slight variations."

2. Introduce the Grumpy Cat meme. Grumpy Cat, as the name suggests, is represented by a picture of a cat that has a grumpy expression. It usually has a two-part caption that is funny because of its negative twist. A popular pattern that the Grumpy Cat meme follows is to start positively at the top of the picture only to become negative in the bottom caption. Examples include the following:

Top	Bottom
Good morning.	No such thing.
People keep thinking I care.	Weird.
Have a nice day.	Don't tell me what to do.

This negative form of humor may not be common in students' cultures, so start by showing a picture of the cat with no captions and eliciting how the cat looks and feels. Show the top caption and ask if it matches the cat's feelings. After students confirm that it doesn't, because it is positive, show the bottom caption and highlight the way a positive message has ended negatively, which creates a humorous twist.

3. Show examples of The Most Interesting Man in the World meme, which uses a picture of a stylish older man who says "I don't usually . . . but when I do. . . ." Explain/elicit why the examples are funny. Examples of captions for this meme include the following:

Top	Bottom
I don't always remember all the scary ghost movies I've ever seen	but when I do, it's 3 a.m.
I don't always look up things on my smartphone	but when I do, it's to prove people wrong.
I don't always play the villain	but when I do, I'm more popular than the hero.

4. Show some examples of Bad Luck Brian. This meme uses a picture of a smiling teenage boy who has braces. It starts with something that might happen to anyone at the top, but ends with an unlucky twist at the bottom. Examples include the following:

Top	Bottom
Spends all night studying	Sleeps through the exam
Gets the highest score	In golf
Goes to a 24-hour store	It's closed

If students already understand the humor in the Grumpy Cat and The Most Interesting Man in the World memes introduced above, the top and bottom sections of the Bad Luck Brian memes could be mixed up and used as a matching task.

5. Repeat with some other preselected memes, and have students try to decipher them in pairs or small groups.

6. Ask the pairs or groups to write captions for some images that they have already discussed. They can access many popular images that have had the captions removed at https://imgflip.com/memetemplates and can use that site to add new captions onto their chosen image, which can then be saved. If they do not have access to the Internet, they can write their captions on paper using images provided by you.

7. Students share their work by posting their files to the class's preferred social networking site or presenting them face to face. They can discuss the new captions in class and/or read and respond to them for homework.

CAVEATS AND OPTIONS

1. Students could introduce memes that are popular in their country and translate them into English or create new English captions for the images. Also, if no Internet access is available, you could print out some worksheets in advance.

2. Some images used in memes have copyright restrictions. You and the students need to be aware of this and should avoid downloading and sharing copyrighted images.

Understanding Humor for Global Marketing

Andrew Reimann

Levels	*Intermediate +*
Contexts	*Business English and general English*
Aims	*Understand how humor can be used to enhance a message or create a connection between groups and across borders for the purpose of creating ideas that spread*
	Gain greater understanding of global marketing and international business communication
Class Time	*20–90 minutes*
Preparation Time	*15–45 minutes*
Resources	*Commercials and advertisements*
	Marketing strategy evaluation worksheet
	Maslow's Hierarchy of Needs (see Appendices for handouts)

The practical aspects of humor extend beyond being a powerful communicative tool for building relationships or entertaining. Humor is also an effective marketing strategy and technique for creating a strong and lasting message or a positive image of a product. Humor is often used in marketing to be fun, memorable, influential, and inspiring. A key benefit of this is that it allows potential customers to let down their defenses and become less apprehensive, more likely to listen, trust, and become open to suggestions. As a result, advertising media is often funny in order to entertain, hook, or identify with potential consumers. Considering that humor requires higher cognitive understanding as well as cultural knowledge, such marketing can be effective in remaining in viewers' memories, creating a connection and positive feeling, or generally developing the brand of the product, within a specific target audience. However, if not done carefully, it can have the opposite effect, by either isolating or offending a potential consumer base. Therefore, humor should focus on supporting a message and not just entertaining.

The goal of humor in advertising is not just producing a big laugh or reaction but rather reaching the audience, promoting the product, and delivering a message by creating a bond, identity, or connection. For this purpose, the message, product, and humor should all be relevant to the audience. Examples of humor

VI

need to be subtle, enhance the goal of the message, and return to business once the viewer is hooked. Humorous stories, images or anecdotes have the power to bring people together and create a strong positive bond or identity with the product. As it involves memory and feelings of euphoria, humor is often remembered, retold, and quoted. This in itself is powerful in marketing, as the message endures long after the advertisement has ended. For both communicating ideas that spread and motivate as well as understanding the intention of a company's message, an awareness of marketing strategies that apply humor is an essential skill and requirement for international media literacy. Like humor, successful marketing requires a deep and comprehensive understanding of the audience. By developing these skills, learners can gain the more complete cross-cultural understanding necessary for communicating ideas in intercultural exchanges, international business, and global marketing.

PROCEDURE

1. *Observation:* Students observe five examples of promotional media or advertisements on their own. (Some examples easily accessible on YouTube include Bridgestone—Squirrel, Doritos—Pug, Berlitz—Why Learn English, and Volkswagen—Beauty Without Common Sense.) These should be analyzed to determine marketing strategies and how humor is used (see Appendix A). In class, you can also show several examples of advertisements that can be further analyzed to show different methods of marketing and humor.

2. *Analysis:* Traditional marketing often applies Maslow's (1954) hierarchy of needs to target an audience's worries, fears, or anxieties. However, this can have a negative impact by seeming dark, depressing, condescending, or even frightening. Humor has a way of taking focus off the severity of some of these elements by generally make light of them or making the most mundane or serious products, such as tires or insurance, seem interesting. Have students apply Maslow's hierarchy (Appendix B) to analyze different media or advertisements. They should consider how humor is used to enhance or diffuse the needs. Are the examples successful or not?

3. *Production:* As a supplemental activity, students can design their own product, company, or logo (see Appendix C). They can then create an advertisement and consider their target audience and subsequent marketing strategy as well as what type of humor may or may not be appropriate in supporting their message.

4. *Reflection:* In conclusion, students can compare, contrast, and reflect on individual and cultural differences in communicating ideas, promoting products, or delivering a lasting message, all of which are essential elements of global marketing.

CAVEATS AND OPTIONS

1. This lesson can be modified for different English proficiency levels by using simple advertisements or local examples from students' own languages.

2. In larger classes this activity can be conducted as pair or group work.

3. If learners find it difficult to understand the message or the humor, use a simple example and focus on identifying patterns, stereotypes, or deviations in logic or expectations.

4. Tell students to keep an open mind and pay close attention to all details.

5. As some marketing is targeted to specific audiences, it can fail to cross cultures. Carefully consider the background and values of all students in the class, and find examples that are appropriate and accessible.

REFERENCES AND FURTHER READING

Byram, M. (1997). *Teaching and assessing intercultural communicative competence*. Clevedon, England: Multilingual Matters.

Maslow, A. (1954). *Motivation and personality*. New York, NY: Harper.

Reimann, A. (2010). Intercultural communication and the essence of humour. *Journal of International Studies* (Utsunomiya University), *29*(1), 23–34.

Reimann, A. (2015). *Culture in context: Critical incidents for raising cultural awareness*. Tokyo, Japan: Intergraphica Press.

APPENDIX A: *Marketing Analysis Worksheet*

Media Survey and Analysis

Choose five brands, products, or companies you like or are familiar with.

- How do they advertise and market their goods or services? (where, when, how)

- What is the target demographic? (age, gender, social status, etc.)

- What is the marketing strategy? (fear, anxiety, inadequacy, comparison, humor, etc.)

- Which do you think are most effective? Why? Is the company foreign or domestic?

- How is humor used to support the message or create a connection?

VI

Brand/Product/ Company	Description	Target Demographic	Date/Time/ Source
1.			

Slogan: Logo:

Marketing strategy/comments:

Brand/Product/ Company	Description	Target Demographic	Date/Time/ Source
2.			

Slogan: Logo:

Marketing strategy/comments:

Brand/Product/ Company	Description	Target Demographic	Date/Time/ Source
3.			

Slogan: Logo:

Marketing strategy/comments:

Brand/Product/ Company	Description	Target Demographic	Date/Time/ Source
4.			

Slogan: Logo:

Marketing strategy/comments:

Brand/Product/ Company	Description	Target Demographic	Date/Time/ Source
5.			

Slogan: Logo:

Marketing strategy/comments:

APPENDIX B: *Maslow's Hierarchy of Needs*

Maslow (1954) highlighted five basic needs that humans work to satisfy. Marketing targets these needs through stimulating our fears and desires, promoting consumption. After viewing several ads, consider how they apply to the hierarchy of needs below.

"Nobody wants to kiss when they are hungry." Dorothea Dix

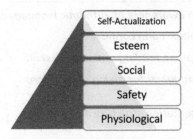

Self-Actualization	Development, improvement, realization (image of satisfaction)
Esteem	Recognition, confidence, status (luxury, designer goods)
Social	
Safety	Love, friendship, belonging (clothes, makeup, vacations)
Physiological	Shelter, security, protection (health products, insurance)
	Food, water, shelter (food, drink, size, taste)

APPENDIX C: *Marketing Project*

Logo	Slogan	Target	Method
E E-Burger	"I'm eatin' it!"	Young men/women, low-income families, students, children	TV commercial, free toys, large portions, discount coupons
Description	Fast food chain. High saturation ads showing happy, young, healthy people enjoying the food. Use sports players to emphasize health.		

Logo	Slogan	Target	Method
Description			

VI

Comical Contraptions

Simon Thomas and Sean Toland

Levels	Low-intermediate to advanced
Contexts	High school, university, language school
Aims	Enhance listening skills and awareness of authentic language
	Improve communicative abilities and confidence
	Expand vocabulary and improve reading and writing skills
	Generate vocabulary and language for giving descriptions of objects and their uses
	Develop awareness of presentation structure and practice presentation skills
Class Time	60–90 minutes depending on expansion activities used
Preparation Time	10 minutes
Resources	Computer and projector (or student mobile devices)
	Downloaded video
	Handouts (see Appendices)

This language learning and use activity uses short video clips of the popular animated characters Wallace and Gromit to introduce "Cracking Contraptions." These videos allow for a light-hearted approach to public speaking, an extremely difficult undertaking that can cause students a tremendous amount of anxiety. Using videos such as these enables learners to incorporate their own creativity and humor into tasks while also employing an embedded focus of structural, language, and communication goals. This independence helps to alleviate the anxiety and stress students can experience. Acquisition of public speaking skills is becoming more important because learners of English as an international language are becoming expected to have not only communicative skills, but also the ability to effectively present information in a professional environment. This activity requires students to think creatively to design an original comical contraption, describe their design and its utility, and give a mini-presentation to their classmates. Expansion activities enable different parts of this activity to focus on language aspects of the instructor's choice and the students' language learning needs.

PROCEDURE

1. Select one or both of the example videos from the references. Other videos are available in the same series. You could also create a script for a listening gap fill exercise.

2. Lead a brainstorming exercise with key words from the title of the chosen video. Instructional focus can be given to vocabulary-building and mind-mapping skills.

3. Introduce the video with accompanying comprehension questions and/or a gap-fill exercise. Give time for watching. Discuss answers and the idea of comical contraptions. Focus can be given to listening comprehension, vocabulary building, and pronunciation.

4. Focus on British English humor in the video. Discuss humor created through character dialogue and actions. You can also discuss differences and similarities between British and American humor and vocabulary.

5. Show students either of the examples in Appendix A. Ask questions to elicit students' ideas about the contraption. Possible questions can be found in Appendix B. Focus can be given to teaching vocabulary and/or grammatical structure of answers. Emphasize that answers can be humorous.

6. Divide the class into groups to brainstorm what kind of comical contraptions they would like to have and what purposes the contraptions would serve. Emphasize comedy and practicality. Distribute the template in Appendix C.

7. Provide sufficient time and language learning support for student groups to complete the template with their ideas.

8. Model an example presentation of a contraption from Appendix A using students' ideas and a structure and presentations skills suitable for the students' language level. Focus and additional time can be given to building and practicing necessary presentation delivery skills.

9. Using a structure appropriate to the classroom setting, students present their comical contraptions to their peers.

CAVEATS AND OPTIONS

1. Students can make posters of their original ideas.

2. The structure and language of a presentation can be taught according to students' language level, giving students awareness of introduction, body, conclusions, and transitions, and giving further opportunity for developing language skills.

3. Presentation delivery skills can be taught, giving students awareness of how physical delivery can enhance information and performance.

4. Students can be instructed to present individually to create greater independence or in groups for greater support and development of collaboration and cooperation skills.

5. Time can be given for students to read, vote on, and discuss the funniest, most useful, and most interesting comical contraption ideas.

6. Time can be given for a final review of language and skills used.

REFERENCES AND FURTHER READING

Autochef—Cracking Contraptions—Wallace & Gromit: https://www.youtube .com/watch?v=2igRcGxlshA&nohtml5=False

The Turbo Dinner—Cracking Contraptions—Wallace & Gromit: https://www .youtube.com/watch?v=eDmwqj6CUOY&nohtml5=False

APPENDIX A: *Comical Contraptions*

Example 1

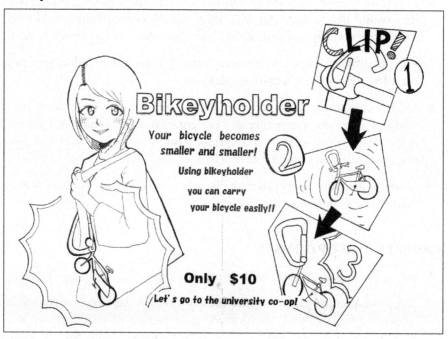

Example 2

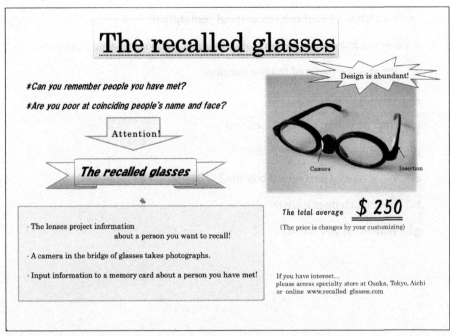

The recalled glasses

Can you remember people you have met?

Are you poor at coinciding people's name and face?

Attention!

The recalled glasses

Design is abundant!

Camera   Insertion

· The lenses project information
    about a person you want to recall!

· A camera in the bridge of glasses takes photographs.

· Input information to a memory card about a person you have met!

The total average **$ 250**
(The price is changes by your customizing)

If you have interest...
please access specialty store at Osaka, Tokyo, Aichi
or online www.recalled glasses.com

APPENDIX B: *Comical Contraption Questions*

1. What is the name of the contraption:

2. What is it used for?

3. How do you use it? (instructions)

4. What are the special features?

5. What type of person will buy it?

6. How much does it cost?

7. Where can you buy it?

VI

APPENDIX C: *Our Comical Contraption Template*

1. Draw a picture of your original comical contraption.

2. Answer the following questions about your original comical contraption.

    a.   What is the name of the contraption?

    b.   What is it used for?

    c.   How do you use it? (instructions)

    d.   What are the special features?

    e.   What type of person will buy this?

    f.   How much does it cost?

    g.   Where can you buy it?

Humorous Online Commercials

Sean H. Toland and Simon Thomas

Levels	**Low intermediate +**
Contexts	**High school, university, job experienced, new immigrants**
Aims	**Enhance critical thinking skills**
	Develop cultural awareness
	Improve speaking, listening, and pronunciation abilities
	Practice presentation skills
	Experience humor in the classroom
Class Time	**60 minutes**
Preparation Time	**10 minutes**
Resources	**Computer and projector or student mobile devices**
	White/blackboard
	Handouts (see appendices)

In nearly every corner of the globe, technological advances have had a profound impact on the way people teach and learn English as an international language (EIL). Nowadays, more and more EIL instructors are using YouTube videos and mobile devices in their classrooms in a variety of innovative ways. Without question, YouTube offers teachers a rich cache of humorous videos that are not only entertaining, but also highly beneficial for English language learners. The use of comical online commercials in an EIL classroom is an effective teaching strategy that can enhance students' listening, pronunciation, and speaking skills. In addition, these amusing videos can ignite learners' critical thinking abilities and act as a springboard to discuss cross-cultural issues.

PROCEDURE

1. Before class, print out the Humorous Online Commercials Chart (Appendix A) and the Our Humorous Commercial Plan (Appendix B).

2. Divide the class into small groups of two to four students.

3. Write terms connected to the theme of commercials on the whiteboard: *viral, marketing, product, setting, celebrity, humorous,* and *target market*. Give groups

5 minutes to think about these terms and discuss the meanings of each one. Lead the class in a brainstorming session and write students' responses on the whiteboard.

4. Tell students they are going to watch four short online commercials. The videos touch on the following subjects: champagne glasses, tablet devices, working in an office, and a movie theater date. Play the videos on a projector or get the students to access them on their mobile devices.

5. When the first viewing is complete, pass out the Humorous Online Commercials Chart (Appendix A) to students.

6. Select student volunteers to read the nine questions on the chart. Review any difficult vocabulary.

7. The students watch the videos a second time. Afterward, give them 15 minutes to discuss the commercials in their group and complete the chart.

8. Students walk around the classroom and discuss their answers with other teams.

9. Distribute the Our Humorous Commercial Plan handout (Appendix B).

10. Ask student volunteers to read the information on the handout. Clarify any questions that learners might have.

11. The teams have 20 minutes to brainstorm ideas for their own comical online video.

12. When the planning stage is completed, model an example presentation with a student volunteer.

13. Give teams time to organize and practice their mini-presentations.

14. Make a brief stop at each group and provide necessary feedback.

15. After the practice session, students rotate around the classroom and give their presentations to several other teams. They also listen to a number of their classmates' presentations.

16. Write the following questions on the whiteboard:

    • What was the funniest idea for a commercial you heard? Why?

    • Do you think it would be interesting to direct a humorous commercial? Why or why not?

    • What are some challenges that directors might have when they direct an online commercial?

17. When the presentations are completed, students once again meet in their small groups to discuss the three questions in the previous step.

CAVEATS AND OPTIONS

1. This lesson can be modified for different proficiency levels. Lower level learners might need more time to brainstorm ideas and practice their presentations.

2. The lesson can be extended over two classes. The presentations can take place during the next lesson.

3. Higher level learners can find their own online humorous commercial for homework and discuss it in small groups during the next class. They can access the video on their mobile devices and play it for their group.

REFERENCES AND FURTHER READING

ALLinADchannel. (2013, March 11). *Le Trefle—Emma*. Retrieved from https://www.youtube.com/watch?v=Wm9iH1VjOFI

Arnell Group. (2011, June 22). *Reebok Terry Tate Episode 1: Terry's World*. Retrieved from https://www.youtube.com/watch?v=k8QziCDf3WA

CarlsbergBE's channel. (2011, September 22). *Carlsberg stunts with bikers in cinema*. Retrieved from https://www.youtube.com/watch?v=RS3iB47nQ6E

MarketingFactory. (2011, July 25). *Champagne Nicolas Feuillatte*. Retrieved from https://www.youtube.com/watch?v=0bciIFs4h7s

VI

APPENDIX A: *Humorous Online Commercials Chart*

Questions	Ad 1	Ad 2	Ad 3	Ad 4
1. What product or service is the online commercial trying to sell? Who will buy the product or service (target market)?				
2. Where does the commercial take place? Describe the setting(s).				
3. Who was in the online commercial? (character roles, famous people)				
4. Describe the objects you noticed in the commercial.				
5. What happened in the commercial?				
6. What is the main message of the commercial? What does the company want the audience to believe about the product?				
7. What was the funniest part of the commercial? Why?				
8. Do you think the commercial was successful? Why or why not?				
9. Which video did you like the best? Why?				

APPENDIX B: *Our Humorous Commercial Plan*

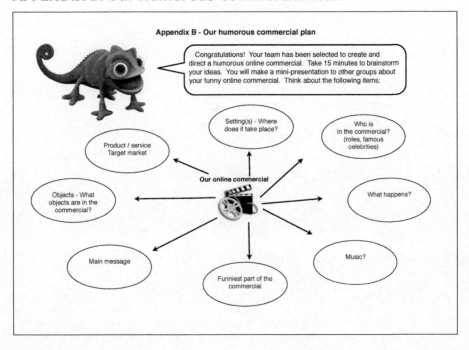

Appendix B - Our humorous commercial plan

Congratulations! Your team has been selected to create and direct a humorous online commercial. Take 15 minutes to brainstorm your ideas. You will make a mini-presentation to other groups about your funny online commercial. Think about the following items:

Setting(s) - Where does it take place?

Who is in the commercial? (roles, famous celebrities)

Product / service Target market

Our online commercial

What happens?

Objects - What objects are in the commercial?

Main message

Funniest part of the commercial

Music?

VI

Part VII

Parody, Satire, and Sarcasm

Integrating Humorous Music and Song in English Language Learning

Diane Boothe

Levels	*Intermediate and advanced (may be adapted to beginning)*
Aims	*Create humorous song lyrics to strengthen comprehension, grammar, pronunciation, and phonological awareness*
Class Time	*30–45 minutes plus follow-up*
Preparation Time	*30 minutes*
Resources	*Sample songs*
	CD player or computer with projector
	Writing paper and pens

The objective of this activity is to use humor and metaphorical semantics to develop learners' skills. Integrating creative language builds a pathway from vocabulary and grammar to expanded learning. Songs are useful for "freeing the speech muscles" (Larsen-Freeman & Anderson, 2011, p. 76) and evoking positive emotion. Music is an excellent resource for ESL/EFL teaching. Combining music with humor provides an additional benefit to stimulate learning.

PROCEDURE

1. Before class, select portions of two or three humorous songs that are age and learner appropriate. Write the lyrics for the students using a PowerPoint presentation, overhead projector, or paper/board depending on resources available. As class begins, play music in the background to set the tone.

2. Introduce the concept of humor and song lyrics. Play a cut of selected songs for students, discussing the humorous meaning of the lyrics. The visual posting of the lyrics reinforces the vocabulary and humorous connotations. Share the idea of song parody with students, and explain about people writing alternate words to already clever lyrics and tunes. Often young people will come up with alternate lyrics to favorite or traditional tunes. Here are two examples of song parody:

   1. From "Pop Goes the Weasel"
      All around the mulberry bush

The monkey chased the weasel
That's the way the money goes
Pop goes the weasel

Alternate lyrics from "Pop Hates the Beatles," by Allan Sherman
(Sherman/Busch, 1964)
My daughter needs a new phonograph
She wore out all the needles
Besides I broke the old one in half
I hate the Beatles!

2. From "Battle Hymn of the Republic"
Glory, Glory Hallelujah
. . .
His truth is marching on

Alternate lyrics (Opie, 1959)
Glory, Glory Hallelujah
Teacher hit me with a ruler
I bopped her in the bean
With a rotten tangerine
And boy did she turn green

3. An original song with alternate lyrics from "The Money Tree,"
both by Jeff West (Jeff West Music BMI, copyright 2003)
Lord knows that I could use some
Can't we all?
Seems like I'm always robbin' Peter
to pay Paul, Dad gum it all

Alternate lyrics
It's not like it's enough
That she's so tall
But she's also got a nose
like Charles DeGaulle, and that's not all

3. After discussing these lyrics and their meanings and rhyming structure, students have 15 minutes to begin writing their own lyrics to the song melody of their choice or an original melody. To start, two to four lines is fine. Then students can share lines in groups of four people. The more outgoing or musical students may even want to sing their lines, post them for others to read, or perform them on a musical instrument.

4. *Follow up/expansion:* This lesson can continue over several days, with students receiving class time to further develop their lyrics and share them with other students. Students can also be assigned groups to design a project involving several students.

CAVEATS AND OPTIONS

1. Depending on age and level of language competency, song lyrics can become more involved or complex. Group discussion builds the comprehension and creativity and elicits laughter and conversation.

2. The lesson can be expanded to encourage students to write and illustrate the lyrics.

3. As a special feature, a musician can visit the class and perform for students.

REFERENCES AND FURTHER READING

Cohen, M. (2013). *Overweight sensation: The life and comedy of Allan Sherman.* Lebanon, NH: Brandeis University Press.

Larson-Freeman, D., & Anderson, M. (2011). *Techniques and principles in language teaching.* Oxford, England: Oxford University Press.

Opie, I., & Opie, P. (1959). *The lore and language of schoolchildren.* New York, NY: Oxford University Press.

WNYC. (2013, July 24). The pioneering parody pop of Allan Sherman. Retrieved from http://www.wnyc.org/story/308561-pioneering-parody-pop -of-allan-sherman

Parody Song Summarizing and Creative Writing

Trisha Dowling

Levels	*High-intermediate, advanced*
Aims	*Increase ability to recognize and understand parody through the use of popular pop music and parody songs*
	Summarize general idea of song lyric meaning through reading and listening to lyrics
	Recognize rhyming words while comparing original song and parody
	Create new song lyrics through the use of recognized rhyming words
Class Time	*30–45 minutes*
Preparation Time	*10–25 minutes*
Resources	*Weird Al Yankovic songs and original versions of songs*
	Graphic organizer (see Appendix)

Music can provide unique insight into both language and culture. It can be beneficial in all areas of language learning. According to Trinick (2011), "there are several areas or domains of mutual benefit for both music and language, including affective, sociocultural, cognitive, and linguistic. Although each domain offers potentially positive outcomes, they are complementary and sometimes inseparable" (p. 6). The benefits of music in the language classroom are plentiful, but popular song parodies can be especially difficult to understand. This activity combines music and humor and aims to support listening, writing, and speaking in the language classroom through structured pair work.

PROCEDURE

1. Select a Weird Al Yankovic parody song. Choices range from 1980s hits like "Eat It" (parody of "Beat It," by Michael Jackson) and "Another One Rides the Bus" (parody of "Another One Bites the Dust," by Queen) to pop music from this decade including "Tacky" (parody of "Happy," by Pharrell Williams).

2. Provide half of the students with a copy of the parody song lyrics and a graphic organizer (see Appendix).

3. Provide the remaining students with a copy of the original song lyrics and a graphic organizer.

4. Play the Weird Al parody song for the class (many of his songs can be found on YouTube).

5. After reading the provided lyrics and listening to the parody, students summarize the alternate meaning of the parody song lyrics using the graphic organizer.

6. Play the original song for the class (these can also be found on YouTube).

7. After reading the provided lyrics and listening to the original song, students summarize the meaning of the song lyrics using the graphic organizer.

8. After students complete the song summary of both songs, they work in pairs and share their written song summary.

9. In pairs, students compare lyrics and make a list of the rhyming words from both songs.

10. For further creative writing practice, students may work in pairs and create new song lyrics (in a serious or spoof style) using the rhyming words as guidelines.

CAVEATS AND OPTIONS

You can choose to not provide song lyrics in order to focus more on listening, especially for more advanced students.

REFERENCES AND FURTHER READING

Trinick, R. (2011). Sound and sight: The use of song to promote language learning. *General Music Today, 25*(2), 5–10.

APPENDIX: *Song Summary Graphic Organizer*

Original song title	Summarize the song meaning
Weird Al song title	

Rhyming words
Creative writing

To You, From Me, With Sarcasm

Raichle Farrelly

Levels	High-intermediate to advanced, adolescent, adult
Aims	Investigate humor in English
Class Time	30–35 minutes
Preparation Time	20 minutes
Resources	Sarcastic online e-postcards

Humor can be easily conveyed across cultures and languages, especially when the humor is based on a shared experience. This shared experience can span countries and cultures as people view trending YouTube videos or laugh about Facebook memes that go viral.

However, one aspect of humor that can be difficult to interpret is sarcasm. Sarcasm is not gentle or kind, but bold and perhaps even bitter. It is often used to mock someone or something and can be both indirect and ironic. But sarcasm can also be fun and playful, especially between friends. Teaching sarcasm to English language learners isn't about teaching them how to ridicule someone, but rather how to identify sarcasm when used in social situations, on social media platforms, and in TV and film. Sarcasm employs both verbal and nonverbal communication strategies and therefore can be a fun aspect of humor to explore with students. Students have to work on their facial expressions, intonation, delivery, and more.

This activity uses online ePostcards or memes to promote critical thinking and creativity through analysis and investigation. You can find many options at www.someecards.com or www.bluntcard.com. The best range of appropriate examples can be found by using the search term "sarcastic ePostcards." Sample ePostcards include a sarcastic text and an image that humorously contradicts the text. For example, one ePostcard depicts a couple at dinner looking at each other lovingly. The text reads, "Just wanted you to know how much I missed you while you were checking your phone during our conversation." (See the Appendix for more examples.)

Prior to the activity, it is necessary to introduce students to the concept of sarcasm and the mechanisms for delivering "lines" sarcastically. There are several ways to do this; for instance, you can show clips from movies and TV shows or deliver some sarcastic examples yourself. In addition, it would be useful to model the activity prior to having students work independently. Show some sample ePost-cards on a screen or print examples on a handout. Then guide students through the procedure below to prepare them for a learner-centered version of the task.

PROCEDURE

1. Print duplicates of each sarcastic ePostcard; however, remove the text from one card in the pair.

2. Have students find their partner by finding the person who has the same picture on his or her postcard.

3. In pairs, ask students to analyze the text of their postcard and determine (a) what makes it funny, (b) what makes it sarcastic, and (c) what makes it confusing. While pairs are sharing their ideas, walk around and see if you can fill in any gaps in understanding the humor.

4. Tell pairs to practice delivering the sarcastic line(s) to each other, considering intonation and facial expressions. Again, help them come up with appropriate gestures, facial expressions, intonation, and pausing for effective delivery.

5. Have each pair turn to another pair and share their sarcastic ePostcard. Each pair should show the blank picture card to the other pair and then deliver the sarcastic line(s) orally. Students listening to the sarcastic delivery should then provide feedback about what made it funny to them.

6. Ask the class to nominate a few pairs who gave a great delivery or who had really funny ePostcards, and invite these students to share with the whole class.

CAVEATS AND OPTIONS

1. After Step 5, you might invite students in their new groups of four to try to write their own sarcastic line(s) for the blank ePostcards. They could then present these to the whole class or to other groups.

2. Sarcasm can be used playfully and in a way that is not harmful; however, sometimes sarcasm can "sting." Choose ePostcards that demonstrate sarcasm without demonstrating rude behavior. Also, as with any online resource, screen carefully for appropriate language. Depending on the level and age of the learners, you can have a critical conversation about harmful sarcasm.

3. To encourage learner inquiry, you might give them additional ePostcards at the end of class and ask them to survey some native speakers to find out what they think makes the ePostcard funny. They can present their findings to the class through mini-presentations or via an online forum.

APPENDIX: *Sample ePostcards Demonstrating Sarcasm (adapted from www.someecards.com)*

Text: Sorry for accidentally having fun at the holiday office party. Cartoon image: Couple dancing	Text: Just wanted you to know how much I missed you while you were checking your phone during our conversation. Cartoon image: Couple at dinner
Text: 100% of people who use statistics in casual conversations are annoying. Cartoon image: Adults at a business meeting	Text: Social media is a great way to reconnect with the people you purposely lost touch with. Cartoon image: Girl working on laptop

Hey! That's Me I'm Laughing At!

Mark Firth

Levels	**Beginner to advanced**
Aims	**Develop skills in analyzing parody and self-depreciative humor**
	Analyze an aspect of culture from an absurd point of view
	Practice using modals
Class Time	**45–90 minutes**
Preparation Time	**10 minutes**
Resources	**Teacher's computer with an Internet connection**
	Projector and screen

Self-deprecation is one of the most difficult forms of humor to successfully achieve, albeit one of the most disarming and effective ways to learn about language and culture. As an intercultural skill, self-deprecation can be a useful tool for nonnative speakers to release tension when making friends in the target language. By using this form of self-parody, learners can also demonstrate their understanding of the idiosyncrasies of culture and potentially a critical stance on issues they feel strongly about.

PROCEDURE

1. Engage students by having them call out some of the words they associate with eating sushi. Students who may not be so familiar with sushi could start by listing words they associate with Japan in general.

2. Set up the following scenario, and have students work in pairs to write their answers to the questions below.

   You live in Japan and one of your friends from England is coming to visit you for the first time. You are going to introduce her to some of the good manners and customs of eating and drinking in Japan. Your friend really wants to enjoy going out to a traditional sushi restaurant (not a revolving sushi bar; they have them in England). Think of all the things you will have to teach her. You should make up your own rules for anything you don't know yourself. Use instructions like *you should, you shouldn't, you can, you have to, _____ means _____ in English,* and so on.

a. How do you enter the sushi restaurant?

b. How do you show the number of guests in your group?

c. How do you get a seat?

d. How do you order?

e. What must you never ask the master?

f. How are the drinks poured?

g. How is the sushi eaten?

h. What is the best and worst tuna?

i. How much soy sauce is the right amount?

j. Why is the sushi served on a wooden board?

k. What is the wet towel for?

l. What is *gari?*

m. Who pays the bill?

n. What is the salt outside the restaurant on the ground for?

o. What other rules can you think of?

3 Encourage students to be creative for anything they don't know. This will make the lesson all the more enjoyable.

4. Call on some students from different pairs to either say their rules for each question, or ask them to write them on the board.

5. Use a search engine using the search terms "The Japanese tradition—sushi," and show the video. Note that the video is spoken in Japanese with English subtitles. There is an adapted English language version of the video; however, it is not suitable for this lesson. (Note: As of this writing, the current YouTube link is www.youtube.com/watch?v=bDL8yu34fz0.)

6. Show the video clip, and have students note any changes they should make to the rules that they wrote down (hopefully it was enjoyable for them).

7. Ask students to share the notes they took, and show the video one more time. Make changes to the rules using the appropriate modals.

VII

8. Discuss students' answers and talk about the various cultural stereotypes and traditions that the video is either poking fun at or over-exaggerating (answers will vary).

CAVEATS AND OPTIONS

1. Students are now ready to send up their own culture and traditions. They could make similar short role-plays or videos highlighting the sociocultural aspects of dining in their own culture.

2. Reflective journals and discussions are useful to develop intercultural understanding. Some questions could include the following:

   • Why do you think we sometimes laugh at the idiosyncrasies of other cultures when we first see them?

   • What are the advantages of using parody to help us understand both our own and different cultures?

   • What are some of the dangers of parody?

   • In what situations can you laugh about yourself and your own culture?

3. Students could investigate some of the different types of self-parody found in their own music, television drama, politics, religion, languages, and dialects. Students should research the intent of the humor and how the targets of the humor would feel about the parody.

Light Bulb Warm-up Jokes for Introducing Satire About Social Issues

James M. Perren

Levels	Intermediate and above
Contexts	Adult
Aims	Develop speaking fluency, motivation to write, and confidence in using humor as a way to connect with others through language learning
Class Time	20 minutes, plus 3–5 minutes for each light bulb warm-up joke throughout the semester
Preparation Time	30 minutes
Resources	Internet access
	Light bulb joke websites
	E-mail account
	Background reading material, either a handout or a website

Jokes can be used in class to ease the stress of language learning. Research suggests that paying attention to the reasons people find something funny is a starting point for discussion, ultimately leading to mediation rather than disagreement and dissonance. Studying the language in jokes also assists in learning about the culture associated with that language. Jokes offer a play on words and require critical thinking skills to decode them and use them with social and cultural sensitivity. Light bulb jokes offer opportunities to augment the classroom social dynamics and atmosphere. Using light bulb warm-up jokes for pragmatic development offers increased opportunities for students to enjoy using English. Finally, light bulb jokes are also a good introduction to how humor is used for social satire in some cultures.

PROCEDURE

1. Introduce the topic of light bulb jokes to the class via the light bulb joke background reading activity (see Appendix). Direct students to complete short reading passages located on several websites to encourage active reading in the form of thoughts, comments, and questions.

2. Provide students with your model list of light bulb jokes in English (e.g., posted on the course website) starting with two of your favorites. Read one of the jokes, and ask for a volunteer to read the next.

3. Demonstrate to students the language from light bulb jokes that assists with course learning objectives: vocabulary, grammar, pronunciation, social issues, and so on.

4. Direct students to several Light Bulb Jokes websites for their selections:

   • http://lightbulbjokes.com

   • www.kidsjokesoftheday.com/Light-Bulb-Jokes-for-Kids_1.html

   • www.funny2.com/bulb.htm

   • www.jokes4us.com/peoplejokes/lightbulbjokes.html

5 Ask students to compile a list of three favorite light bulb jokes. Require that students type their light bulb jokes and submit them by e-mail 2 days before the due date for your approval and feedback.

6. Ask students to share one light bulb joke (one joke in English, one from the home culture) with the members of their daily warm-up group. Explain the need to share their light bulb jokes with classmates. Instruct students to store their past English light bulb joke Internet links on the course website to avoid recycling.

CAVEATS AND OPTIONS

1. This activity can be modified for beginning students by asking them to write about very specific aspects of a light bulb joke, breaking the task down to more manageable segments. They can also work independently and write a reflective journal entry based on connecting the light bulb joke to the social issues discussed in other assignments.

2. Invite student questions and discussion related to the general use of light bulb jokes for learning English, and have students write key discussion points on the board. Students could also discuss the stereotypes found in light bulb jokes and consider where they come from. In addition, they could discuss how new light bulb jokes are created to satirize current social issues or public figures.

3. For students with less access to and experience using technology, pair work can also be required to facilitate using library or learning center resources in an educational institution or community library. Students with advanced technology skills can write their light bulb joke entries directly into mobile devices and immediately post reflections on blogs.

REFERENCES AND FURTHER READING

Bell, N. (2012). Comparing playful and non-playful incidental attention to form. *Language Learning, 62*(1), 236–265.

Flamson, T., Bryant, G., & Barrett, H. (2011). Prosody in spontaneous humor: Evidence for encryption. *Pragmatics & Cognition, 19*(2), 248–267.

Wikipedia. (n.d.). Lightbulb joke. Retrieved from http://en.wikipedia.org/wiki /Lightbulb_joke

APPENDIX: *Light Bulb Joke Background Reading Activity*

Find and read information about light bulb jokes from North American culture. Use either Google or Wikipedia. Please look up the word *satire* in an online American English dictionary to understand the meaning.

Write answers to these questions before coming to class:

1. What is the basic form of a light bulb joke?

2. What does a light bulb joke ask?

3. How does the punch line answer highlight a stereotype of a target group?

4. What versions of the light bulb joke satirize a wide range of cultures, beliefs, and occupations?

5. How might light bulb jokes be connected to current news events, particularly those related to local and international politics or social issues?

Fake News for Recognizing Satire and Developing Media Literacy

Caleb Prichard

Levels	Intermediate and advanced
Aims	Develop media literacy
	Recognize and enjoy satire
Class Time	1 hour
Preparation Time	1 hour
Resources	Articles from satirical news sources and off-beat news sources

Satirical websites, such as *The Onion* (www.theonion.com) and *News Thump* (http://newsthump.com), are very popular in the United States, the United Kingdom, and other English-speaking countries. Frequent exposure to satire and fake news shows (e.g., *The Daily Show*) develops one's media literacy so that people can recognize satire and perhaps enjoy the humor. The articles are frequently shared on social networking sites like Facebook.

Nevertheless, many people mistake fake news for real news, as these sites mimic real news and often comment on current events. This may lead to confusion or embarrassing misunderstandings. This happens so frequently that a website has been created (http://literallyunbelievable.org) that documents the Facebook comments of mystified or angered people who thought a shared (fake) news story was real. Facebook even introduced a "satire" tag in 2014 to warn users of fake news. Another website (http://realorsatire.com) offers users the ability to find out if a website is satirical or not.

Language learners less accustomed to satire may be particularly prone to being fooled into thinking the news is real. However, by reading and discussing fake news stories in class, learners can develop media literacy and learn to appreciate this form of humor. Moreover, since the articles can be enjoyable to read, they provide a good source for practicing reading and summary skills. This activity uses both satirical news articles and offbeat news stories to challenge learners to guess whether articles are real or not.

PROCEDURE

1. Briefly explain to students about fake news sites and the concept of offbeat news. As a warm-up activity, show headlines to students and have them guess whether each is real or fake. Here are examples:

   a. Man Rolls in Dog Waste to Try Avoiding Arrest; Plan Fails

   b. Death Row Inmate Dies of Natural Causes 3 Days Into Execution

   c. Man Who Stopped Dieting Already Seeing Results

   d. Woman Admits Digging Up Dad's Grave in Search of "Real Will"

   e. Raccoon's Freedom Costs San Francisco Carpenter His Job

   f. Passengers Feel Sorry For Flustered Toddler Traveling With Loud, Obnoxious Parents

   g. Oregon Man Accused of Stealing Bikes, Goat Too

   h. Fast Food Customers Less Appealing Than in Commercial

   i. Ireland Rushes Through New Law After Inadvertently Legalizing Ecstasy

2. Students discuss in groups which articles they think are real and which are fake. Have students vote as a class, and then give the answers. (The headlines above that are from real news stories [http://news.yahoo.com/odd-news] are a, d, e, g, and i. The rest are fake news stories from *The Onion*.)

3. Give students one satirical news story and one offbeat story. Cut out the source (unless you want to stress the importance of previewing skills). Ask students to read silently (for a reading class) or out loud in groups (for a speaking class).

4. In small groups, students summarize each story in their own words. They then discuss which story they think is the real one. They also discuss whether they think the stories are funny.

5. Ask for volunteers to share their summary. The class takes a vote on which one they think is real. Give the answers and provide clues to help students recognize satire. This may include the following:

   • Fake news stories often feature a "local man or woman" who does something that is not newsworthy; the satire makes fun of society or a group of people. Offbeat (real) news stories frequently involve someone doing a stupid thing, and the person usually gets into some trouble for it (e.g., gets arrested, gets in an accident).

VII

- Fake news is often too crazy to be real, but it may mimic some recent news story. Offbeat news may seem *almost* too crazy to be real, but it is possible.

- Fake news stories often use profanity and slang, while offbeat news usually does not (Burfoot & Baldwin, 2009).

6. This activity should be repeated in future classes until students seem to have developed the ability to recognize satirical news stories. Of course, if students enjoy it, such stories can continue to be used to practice language skills.

CAVEATS AND OPTIONS

1. Choose articles that you think students will enjoy, and be sure to select ones that are appropriate for the class in terms of content and level. Depending on the students, you may want to simplify the language or edit inappropriate language.

2. As a follow-up assignment, students can search for offbeat or satirical news stories on their own. They can summarize or share ones they enjoy.

3. Students can try to create a humorous fake news story. They can share with the class, which then votes on the funniest story.

4. For listening classes, show satirical and offbeat news videos. These are also available on *The Onion* and *Yahoo* websites.

REFERENCES AND FURTHER READING

Burfoot, C., & Baldwin, T. (2009). Automatic satire detection: Are you having a laugh? In *Proceedings of the ACL-IJCNLP 2009 conference short papers* (pp. 161–164). Stroudsburg, PA: Association for Computational Linguistics.

Understanding Sarcasm Through Memes

Caleb Prichard

Levels	All
Aims	*Develop cross-cultural understanding, ability to recognize sarcasm, and language skills*
Class Time	*1 hour*
Preparation Time	*1 hour*
Resources	*Memes shared on paper, via projector, or on a learner management system*

Sarcasm is a common form of humor and criticism in English-language media and interpersonal communication. While the literal meaning of a sarcastic statement does not match the intended meaning, sarcasm can be detected based on cues such as context, facial expression, and inflection (Attardo, Eisterhold, Hay, & Poggi, 2003; Rockwell, 2000). Sarcasm is often intended to be humorous, but it can leave English language learners confused and frustrated if they cannot recognize it.

This lesson utilizes Internet memes, specifically image macros, to teach English language learners how to detect sarcasm. Creators of memes remix trending images, phrases, or ideas to express their feelings and to be humorous. Sarcasm is very present in memes. "Condescending Wonka" memes, based on a still image of Gene Wilder in the 1971 film *Willy Wonka & the Chocolate Factory*, may be the most popular example. Nearly a half-million unique memes have been created using this image on the site Meme Generator (https://memegenerator.net).

Image macros provide a clear way to present sarcasm because these memes include both a still image and text. This allows learners to evaluate the key feature of sarcasm, namely the mismatch of language and context. Moreover, the lesson can be enjoyable. Memes are very common on popular social networking sites, so learners may find the lesson both authentic and humorous.

PROCEDURE

1. Have students look at several different memes, including a number that use sarcasm. In addition to "Condescending Wonka," you could do an image search for "sarcastic memes." (The images should be carefully preselected by you for appropriateness and comprehensibility. Many sarcastic memes use profanity or offensive humor.) Individually, students rank each meme based on how much they understand it and how humorous they think it is.

2. Students get together in pairs or small groups to compare their rankings and to help each other try to understand each meme.

3. Elicit from students the point of each meme. Especially for the sarcastic memes, draw attention to the visual, linguistic, and contextual aspects of each.

4. Introduces the main strategies for detecting sarcasm:

   • looking for gaps between literal utterance and expected message

   • recognizing a "blank face" (Attardo et al., 2003) or an expression that does not match the utterance

   • (in oral contexts) noticing lower, slower, and louder inflection (Rockwell, 2000)

5. Students practice reading the memes in a sarcastic way (with the appropriate intonation and expression). You may need to model this.

6. Show students more memes. In groups, they guess whether each is sarcastic. They get points for each correct answer. They can then vote for their favorite meme and discuss their choice.

CAVEATS AND OPTIONS

1. Memes often include content that is unsuitable for certain student groups, and sarcasm is often considered rude and hurtful. You should, of course, avoid selecting offensive and inappropriate memes. Moreover, you may need to warn students about the potential harm of sharing offensive content and being sarcastic in a condescending way.

2. As a follow-up assignment, more mature classes could search for memes (or even create their own) online to share their observations and opinions about what they feel is disappointing, annoying, frustrating, and so on.

3. Students can write comments on the memes to practice digital literacy. They can start with simple comments such as "LOL" or "I hate it when that happens!"

REFERENCES AND FURTHER READING

Attardo, S., Eisterhold, J., Hay, J., & Poggi, I. (2003). Multimodal markers of irony and sarcasm. *Humor, 16*, 243–260.

Rockwell, P. (2000). Lower, slower, louder: Vocal cues of sarcasm. *Journal of Psycholinguistic Research, 29*, 483–495.

Understanding Parody

Ted Quock

Levels	*Intermediate and above (can be simplified for lower level and younger learners)*
Aims	*Study humor in a cognitive and critical way*
	Learn about parody as a form of humor
	Communicate orally and/or in writing about concrete and abstract concepts
	Learn about categorizing
Class Time	*From 15 minutes to a full lesson or more*
Preparation Time	*10–15 minutes*
Resources	*Internet access*
	Projector/screen/monitors or a printer (preferably color) or Overhead camera

Parody is among the easiest kinds of humor to understand because the original, by definition, should be easily recognizable. This can then serve as a baseline for guiding students to go beyond instinctive and emotional reactions, such as enjoying parody, to being able to analyze it critically based on measured intellectual reactions. This approach can transfer to a study of other kinds of parody (movie scenes, songs, and advertisements) or serve as a springboard for studying other kinds of humor, or even parody and other kinds of humor in foreign cultures (e.g., through a contrastive analysis of Japanese and Western parody).

PROCEDURE

1. Display Leonardo da Vinci's "Mona Lisa" and elicit from students the title and artist.

2. Display two parodies of "Mona Lisa" using recognizable figures (e.g., Mickey Mouse and Aung San Suu Kyi). Have students name the character and what kind of picture it is (parody; if they don't know the word *parody*, it's a teaching opportunity).

3. Elicit the category "Mona Lisa replaced by another person/character" from the list below (Caveats and Options 2b), and have students identify pictures that fall into that category. Then give them other categories to match pictures with, or have them use other pictures to brainstorm additional categories.

CAVEATS AND OPTIONS

Preparation

1. Go to Google or another search engine, enter "Mona Lisa parody image."

2. Choose several pictures from the following categories:

   a. Mona Lisa replaced by another person/character (e.g., Pikachu, a movie star)

   b. Mona Lisa appearing in a different setting (e.g., in a speeding car, on Mount Rushmore)

   c. Mona Lisa with a different pose (e.g., sleeping, making a funny face)

   d. Mona Lisa with different costuming or props (e.g., wearing a kimono, holding a Starbucks mug)

   e. Mona Lisa with surrealistic changes (e.g., headless, morphed face)

3. Categories a–d are the easiest to work with; d–e could be combined into one to save time. Many students may not understand surrealism well, but this can be a teaching opportunity involving abstract concepts. Other tasks can involve more subtle categorizations.

Execution

1. Pictures can be either displayed on a screen or distributed as handouts.

   a. Displaying pictures one by one can ensure that everyone is working at the same pace, learns relevant new vocabulary, and receives the same feedback, including error correction.

   b. Having students work in groups gives them more autonomy, opens the door for agreeing/disagreeing and other functions, and fosters teamwork and leadership.

   c. Having students work individually in class or for homework allows them to work at their own pace.

2. Giving the categories first and then assigning groups to work on specific categories gives them a more focused task with less ambiguity, and groups can prepare and deliver mini-presentations of their findings.

3. As humor and art are subjective, some pictures can arguably fall into more than one category.

Other Options

1. Besides "Mona Lisa," other widely parodied works of art include Vincent Van Gogh's "Starry Night" and Edvard Munch's "The Scream."

2. An alternative activity can focus on parody in other media (movie scenes, songs, advertisements, logos).

3. To foster greater general knowledge and familiarity with pop culture, the "Mona Lisa" can be introduced together with other famous works of art. This can also be a matching activity using titles and artists.

4. For more advanced learners, this activity can include the following:

   a. discussion on why students find particular pictures more humorous than others (including discussion on target audience)

   b. discussion on criteria for parody (well-known original with humorous changes, but still recognizable)

   c. presentations introducing their own original parodies

   d. oral or written work about the purpose of parody (benign or malignant? mockery or homage?)

Irony in Everyday Language Use

Vander Viana and Sonia Zyngier

Levels	Intermediate+
Contexts	English language school, teenager to adult
Aims	*Learn about the differences between literal and ironic utterances*
	Employ resources that may enhance the irony of a situation
	Develop awareness of the appropriateness of irony in different contexts
	Identify instances of irony in everyday situations
Class Time	*30 minutes*
Preparation Time	*3 minutes*
Resources	*Slips of paper with two sentences on each*

Irony, or verbalizing what is contrary or different from what is actually meant, has always been part and parcel of human interactions and depends on the shared knowledge of the speakers for its understanding. Far from being a new linguistic strategy, its history is broad and diverse, covering a gamut of different areas (cf. Colbrook, 2004; Gibbs & Colson, 2007). Appropriate ironic remarks may help one bond socially with peers, while inappropriate use may eventually lead to social exclusion. Irony can be easily misunderstood by speakers who do not share common ground. In order to recognize ironic remarks, be able to use irony, and be understood as intended, English language learners must be aware of the cultural context. As explained by Ross (1998),

> Understanding the force of irony involves awareness of the language used and knowledge about the world. Attention is brought to the form because there is something incongruous about its use in that context. The mismatch between the language use and intended meaning is often subtle, which means that irony may not be perceived as such. (pp. 50–51)

This activity is aimed at introducing students to a more conscious recognition, understanding, and use of irony in their daily interactions.

PROCEDURE

1. Ask students to create a literal dialogue in which the sentences on their specific slip of paper (either A or B) could be said by one of the speakers.

Group A	Group B
"Is this my grade? Fantastic!"	"You look great in this outfit!"
"This party is really exciting, isn't it?"	"What lovely weather!"

2. Pair students from the same group, and ask each pair to compare their answers.

3. Walk around, check their answers, and provide guidance as needed.

4. In pairs, have students choose one of the sentences and think of a context in which the chosen sentence would indicate exactly the opposite of the speaker's intention.

5. Ask students to create a short dialogue and to practice it orally.

6. Invite students to present their ironic interactions to the class.

7. After the presentations, ask students to consider (a) how different the dialogues they acted out are from the ones they created in Step 1 (e.g., mismatch between what the sentence means literally and the context in which it was said) and (b) which resources they used to enhance the ironic aspect of the dialogue (e.g., contextual features, intonation, facial expressions, body language).

8. Have students consider the contexts in which it would be appropriate or inappropriate to be ironic.

9. Allow students to personalize what they have just learned by asking whether they have ever experienced a situation in which they said or were told these sentences (or similar ones). During the discussion, get them to consider the effect that the use of irony had in the interaction and/or in the relationship among the speakers.

CAVEATS AND OPTIONS

1. If time is an issue, each group could be given only one sentence, and you could skip Step 6. In the latter case, Step 5 could also be slightly changed so that students do not practice the dialogue orally.

2. It is important to realize that not all students will be comfortable acting out in front of the class. Take care not to embarrass anyone. In large classes, you might want to ask for a few volunteers instead of having all the students act out their dialogues.

3. The level of student participation in Steps 7–9 is directly related to their proficiency level. It might be more difficult for them to express their ideas in English if they are at lower intermediate level, for instance. In this case, either conduct a less detailed discussion in English or allow students to express themselves in their mother tongue.

4. When working with more advanced students, instead of providing them with slips of paper, you could illustrate what is meant by an ironic statement and ask them to come up with their own examples. These examples could then be used as the springboard for the activity.

5. If you are teaching a multicultural class, Steps 8–9 can be usefully enriched by teasing out the differences/similarities in diverse national groups.

REFERENCES AND FURTHER READING

Colbrook, C. (2004). *Irony*. London, England: Routledge.

Gibbs, R., & Colston, H. L. (Eds.). (2007). *Irony in language and thought: A cognitive science reader*. New York, NY: Taylor & Francis.

Ross, A. (1998). *The language of humour*. London, England: Routledge.

Flight of the Conchords: "Carol Brown"

Max Watson

Levels	Advanced
Contexts	High school through adult
Aims	Observe and learn to distinguish several common elements of satire while engaging in English conversation with classmates
Class Time	45 minutes
Preparation Time	15 minutes
Resources	Audio or video recording of "Carol Brown" by Flight of the Conchords (available on CD or YouTube)
	Copy of lyrics to the song
	Audiovisual equipment
	Handout (see Appendix)

Humor can be challenging to understand across cultures. This lesson uses a popular Emmy-nominated song by Flight of the Conchords, a New Zealand comedy band, along with the "into, through, and beyond" approach to get students thinking and talking about humor.

PROCEDURE

1. Give students handouts with the song lyrics and the vocabulary and discussion questions from the Appendix.

2. Go through the vocabulary with students.

3. Play the song while students follow the lyrics on the handout.

4. Play the music video.

5. In small groups, have students use the discussion questions to guide their conversations. Circulate and answer questions as they come up.

CAVEATS AND OPTIONS

1. The lesson can be adapted for television-free classrooms by removing a few video-specific questions.

2. This song is homage to Paul Simon's "50 Ways to Leave Your Lover"; a connected lesson could be created around it to give students a better understanding of song parody.

REFERENCES AND FURTHER READING

Brinton, D., Goodwin, J., & Ranks, L. (1994). Helping language minority students read and write analytically: The journey into, through and beyond. In F. Peitzman & G. Gadda (Eds.), *With different eyes: Insights into teaching language minority students across the disciplines* (pp. 57–88). White Plains, NY: Longman.

APPENDIX: *Class Handout*

Humor Vocabulary

Anecdote: funny personal stories that may be true or partly true but exaggerated.

Deadpan: humor that is said in a serious, often expressionless manner.

Irony: something that is opposite of what is expected, resulting in a funny situation.

Pun: a humorous way of creating different meanings by using words that sound alike but that have different meanings.

Self-deprecating humor: comedy wherein the self is the target.

Slapstick: a kind of humor that focuses on ridiculous or exaggerated physical activity.

Lyrical Vocabulary (in order of appearance)

"Broke it off": to end a relationship.

"After the tone": the "tone" refers to the beep you hear before you leave voicemail.

"See me again": to go on another date with someone.

Amnesia: a medical condition where you can't remember things because of injury, shock, or illness.

Electricity: a feeling of excitement.

Chemistry: a strong attraction between people.

"Go with the flow": to be relaxed and accept a situation, rather than trying to change or control it.

"Stick around": remain in or near a place or person.

"Boyfriend material": a guy who would be a good boyfriend.

Choir: a group of singers.

Coma: a state in which a sick or injured person is unconscious for a long time.

Epiphany: a moment during which you suddenly understand something in a new or very clear way.

Sample Discussion Questions

1. How does irony work in the verse about Jen?

2. How do deadpan humor and irony work together in the verse about Bruce? (Understand that Bruce is considered a man's name.)

3. What is the pun in the verse about Flo?

4. Jemaine (the lead singer) offers cereal after the choir states that he cannot cook. What is it about the preparation of cereal that makes this funny?

5. Compared to typical songs, how is the choir here ironic?

6. "Britney hit me" is a pun because it is also a reference to which Britney Spears song?

7. Mona told Jemaine that she was in a coma. How is that ironic?

8. Based on what the choir says about Jemaine, what do you think was Tiffany's epiphany?

9. Jemaine and Bret play musical instruments made with old video-editing equipment that affects the other. How is this both ironic and slapstick?

10. Many of the song's verses are funny because they rhyme. What are your favorite verses and why do you like them?

11. Some of the comedy in the video relies on visual puns that work in conjunction with the lyrics. For example, Felicity is shown with an unlit light bulb, representing "no electricity." Which others did you notice?

12. Does this song use anecdotal humor? If so, how do you think it has been exaggerated?

13. How would you summarize the theme of self-deprecating humor in the song?

Sample Expansion Questions/Activities

1. Many of the reasons for breaking up in the song are excuses. What's the most ridiculous excuse you've ever used or heard for breaking up?

2. Working together, write two more verses for the song using irony and puns.

3. Practice deadpan. Turn to someone in your group and say something surprising or strange.

4. Try to make a joke using self-deprecating humor.

5. Do you watch any TV shows that use slapstick humor? Explain how slapstick humor was used effectively.